"Krippendorf and now Goodwin are the architects of modern responsible tourism. A challenging and inspiring read that defines the agenda for the next decade".

Justin Francis CEO, responsibletravel.com

"Harold Goodwin takes us on a travelogue of a change agent who stumbled into an issue by following his delight in visiting foreign places and then learning about the complexity of the industry and what it means to take responsibility by being part of it. This fascinating story will be of interest to anyone who goes on holiday and cares about living responsibly. This humane book is also profoundly relevant to any industry, activity or academic discipline concerned about practical wisdom (what Aristotle called phronesis), the socially useful knowledge that helps us live sustainably on this beautiful planet".

Titus Alexander, Author and Head of Policy and Research, NovasScarman Group

"Tourism is undergoing the greatest revolution since the package holiday first became popular in the 1960's, attracting millions to seek new sights and experiences. Hotels, resorts, airports blossomed overnight. Travel was exciting, addictive and cheap. But how long can the march for advancement continue without thought or care? Can this brilliant, pervasive, highly successful industry continue as before without destroying the 'golden goose'. Can the industry adapt to the dawning of a vital new era of responsible tourism, where consumers still enjoy the benefits of travel but at the same time, ensure a sustainable world. Where we are held to account for our actions, ensure communities gain real benefit and where we focus - and act on - key issues such as the appalling scarcity of water, carbon emissions and poverty.

Harold Goodwin's book considers sweeping, life-changing decisions that affect us all. His findings are critical for the industry, our children and future generations.This should be required reading for anyone who, like me, loves and works in the industry, as well as consumers who believe a holiday is a must".

Fiona Jeffery, Chairman and Founder, WTM World Responsible Tourism Day

Taking Responsibility for Tourism

"This is a vitally important book for academics, practitioners and policy makers. It eschews some of the formality of conventional academic publishing in order to strengthen and clarify the arguments about the concept of taking responsibility for tourism and its effects. The author uses his vast experience in this area to good effect, making a powerful argument about the ways in which we should manage and develop tourism and deal with this powerful force.

This volume represents a powerful and articulate argument about the issues resulting from tourism's expansion into all parts of the world and presents a strong case about how we might manage the challenges which result from this development. It should be mandatory reading for all those interested in, studying, and producing policy relating to tourism development. It draws on the author's vast experience in studying the effects of tourism on environments and peoples and expresses clearly his challenging views on appropriate management procedures."

Richard Butler, Professor Emeritus, Strathclyde Business School, Strathclyde University

"Harold Goodwin's book is a much-needed piece of research that goes to the heart of the development of what has become known as responsible tourism. It combines solid research and academic precision with the fluency and persuasion that make it an enlightening and absorbing read - of interest to the travelling public and research student alike.

That an increasing number of specialist travel companies now place such responsibility as an automatic part of the commercial process is, in no short measure, due to Goodwin's thinking".

Richard Hearn, Chair (2005-6), Association of Independent Tour Operators (AITO), Founder director, Inntravel, Founder director, Village Ways

"In principle, the need for all stakeholders to adopt a more responsible approach to tourism is undeniable; in practice, however, the concept of responsible tourism remains highly contested. In this book, Harold Goodwin, who for many years has been at the vanguard of the responsible tourism movement, charts a clear path through the debate. Writing coherently, passionately and, at times, controversially, he presents a powerful argument in support in the case for responsible tourism, explaining its evolution, principles and objectives before exploring its practical implementation. The book is, therefore, a 'must read' for anyone with an interest in the responsible tourism debate and, more importantly, an interest in the future of tourism itself."

Richard Sharpley, Professor of Tourism & Development, University of Central Lancashire

Taking Responsibility for Tourism

Responsible Tourism Management

Harold Goodwin

Goodfellow Publishers Ltd

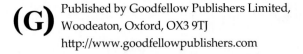 Published by Goodfellow Publishers Limited,
Woodeaton, Oxford, OX3 9TJ
http://www.goodfellowpublishers.com

British Library Cataloguing in Publication Data: a catalogue record
for this title is available from the British Library.

Library of Congress Catalog Card Number: on file.

ISBN: 978-1-906884-39-0

 Design and typesetting by P.K. McBride, www.macbride.org.uk

Printed by Marston Book Services, www.marston.co.uk

Cover design by Cylinder, www.cylindermedia.com

Contents

Foreword

In 1987 Jost Krippendorf wrote *The Holiday Makers – Understanding the Impact of Leisure and Travel*, the defining text of the Responsible Tourism movement. That text reflects the first 40 years of postwar tourism.

Now Harold Goodwin has stepped in to fill the space left by the ever-accelerating development of tourism and the Responsible Tourism movement, bringing us into the 21st century.

He has found the right formula for this work, by not seeking to supersede or replace Krippendorf. Goodwin charts the intervening development in learning, knowledge, experience and research – the great disappointments and missed opportunities, as well as the many reasons to be hopeful. The Responsible Tourism glass is more than half full.

Tourism's capacity for economic development in some of the world's poorest communities is certain. Our ability to manage tourism to deliver good outcomes for those in the host communities is the real question. The purpose of the Responsible Tourism movement is to help deliver those good outcomes – not to criticise or constrain – unless tourism is itself irresponsible.

Goodwin's practical approach clearly shows his unique background as an academic with considerable exposure to the worlds of industry, NGO and consultancy work. He has pulled off a master stroke in style – engaging the interested industry reader, students of tourism, Responsible Tourism and sustainability, as well as academics.

This text is a must for all those interested in a substantial but digestible summation of the state of Responsible Tourism. It reflects the author's complex make-up as academic, practitioner, campaigner and advocate for, and agent of, change.

It is a true academic work, but it is a practical one and one with a clear cause. I commend this text to industry and academia alike.

John de Vial

Director, ABTA and FTO
Trustee, The Travel Foundation
Director, Travelife Sustainability System
Chair, Advisory Group, Leeds Metropolitan University, International Centre for Responsible Tourism
Member, Visit England, Sustainable Tourism Action Group, Steering Committee

Preface

Treat the Earth well. It was not given to you by your parents.

It was loaned to you by your children.

Proverb heard in Kenya

This is the story of a journey, my journey – a journey of discovery, though not a travelogue. I discovered travel later than many of my generation, first as a tourist then as a tour leader, but I became uneasy about how much tourists take and how little they contribute to the people and places they visit. Seeking answers, I became a tourism academic and discovered and explored Responsible Tourism. This book is about the journey and about a movement which is gathering strength. It has been written in the hope that you will respond and be encouraged by it. Responsible Tourism is not a negative approach, it is not about what you shouldn't do, it is about how we can make, and enjoy, real holidays. It is about how we can make better holidays for ourselves and for others, how we make better places for people to live in and for us, as travellers and tourists, to visit.

My father had travelled, like so many of his generation, for war. My first visit abroad was a day trip from Ramsgate to Boulogne and then the school trip to France. To my current students none of this counts as real travel; they have higher expectations and more experience. It was in the winter of 1979, when I was already 27, that I first travelled anywhere that our students might regard as exotic: I took a Thomson's package to Moscow and what was then Leningrad. Later, working in adult education, I was challenged by the people I taught to create an opportunity for them, and I discovered that I could travel anywhere in the world for free if I could persuade a group to travel with me. Tour leading in Siberia, India, Greece, Germany, Albania, Vietnam, Czechoslovakia and China followed, throughout the 1980s. I was having a great time in every vacation – summer, Easter and Christmas – travelling with interesting people to some of the world's most fascinating places, meeting doctors, trade unionists, political activists, historians and naturalists. As a group we were able to travel as we wished, and had the collective economic power to receive the special interest visits we requested, at least most of the time.

But I was uneasy. The ecotourism aphorism 'Leave only footprints, take only photographs' that we were encountering on our travels, often lovingly embroidered or hand-painted, seemed to me to be in truth a licence to exploit. Even as an entreaty or exhortation I thought it was misleading. The slogan is predicated on the assumption that these special environments are for free, that there is no reason to make a contribution to their maintenance nor to compensate local people for their loss of access to natural resources – whether they used them for hunting or gathering for the table, for building materials or for saleable raw materials like timber, honey or perfumes. Research which I undertook later at the Durrell Institute of Conservation and Ecology, and to which we shall return, demonstrated that we were often not meeting the full cost of our visits, let alone contributing to the maintenance of the resource. We were enjoying it at a cost so low that our visits were being subsidised by locals who earned on average a fraction of what we did.

There is an inherent inequality in the tourism experience. As tourists we are *free-riders*[1] *or freeloaders*, rarely do we meet the full costs of our visits, we enjoy the natural and cultural heritage, the beaches and public squares, the buildings, museums and flora and fauna of the places we visit, most often without putting anything back. There are alternative forms of tourism, which are often assumed to be inherently superior to 'normal' or mass tourism – for example ecotourism or community-based tourism – but, as we shall see, there is often little or no evidence to back this up. When I discuss these alternatives with students, I am reminded of Gandhi, who, when asked what he thought about British civilisation, responded: 'I think it would be a good idea'. Ecotourism and community-based tourism are tenacious and seductive ideas – they *are* good ideas – but the road to hell is paved with good intentions. The idea is not enough.

The development of Responsible Tourism as a movement has been a personal journey, but not one which I have felt in control of. Rather, a journey which has been undertaken with many different people, moving in a broadly similar direction. Over the last 15 years I have had the privilege to learn with a committed and often richly talented groups of learners on Masters courses at three universities; and to work with professionals in companies, governments, NGOs and in education around the world, many of whom have contributed to the development of the Responsible Tourism movement and to the ideas presented here. In a movement it is important that ideas are viral, that they are taken up and used, ownership is not as important as their application and the fruit they bear.

---

1   Free-rider meaning someone who uses public transport without paying the fare, they benefit at the cost of those who do pay. The free-rider problem is how to reduce or eliminate it.

Responsible Tourism is a broad movement. The priorities and issues are different in different destinations and originating markets. The idea is simple, the principles only a little less so and yet the application is often complex and difficult, requiring as it does action by a wide variety of stakeholders, often with divergent interests and priorities. The idea of sustainability began to emerge in the 1960s. The publication of Rachel Carson's *Silent Spring* in 1962 and the Club of Rome's *Limits to Growth* 10 years later caused controversy and made headlines in the Sunday papers, challenging as they did the scientific orthodoxy of the green revolution and the 19th- and 20th-century assumptions about the inevitability of human progress. The controversy continues. While, for some, awareness of the finite world leads them to place emphasis on the limits of growth, others, including many of those who remain unconvinced about the human contribution to climate change, are more sanguine about our ability as a species to solve the problems which we confront.

At the heart of sustainability is the idea of human life enduring. The concept is fundamentally anthropocentric; as a species we are very unlikely to destroy the earth, although we have the capacity to make it less habitable for ourselves and for other species. There is still no universally accepted definition of sustainability and certainly not one that can be used to measure our global performance. Global definitions are bound to be inadequate: the issues and the remedies are local, and there is no choice but to 'dig where you stand'. The Brundtland Commission defined sustainable development as, "development that meets the needs of the present without compromising the ability of future generations to meet their own needs." This definition is profoundly unsatisfactory as it defines neither these 'needs', nor the constraints which might compromise the ability of our descendants to meet their own needs and which would preclude their sustainable development. To take but two examples: airlines are prone to being unreasonably optimistic about magic fuels which will dramatically reduce carbon emissions from flights and allow them to continue to grow; and environmentalists often ignore the importance of development to the world's poor and the developing countries in which they live. The Earth Summit in Rio in 1992 was about environment and development. The United Nations objective is sustainable development, not merely a green agenda.

At the heart of the problem of sustainability is its complexity. There is a triple bottom line: the challenge is economic, social and environmental. Yet we are still unable to define sustainability in a way that secures its attainment. There has been a widespread failure to accept responsibility for achieving sustainability. It has been all too easy for businesses, environmentalists, governments, all of us, to expect others to deal with it, to expect others to make sacrifices so that we can continue irresponsibly with our lives and our unsustainable patterns of consumption. Responsible Tourism emerged as a way of addressing this challenge. It poses the question: 'How can all forms of tourism be made more sustainable?' Its ambition is to tackle the mainstream: to engage tourists and to encourage them to change the way they travel; to engage the industry to encourage them to make sustainability part of the way they do business, to take responsibility and to mainstream sustainability into their business models, to challenge government to do what only it can.

My purpose in writing this book is to look at what has been done, to argue the case that some progress has been made and to encourage you to do more. There is much more to be done and it needs to be done faster. In the wake of Copenhagen and our seeming inability to even begin to meet the challenge of the 'perfect storm' of climate change, peak oil, water shortages, food shortages and population growth – in short, our failure as a species to come to terms with the finite world, the spaceship,[2] on which we live – this is an account of efforts to address sustainability by encouraging consumers and producers to make changes and to take responsibility. Travelling in the Indus Valley and on the coast of northern Peru, where evidently great civilisations perished almost without trace,[3] it is difficult to escape the realisation that these civilisations too believed that they would endure and that they were wrong. I used to ponder how it was that the last tree was cut down on Easter Island; over the last ten years I have begun to understand. Individuals pursued their own self-interest, felling those trees to make a canoe, which, in a finite world like Easter Island, culminates in the destruction of the environment upon which their survival depended. This is also our situation. The 'tragedy of the commons' is a very human tragedy.

The work I will describe is only a beginning. Change does not come through top-down prescription. It comes when individuals work with others to identify local problems and priorities, and develop solutions which deliver in particular places. I hope that the experiences shared here will inspire you

2   Buckminster Fuller published an *Operating Manual for Spaceship Earth* in 1969.

3   'All civilisations, so far, have decayed and died, however magnificent they have been in their glory, however difficult it is to believe that they can vanish and be replaced by desert or jungle" Zeldin 1998: 47–48. Fernandez-Armesto argues that all civilisations have in common: 'their programmes for the systematic refashioning of nature' (2000:18). In that perhaps is the seed of their demise. Will our industrial civilisation be different?

to engage and to make your contribution. Tackling tourism's polluting effects, and its dependence on fossil fuels are the major challenges, but there are others too. There is so much more to do and we are running out of time.

Responsible Tourism originated in the work of Jost Krippendorf who, in his seminal text, *The Holiday Makers*, called for 'rebellious tourists and rebellious locals'. Will you heed the call? Will you be part of the solution or remain part of the problem, irresponsibly exacerbating it?

Harold Goodwin
Faversham, March 2011

Dedicated to the memory of
Jost Krippendorf
who understood the significance of responsibility
and called for
'rebellious tourists and rebellious locals'.

Acknowledgements

The ideas and arguments presented here have been voiced and honed, provoked and informed by discussions and arguments with owners, managers and workers in tourism businesses in many countries in the developing and developed world, with communities affected by tourism, with policy makers and government officials, with ICRT associates and students, colleagues and friends too numerous to mention. Many people have contributed to the development of the ideas presented here; some may hear the echoes, others may not realise the contribution they have made. To learn through teaching engaged and experienced students is a privilege.

A small number of friends and colleagues have read all the chapters and found weaknesses and errors which they have generously spent time giving advice on strengthening and correcting: Justin Francis, Richard Hearn, Max Leonard, Kate Stefanko, John de Vial, and Caroline Warburton. Others have read parts and provided valuable criticism or evidence: Titus Alexander, Jane Ashton, Jo Baddeley, Manda Brookman, Xavier Font, Jason Freezer, Sallie Grayson, Nicole Haeusler, Ruth Holroyd, Heidi Keyser, Kylie McCabe, Sean Owen, Andreas Walmsley and Alison White. The responsibility for any weaknesses of argument or errors of fact is mine alone.

Finally I would like to thank Tim Goodfellow and Sally North who are as passionate as I am, to communicate these ideas. Goodfellow is a 21st-century publisher.

There is a website associated with this book where you will find further resources and a forum for discussion and debate. Find it at:

www.takingresponsibilityfortourism.info

Abbreviations and acronyms

ABTA   Association of British Travel Agents (The Travel Association)

AITO   Association of Independent Tour Operators

ATOL   Air Travel Organiser's Licence

BBBEE   Broad-Based Black Economic Empowerment

CBT   Community-Based Tourism

CITES   Convention on International Trade in Endangered Species

DCMS   Department for Culture, Media and Sport, UK

DEAT   Department for Environmental Affairs and Tourism

DFID   Department for International Development

ECPAT   End Child Prostitution, Child Pornography and the Trafficking of Children for Sexual Purposes

IHG   Intercontinental Hotels Group

ICRT   International Centre for Responsible Tourism

IPCC   International Panel on Climate Change

IUCN   International Union for the Conservation of Nature

LOST   Local Option Sales Tax

NTB   National Tourist Board

TALC   Tourism Area Life Cycle

SNV   Netherlands Development Organisation

TOMM   Tourism Optimisation Management Model

TSA   Tourism Satellite Account

UNEP   United Nations Environment Programme

UNWTO United Nations World Tourism Organization

VSO   Voluntary Service Overseas

WCED   World Commission on Environment and Development (the Brundtland Commission)

WEF   World Economic Forum

WMO   World Meteorological Organization

WTO   World Tourism Organization

WTTC   World Travel and Tourism Council

WWF   World Wide Fund for Nature

Part 1
Why Responsible Tourism?

Ah but a man's reach should exceed his grasp,
Or what's a heaven for?

    Robert Browning

Tourism is inherently neither good nor bad – though the word 'tourist' has a pejorative edge to it and most of us would rather see ourselves as travellers or visitors.[1] Tourism is used to describe both the human activity, the experience, and the services which facilitate it. And tourism is what we make of it – individually and collectively, as businesses and as tourists. In buying a tourism experience, whether as a package or constructing it ourselves, we purchase accommodation, transport and activities which allow us to experience another place. Then there are the consumer goods: accommodation, food and beverage, entertainment, souvenirs, entrance fees, guiding and a wide range of other goods and services. Responsible Tourism is one response to the challenge of sustainability for a particular area of consumption; it is about taking responsibility for making the consumption and production of tourism more sustainable.

Responsible Tourism is in principle inherently optimistic: at its heart, the imperative to make tourism better. This is not about a niche. All forms of tourism can be better and more responsible if we, individually and collectively, take responsibility. The converse of Responsible Tourism is irresponsible tourism. Most of us do not wish to be, or be thought of as being, irresponsible. Some will counter that to advocate Responsible Tourism is to be a killjoy, a naysayer, that urging people to behave responsibly when they seek irresponsible self-indulgence is elitist and unlikely to be successful. As we shall see the evidence does not support that generalisation. It is of course, partially true: there is plenty of irresponsibility to work on. There is a substantial critique

---

1   'I am a traveller. You are a visitor. They are tourists.' Quoted by Adrian Phillips in his foreword to Ceballos-Lascurain (1996): xi

of tourism as a form of unsustainable, inequitable and exploitative consumption, a plague.[2] We shall return to this critique. Useful as it is in pointing to the issues, it tells us little about how to address the specific problems associated with tourism in particular places other than to suggest that it should cease. In many small-island developing states and least-developed countries there are few, if any, alternatives to tourism, their only viable export sector. The argument that tourism should cease raises the questions of how it might be stopped, and what would be the impacts on local livelihoods if it were.

As prosperity spreads there is a growth in expenditure on leisure and recreation; domestic and outbound tourism has been growing very rapidly in the tiger economies of the Pacific Rim, and more recently in China and India. Since the fall of the wall in 1989 we have seen significant changes in mass tourism flows from Russia and Eastern Europe. Tourism is no longer a phenomenon of the developed countries of the North. Britain used to be a very significant source market for Kerala in southern India, by 2009 Kerala had just over 100,000 UK visitors and around 7.5 million domestic tourists. Both the scale and the composition of tourism are changing rapidly.

The idea of Responsible Tourism has at its core an imperative to take responsibility, to take action; consumers, suppliers and governments all have responsibilities. The ambition of Responsible Tourism is to address the impacts of mainstream tourism, to enhance the positive and to reduce the negative, recognising that in the destination it can be very difficult to tell apart the mass and ecotourists; that it is particular impacts which need to be managed and accepting that part of the challenge is to enable destinations to cope with the numbers of people who are likely to continue to arrive.

In Part I we look at what Responsible Tourism is, at the market and the business case and at what it means in destinations. The first chapter is about the challenge and about the context in which we as travellers should change the way we travel and take our holidays. And, because tourism is an industry, it is about us as individuals changing the way we run the businesses we work for. The second chapter describes the emergence of the Responsible Tourism movement in the UK, looks at the role of the consumer and at market-based approaches to securing change. The third chapter explores the business case for engagement, addressing the issue of whether or not Responsible Tourism makes business sense. The fourth looks at how a Responsible Tourism

---

2   Wheeller (1992); Boissevain (1996); Broham (1996); Diamond (1977); Wall and Mathieson (2006)

approach can be used in destinations, in the words of the Cape Town Declaration, to 'create better places for people to live in and for people to visit.'[3]

In Part II we look at the three elements – social, economic and environmental – of sustainability. John Elkington coined the term 'triple bottom line' in 1998 to refer to the economic, social and environmental sustainability of a business, providing a convenient shorthand for those wishing to challenge approaches to sustainability which are narrowly environmental. Its utility has ensured its dissemination. The fifth chapter addresses social responsibility: heritage and authenticity; the host-guest encounter; hedonism; and giving back through philanthropy and volunteering. Chapter 6 explores some of the issues of economic responsibility, and looks in particular at all-inclusives, oversupply, community-based tourism and poverty reduction though tourism. Chapter 7 turns to the environmental issues and measures the scale of the challenge – including greening businesses, responsible aviation and two cul-de-sacs: ecotourism and certification.

The book concludes with some reflections on the Responsible Tourism movement and the ethic of responsibility. Finally, it suggests an agenda for change.

One last note. I have capitalised the phrase 'Responsible Tourism', throughout, to help denote its status as a movement. I hope this makes sense to the reader.

---

3   Cape Town Declaration (2002) www.responsibletourismpartnership.org/
    CapeTown.html

References

Boissevain, J. (ed.) (1996) *Coping with Tourists: European Reactions to Mass Tourism*, Oxford: Berghahn.

Broham, J. (1996) 'New directions in tourism for Third World development', *Annals of Tourism Research*, **23**, 48–70.

Cape Town Conference (International Conference on Responsible Tourism in Destinations – ICRT) (2002) *Cape Town Declaration*, Cape Town: ICRT and Western Cape Tourism.

Ceballos-Lascurain, H. (1996) *Tourism, Ecotourism and Protected Areas: the State of Nature-based Tourism around the World and Guidelines for its Development*, Gland, Switzerland: IUCN.

Diamond, J. (1977) 'Tourism's role in economic development: the case re-examined', *Economic Development and Cultural Change*, **25** (30), 539–553.

Elkington, J. (1997) *Cannibals with Forks: Triple Bottom Line of 21st Century Business*, Oxford: Capstone.

Wall, G. and Mathieson, A. (2006) *Tourism Change, Impacts and Opportunities*, Harlow: Pearson.

1   What is Responsible Tourism?

Tourism is like a fire, you can cook your food on it, or it can burn your house down.

> *Asian proverb*

Tourism is a human activity, albeit with consequences for the natural world. Tourism businesses, governments and tourists make choices every day which shape the social phenomenon of tourism – it does not have to be the way it is. We can change it. As Jost Krippendorf pointed out in his seminal work, *The Holiday Makers*, 'every individual tourist builds up or destroys human values while travelling'.[1] We all make choices about how we travel. Responsible Tourism is about taking responsibility and recognising that tourism is what we make of it. We can use Responsible Tourism to enhance the experience, to make it more real and authentic. The Responsible Tourism approach works best when it engages the consumer, enabling the traveller, the holidaymaker, to have a better experience, and the community to have tourism on their terms.

Tourism is not a new phenomenon. It continues to evolve, shaped by economic development and technological change. Now often referred to erroneously[2] as the world's largest industry, it has some specific advantages but poses particular sustainability challenges. Issues of irresponsibility and the challenges of sustainable development are not new, nor are they specific to tourism. This chapter begins with a broad discussion of tourism, and then considers whether sustainable development is an oxymoron. The 'tragedy of the commons' has received some attention in tourism literature; it is explored further here, framing the distinction between individual and collective responsibility, and emphasising the necessity for regulation. After an introduction to Krippendorf and the development of Responsible Tourism, the chapter concludes by addressing some of the myths about responsible and alternative forms of tourism.

---

1   Krippendorf (1987): 109
2   See below p. 9, 129-30

Tourism

Tourism takes place in destinations, in the places where tourists interact with the people who live and work there. It is a social experience for the visited and the visitors, an interaction often characterised by substantial inequality. The tourists are at leisure, away from home, eating out, on holiday, indulging themselves, generally spending and consuming more each day than they would at home. Yet we take our holidays in other people's places, other people's homes.[3] The local resident or worker encounters tourists as customers, or crowding streets and squares, museums and public transport, or in and around their church or temple. They may be welcome as customers but they are often 'in the way'. In this sense they can be compared to weeds: plants which, however attractive are in the wrong place, and therefore seen as undesirable or troublesome. Tourists of whatever nationality often strike us as being different from the people we meet when we visit them, when we are the tourists in their place. At the heart of the subject of tourism is the tourist.

It is relatively simple to define a tourist as someone who is 'travelling to and staying in places outside their usual environment', and the United Nations definition describes a tourist as someone staying somewhere else for at least one night.[4] However, the diverse demographics of tourists and the diversity of their motivations for travel: leisure, recreation, holidays, business meeting, conferences, scientific study, pilgrimage, health treatment, account for the complexity of the phenomenon. A complexity compounded by their impacts on the people and places they visit. We simplify when we think about tourists and tourism, but we need to be wary of the consequences of that simplification: Tourism is not only about international visitors, domestic tourism is important too. Tourism includes people staying with friends and relatives, camping, caravanning, staying in hotels, apartments, guest houses and sleeping on the beach – tourism occurs when we stay overnight in someone else's place. In the museum or on the beach, day excursionists may be indistinguishable from tourists, but they do not stay overnight.

When we study tourism, then, we study how we behave when we are away from home, the services which meet our needs as tourists for accom-

---

3   The UK NGO, Tourism Concern's campaign 'Our Holidays, Their Homes' established the point.

4   This is the definition used by the UN World Tourism Organization – it involves a stay of at least 24 hours and a maximum duration of one year. 'Tourism' is used more broadly to include the activities of tourists, 'overnight visitors', and 'same-day visitors'.

modation, board and activities and the impacts of our activities as tourists on those who live and work in the places we visit, on their natural and cultural heritage, on their economy and on the environment. This is why the study of the phenomenon of tourism is challenging – it is complex and requires an interdisciplinary approach.

Tourism has been a pervasive influence in our world, in the originating markets and in destinations. The growth in travel and tourism relies upon the availability of funded leisure time and improvements in transport. There have been travellers of one sort or another for millennia – soldiers, sailors, scientists, traders, pilgrims – but travel for leisure and pleasure, the popular experience of tourism, is a relatively recent mass phenomenon, largely a consequence of raised standards of living and improvements in transport which resulted from the Industrial Revolution and the burning of fossil fuels. The growth of tourism is a consequence of increasing prosperity first in Europe, in the countries of the North, and increasingly in the richer countries of the South.

There has been dramatic growth since the Second World War. Particular changes in the economy and in society have facilitated the growth of the mass tourism sector – a new and defining part of the modern consumer world. 'Travel' comes from the Middle English '*travail*' originally meaning to engage in painful effort. In the medieval period it was used to refer to journeying through a country. In 1556 'traveller' was used to refer to someone who had travelled abroad, a significantly more onerous challenge then than it is now – although the queues at airport check-ins and security lead to reflection about how short was the golden age of relatively stress-free travel, if it ever existed. The respect associated with the Arabic term 'Haji', used to refer to someone who has made the pilgrimage to Mecca, and 'pilgrim', when used to refer to people who travel to a sacred place as an act of religious devotion, differentiates this kind of devotional *travail* from leisure tourism.[5]

The services which accommodated traders, pilgrims and travellers – originally caravanserai, inns, monastery guest-houses and hospitals[6] – have evolved into the diversity of tourist accommodation that we have today. 'Hotel' comes from the French '*hôtel*', a town house which frequently hosted guests; paying guests stayed in guest houses. These facilities grew to accommodate tourists. The word 'tour' derives from the Greek '*tornos*' (lathe), hence the strong con-

---

5   The Saudis in particular, insist that the Haj is not tourism, tourism being associated with discretionary, indulgent, leisure travel.

6   Meaning a place of shelter and rest for travellers, this usage is now obsolete. The root of our contemporary word for the hospitality industry.

notation of travelling circuitously to return to where the journey began. Those with the time and money took the 'Grand Tour'[7] in the 18th century, justified as educational in purpose. As Withey has pointed out, the Grand Tour was largely a British invention because, in the 18th century, its elite had leisure and money enough to travel.[8] Young men explored the continent in order to become part of the elite and fashionable society. This conspicuous consumption also created opportunity for uninhibited indulgence in leisure and 'the pleasures of the flesh'.[9] By the end of the 18th century British consuls as far east as Dresden and Vienna were reporting on the inundation of tourists: 'the rage for travelling' had reached 'an amazing pitch of folly'.[10] The concern about irresponsible behaviour and licentiousness associated with travel is not new and not restricted to international travel – consider the role of Blackpool and Brighton for generations of British domestic tourists and reflected in the adage, 'What happens in Vegas, stays in Vegas.'

It was not the Industrial Revolution, then, that invented the anxieties associated with travelling, though it did create the conditions necessary for mass tourism: increased prosperity and leisure for labouring people, and more reliable and affordable transport, thanks to steam. Upper class men who travelled in the 18th century did not hold jobs from which they might be fired if their return was delayed; but when the working classes began to travel they needed to be able to travel cheaply, rapidly and reliably. The coming of the railways, and the annual holidays which came with trade union organisation and industrialisation, created the conditions necessary for the development of seaside resorts. Places that had served the requirements of the wealthy travelling by coach to a spa, to take the sea air or to bathe in sea water for medicinal purposes, evolved to provide recreation and entertainment for the masses. Thomas Cook organised the first mass tour in 1841, taking 570 people by rail for the day from Leicester to Loughborough. By 1855 Cook was organising tours to Europe; by 1869 to Egypt.

In both historical and current popular usage, tourism is clearly perceived as primarily leisure, a recreational activity characterised by indulgence with frivolous overtones; a connotation which still bedevils the study of tourism and attitudes to it. The word 'tourist' was first used in 1800 to refer to a person

---

7   Thomas Nugent's Grand Tour was first published in 1749

8   Withey (1997): 6–7

9   Withey (1997): 8

10   Withey (1997): 6

travelling for recreation, for pleasure or culture, visiting a number of places of interest. In popular usage a tourist travels on holiday, a concept which comes from 'holy day', a day on which work was suspended. As early as 1440 it was being used to mean 'suited only for a holiday; dainty idle, trifling.'[11] Thus tourism is frivolous and irresponsible, to be distinguished from the religious act of pilgrimage.

The tourism industry is demand led. Greater disposable income, leisure[12] and cheaper reliable transport, from the steam engine to the jet aeroplane, created the demand that then generated supply in the destinations.[13] There has been a rapid growth in all three, particularly since the 1950s. Its growth has depended upon fossil fuels. A decline in prosperity, in effective discretionary spend, reductions in holiday entitlements or an increase in the costs of travel, whether through congestion, the impacts of rising costs or regulatory efforts to reduce greenhouse gas emissions, could reduce the volume of tourism from particular source markets or globally. Continued rapid growth is not inevitable.

For now tourism is often described as the world's largest industry. This claim is based on extensive work by the World Travel and Tourism Council,[14] an association of around a hundred leaders of the world's largest travel and tourism companies. Its estimate is that the economic importance of the industry at close to 10% of global GDP.[15] The term 'industry' is generally used either to describe an attitude to work (diligence, assiduity, energy) or the commercial production and sale of goods and more recently services (for example, the steel or film industries). These industries are defined by the product; tourism is defined by the consumer. Tourism is what tourists buy; as an economic activity it is not tourism until it is sold.

The term 'tourism' is thus used to describe a set of experiences and activities enjoyed by tourists; the market created by tourists for goods and services;

---

11 *Shorter Oxford English Dictionary*, 1983

12 Contiguous blocks of planned leisure time which enable the planning and booking of a holiday not unplanned leisure or idleness

13 For foreign travel purchased in another currency exchange rate changes can have significant effects on patterns of holiday making.

14 www.wttc.org. Established in 1990 to counter the view that the industry was frivolous or non-essential, it achieved its target membership of 100 in 1997 and established Tourism Satellite Accounting, which was recognised by the United Nations at the World Conference on the Measurement of the Economic Impact of Tourism.

15 9.2% www.wttc.org, accessed 24 August 2010, the WTTC is now referring to tourism as one of the world's largest industries.

the organisations and businesses that meet the needs of tourists. Not all of those involved in providing goods and services for tourists, and whose economic value is included in satellite accounts, will see themselves as part of the tourism industry: think for example of train and taxi drivers, bakers, newsagents, horticulturalists and museum curators.

Tourism has a number of advantages for local economic development (explored in Chapter 6). For the tourist, tourism is about experiencing other people's places, environments and cultures, but tourism is primarily a traded activity, like any other. As a business, tourism is about selling goods and services to tourists. Tourists and day excursionists constitute the visitor economy, an addition to the resident and commuting population, and an additional market for a broad range of local goods and services. Tourism can bring relatively wealthy consumers to marginal and economically poor areas, providing an opportunity for local economic development in areas where there is no other opportunity for the community to move beyond subsistence.

One of the advantages of tourism as an economic activity is that the consumers travel to the factory to consume the product: the day excursionist comes to visit; the tourist to stay for a few nights. If a village has a lodge, the end consumer travels to the lodge and there are opportunities for the local community to make sales to the tourists. If there is only, for example, a shoe factory in the village, there are very few visitors and very limited opportunities for the sale of farm produce, meals, crafts and souvenirs; the market does not come to the village. Of course, if you have a shoe factory and a lodge, guests may buy the shoes, as they buy carpets in Nepal and pottery in Staffordshire.

Even on a micro level, lodges and shoe factories both have positive and negative impacts on the village. The balance of positive and negative impacts will vary from place to place, a consequence of the interaction between visitors and locals, their cultures, the forms of tourism and the environment in which it takes place. If we accept that the tourism sector is indeed one of the world's largest industries – one in which the social and economic challenges of the lodges and shoe factories are played out globally a million times over, and with an additional set of environmental problems – it cannot expect not to be challenged on its sustainability.

And that means that we, all of us, are being challenged. The choices we make, as hosts, visitors, planners or academics shape tourism. This means that we can take responsibility for making a better form of tourism. We must, however, accept that what constitutes a 'better' form of tourism will vary from place to place and that it may well be contested. With the opportunity and ability comes the responsibility to change it: because we can make tourism better, we should. To begin to understand these challenges, we should first look at issues of sustainability and development as they relate to tourism.

Sustainable Development: an oxymoron?

Bluntly, sustainability is a challenge for us as a species. If we do not individually and collectively modify our behaviour, whether we are at work or play, we will contribute to keeping billions of people in poverty and imperil humanity's survival. Tourism poses some particular environmental, social and economic sustainability issues because of our travel choices and our interactions with the people we encounter. When we travel to stay in other people's places, for their culture and environment or simply to enjoy their sunshine, we travel where the experiences we seek are produced. Production and consumption take place in the destination where tourists, locals and workers meet. Holidaymakers and travellers may not notice the conditions under which their experience is created but there is a greater chance, and an opportunity, to realise the environmental impacts and labour conditions of the workers they encounter, to be aware of the impacts, positive and negative, of their holiday. They may also experience a heightened level of concern because of the disparity in living conditions, the inequality, between those employed in the industry, encountered in the streets and themselves – with leisure and wealth to expend on travel.

The UN's concern about man's impact on the environment goes back at least 40 years, to its first major conference on the subject, the Conference on the Human Environment in 1972.[16] The Secretary-General of the conference, Maurice Strong, has said, 'the Conference was launching a new liberation movement to free men from the threat of their thraldom to environmental perils of their own making.' He went on to say that success was only possible, 'if there was a new commitment to liberation from the destructive forces of mass poverty, racial prejudice, economic injustice, and the technologies of modern warfare'.[17] Strong argued that 'the physical interdependence of all people required new dimensions of economic, social and political interde-

---

16 Report of the United Nations Conference on the Human Environment, Stockholm, June 1972 accessible at www.un-documents.net/aphe-b5.htm

17 Strong (1972): para 34.

pendence'[18] and that 'developing countries could ill afford to put uncertain future needs ahead of their immediate needs for food, shelter, work, education and health care.'[19] 'No growth' was not an option. The problem was 'how to reconcile … legitimate immediate requirements with the interests of generations yet unborn.'[20]

Strong foresaw the issues of inter-generational and intra-generational equity and recognised that the challenge of managing the human environment would require 'new concepts of sovereignty, based not on the surrender of national sovereignties but on better means of exercising them collectively, and with a greater sense of responsibility for the common good… [as well as] …new international means for better management of the world's common property resources'.[21] The problem of reconciling the maintenance of a healthy human environment with growth and development remains as intractable now as it was then. This is the problem we are yet to properly confront, let alone solve, though many have repeatedly tried to start a meaningful process. It is easy to be disheartened and suspect that 'sustainable development' is a contradiction in terms. Each of us, severally and collectively, will need to take responsibility, to respond to the multiple problems we confront, if we are to become sustainable.

The World Commission on Environment and Development (WCED) is more popularly known as the Brundtland Commission from the name of its chair, Gro Harlem Brundtland. The Commission was convened by the United Nations in 1983 to address growing concern 'about the accelerating deterioration of the human environment and natural resources and the consequences of that deterioration for economic and social development.'[22] By 1983, the UN had reached a consensus that the environmental problems confronting our species were global in nature and that long-term environmental strategies for achieving sustainable development were required. The solution to the problem of permitting development in a finite world was (and is) sustainable development.

The Brundtland Commission's report was published as *Our Common Future* in 1983. In her foreword, Brundtland pointed out that the period had

---

18 Strong (1972): para 35

19 Strong (1972): para 36

20 Strong (1972): para 36

21 Strong (1972): para 41 a and c

22 UN General Assembly 38th Session Resolution A/RES/38/161, 19 December 1983 accessible at http://www.un-documents.net/a38r161

been 'marked by a retreat from social concerns'[23] and that there had been 'a decade and a half of a standstill or even deterioration in global co-operation'.[24] When the terms of reference were being discussed in 1982, some had wanted the commission only to deal with the environment. Brundtland's critique of this position is trenchant and should not be forgotten:

> The environment does not exist as a sphere separate from
> human actions, ambitions, and needs, and attempts to defend
> it in isolation from human concerns have given the very word
> 'environment' a connotation of naivety in some political circles.
> … the 'environment' is where we all live; and 'development' is
> what we are all doing to improve our lot within that abode. The
> two are inseparable.[25]

It is indicative of how little progress has been made that Brundtland's recognition that '[m]any critical survival issues are related to uneven development, poverty, and population growth'[26] still sounds fresh. Her, and the WCED's, solution to the problem of 'poverty, inequality, and environmental degradation' was a 'new era of economic growth – growth that is forceful and at the same time socially and environmentally sustainable'.[27] The Brundtland solution was sustainable development and the commission was optimistic: 'Humanity has the ability to ensure that it meets the needs of the present without compromising the ability of future generations to meet their own needs.'[28] This aspirational definition may be an oxymoron, but Brundtland clearly revealed the political dimension and the issues of inter- and inter-generational equity in a finite world which continue to bedevil progress.

The United Nations Conference on Environment and Development (UNCED), informally known as the Earth Summit, took place in Rio in 1992 and recognised amongst other things that 'human beings are at the centre of concern for sustainable development' and that 'the right to development must be fulfilled so as to equitably meet developmental and environmental needs

---

23 WCED (1983): xi

24 WCED (1983): x

25 WCED (1983): xi

26 WCED (1983): xii

27 WCED (1983): xii

28 WCED (1983): 8. This thinking echoes the oft quoted 'We do not inherit the earth from your ancestors: you borrow it from your children' which is variously referenced to sources in a number of cultures.

of present and future generations'.[29] The United Nations Framework Convention on Climate Change was also agreed at the conference with the objective of stabilizing greenhouse gas concentrations in the atmosphere at a level that would prevent dangerous anthropogenic interference with the climate system but it lacked mandatory limits or enforcement mechanisms.[30]

The Earth Summit was important in linking the prevention of environmental degradation through our unsustainable use of it with the need to allow sustainable growth particularly to enable development out of poverty for a large part of the world's population. The contradiction between avoiding environmental degradation and reducing poverty through economic growth is resolved through sustainable development; the circle is squared by linking the carrying capacity of natural systems with development of human societies. The publication of *Limits to Growth*[31] in 1972 was controversial. It drew attention to the likely consequences of a growing world population in the context of finite resources. More recently has come concern about peak oil[32] and water.[33] There is increasing awareness of the challenge of achieving sustainable development in a finite world – and one with a rapidly growing population seeking a higher material standard of living. In the 1970s, sustainability was used to describe an economy in equilibrium with the environment.[34] We are a long way from achieving this, and the problem becomes more acute each year.

In 1992, the World Wildlife Fund (WWF – now the World Wide Fund for Nature) commissioned a discussion paper from Tourism Concern on sustainable tourism, which identified 10 key elements.[35] There were four prin-

---

29   Rio Declaration on Environment and Development, Principles 1 and 3 accessible at www.n.org/documents/ga/conf151/aconf15126-1annex1.htm. The right to development was proclaimed by the United Nations in 1986 in the 'Declaration on the Right to Development', which was adopted by the United Nations General Assembly resolution 41/128

30   In 1997, the Kyoto Protocol established legally binding obligations for developed countries to reduce their greenhouse gas emissions.

31   Meadows et al. (1972)

32   Hubbert (1956); Deffeyes (2006); Simmons (2000). I am aware that this is contested science but a precautionary approach would be prudent

33   Bell (2009) and Solomon (2010)

34   See for example Stivers (1976). This is also often described as a steady state economy, one constrained by the physical environmental limits to growth, see for example Boulding (1996). Hardy et al. (2002) produced a useful analysis of sustainable development and its application to tourism, arguing that sustainable tourism is a reactive concept, one which has 'largely been developed in reaction to prevailing economic theories and environmental problems' (p.90)

35   Eber (1992)

ciples (sustainable use of resources; reducing over-consumption and waste; maintaining diversity; supporting local communities) and six processes (integrating tourism into planning; involving local communities; consulting stakeholders and the public; training staff; marketing tourism responsibly; undertaking research). The agenda for the 21st century, *Agenda 21*, adopted at the Earth Summit, focused on sustainability actions appropriate to groups at international, national and local levels. The programme called on countries to 'promote, as appropriate, environmentally sound leisure and tourism activities', as well as 'the formulation of environmentally sound and culturally sensitive tourism programmes as a strategy for sustainable development of urban and rural settlements, and as a way of decentralizing urban development and reducing discrepancies among regions'.[36] Green Globe, a certification programme for tourism businesses, was established through *Agenda 21 for the Travel and Tourism Industry: Towards Environmentally Sustainable Development.*[37] It too identified areas for action including waste, energy, water, hazardous substances and transport. It also identified some approaches: land-use planning, design, partnerships, corporate social responsibility and involving staff, customers and communities. Green Globe's focus was almost exclusively on the environment rather than on development.

By the time tourism was considered at the Commission on Sustainable Development (the post-Rio process) at the United Nations in New York in 1999, Ministers of Tourism were reminding those present that Rio had been about environment *and* development. Subsequently the World Tourism Organization (WTO) launched its *Tourism and Poverty Alleviation* report at the World Summit on Sustainable Development in Johannesburg in 2002.[38]

In 1993, the WTO, now UNWTO,[39] defined sustainable tourism development very generally as meeting 'the needs of present tourists and host regions while protecting and enhancing opportunity for the future',[40] The WTO's definition was more technical by 2001 it was 'envisaged as 'leading to management of all resources in such a way that economic, social and aesthetic

36 United Nations Department of Economic and Social Affairs: §36.10 g 7.20 e

37 WTO and WTTC

38 Tourism and poverty reduction was endorsed by the United Nations at CSD 7(the seventh session of the Commission on Sustainable Development at the UN in New York 19–30 April 1999. www.un.org/esa/dsd/csd/csd_csd07.shtml) see below Chapter 6, 207-209.

39 The World Tourism Organization dates from 1970 though there were predecessors. It became a specialized agency of the UN in 2003 and from 1 December 2005 it was renamed the UNWTO. I have followed the convention of using the contemporary name in citing publications.

40 Sharpley (2000): 9–10

needs can be fulfilled while maintaining cultural integrity, essential ecological processes, biological diversity and life support systems'.[41] Their approach has been consistently 'triple bottom line' in its focus on economic, social and environmental sustainability.

The Lanzarote Declaration, a Charter for Sustainable Development, agreed by the World Conference on Sustainable Tourism in 1995, also addressed the issues with a firmly triple-bottom-line perspective; tourism development should be 'ecologically bearable in the long term, economically viable as well as ethically and socially equitable for the local communities'. The Lanzarote Declaration argued that the 'active contribution of tourism to sustainable development necessarily presupposes the solidarity, mutual respect, and participation of all the actors implicated in the process' and asserted that all 'options for tourism development must serve effectively to improve the quality of life of all people.'[42] The Responsible Tourism agenda is broader than the environmental and, in common with these early definitions of sustainable tourism, recognises the importance of cultural integrity, ethics, equity, solidarity and mutual respect placing quality of life at its core. The WTO recognised the importance of politics in its 2004 definition (see Box 1.1).

As the history demonstrates, it has long been recognised that environment and development are inseparable challenges. They are combined and magnified in the oxymoronic concept of sustainable development. Sustainable development lacks definition and measurable indicators to determine whether or not tourism is being successfully managed towards sustainability by government. Lip service is paid to the concept: it is used to generate work for consultants and NGOs, to bolster the reputation of companies and governments, but rarely are the outcomes measured or reported. We are not able to demonstrate whether tourism is becoming more or less sustainable, the concept is widely used but is difficult to determine whether the ideas are operative or inoperative.[43] The concept appears to be operative and is often used to secure resources and support, but in practice the principles are not applied, the concept is inoperative, the objectives are not achieved. It is left to someone else. Responsibility is not taken.

---

41   Quoted in Liu (2003): 460

42   Lanzarote Declaration 1–2.

43   Harris (1971): 49

Box 1.1: WTO Sustainable Development of Tourism

Sustainable tourism development guidelines and management practices are applicable to all forms of tourism in all types of destinations, including mass tourism and the various niche tourism segments. Sustainability principles refer to the environmental, economic and socio-cultural aspects of tourism development, and a suitable balance must be established between these three dimensions to guarantee its long-term sustainability.

Thus, sustainable tourism should:

1. Make optimal use of environmental resources that constitute a key element in tourism development, maintaining essential ecological processes and helping to conserve natural heritage and biodiversity.

2. Respect the socio-cultural authenticity of host communities, conserve their built and living cultural heritage and traditional values, and contribute to inter-cultural understanding and tolerance.

3. Ensure viable, long-term economic operations, providing socio-economic benefits to all stakeholders that are fairly distributed, including stable employment and income-earning opportunities and social services to host communities, and contributing to poverty alleviation.

Sustainable tourism development requires the informed participation of all relevant stakeholders, as well as strong political leadership to ensure wide participation and consensus building. Achieving sustainable tourism is a continuous process and it requires constant monitoring of impacts, introducing the necessary preventive and/or corrective measures whenever necessary.

Sustainable tourism should also maintain a high level of tourist satisfaction and ensure a meaningful experience to the tourists, raising their awareness about sustainability issues and promoting sustainable tourism practices amongst them.

Source: WTO 2004:7

Tourism may be unsustainable for many reasons, some of which are more easily addressed than others. Some can be resolved through individual decisions by consumers and producers, if sufficient individuals make the change. But some of the causes are more intractable. The world's population continues to grow rapidly and more of those individuals have time and financial resources to travel, at least for the foreseeable future.[44] Often suggestions to deal with fossil fuels by growing biofuels are adopted without thinking about the consequences for food production and water supply. There is a tendency to focus on one issue rather than to seek to address, in an integrated way, the major issues which confront us. Individual action by consumers and businesses can contribute, but such initiatives are vulnerable to freeloading, which undermines the efficacy of any individual contribution. The tourism sector's responsibility for addressing its contribution to anthropogenic climate change is given close attention in Chapter 7.

The Tragedy of the Commons

Close to Lake Koronia on the northern coast of Greece, the local mayor, over a good lunch, described at length to me what was on his mind. He was receiving increasing numbers of complaints from hoteliers and guest-house owners because of falling occupancy rates, lowering prices and revenues. The problem was an oversupply of beds. As I went to leave he invited me to see his new guest house in the process of being converted. He had correctly calculated that with his connections, and a modern newly decorated property with good facilities, he would capture enough of the market to have a profitable business. He would benefit to the detriment of all the other accommodation providers. Of course, in time, others will develop new rooms which will be to his detriment – the tragedy plays out in Greece and around the world.

Tourism is dogged by the 'tragedy of the commons', a phrase which describes how the individual pursuit of self-interest does not necessarily result in the common good, and, moreover, in a finite world may result in ruin for all. In an influential paper that appeared in the journal *Science* in 1968, Garrett Hardin described how individuals who rationally and independently pursue their own self-interest will ultimately deplete and degrade a shared limited resource even though this is not in the long-term interest of the group or society.

As Hardin writes:

Therein is the tragedy. Each man is locked into a system that compels him to increase his herd without limit – in a world that is limited. Ruin is the destination toward which all men rush, each pursuing

---

44 The 'perfect storm' which we confront as a species in a finite world is likely to begin to restrict growth later this century.

his own best interest in a society that believes in the freedom of the commons.[45]

Writing more than a decade before Hardin, Gordon described the same issue in the context of fishing:

> There appears … to be some truth in the conservative dictum that everybody's property is nobody's property. Wealth that is free for all is valued by no one because he who is foolhardy enough to wait for its proper time of use will only find that it has been taken by another. The fish in the sea are valueless to the fisherman, because there is no assurance that they will be there for him tomorrow if they are left behind today.[46]

This is an elegant description of the problem of common pool resources,[47] where the common pool resource is a fugitive, migratory, resource. In Hardin's view, it was a tragedy because overexploitation and ruin follow predictably from the rational behaviour of individuals pursuing their individual self-interest in an unregulated commons. Hardin's tragedy of the commons was developed to argue for restraint in the growth of population, but it is far more widely applicable. The tourist, like the fish, is a fugitive migratory resource. Hardin's view contradicts that of the economist Adam Smith, who believed that although a free market may appear unrestrained and chaotic, it is in fact self-regulating, and that the 'invisible hand' of the market ensures that individuals acting in their own self-interest benefit society as a whole.

> In spite of their natural selfishness and rapacity, though they mean only their own conveniency, though the sole end which they propose … be the gratification of their own vain and insatiable desires, they divide with the poor the produce of all their improvements. They are led by an invisible hand to make nearly the same distribution of the necessaries of life, which would have been made, had the earth been divided into equal portions among all its inhabitants, and thus without intending it, without knowing it, advance the interest of the

---

45 Hardin (1968): 1244

46 Gordon (1954): 124

47 Common pool resources, sometimes called common property resources, are those where users diminish the resource and the amount available for others, but where users cannot be excluded, this results in over use and an unwillingness by users to maintain them since they cannot be sure to capture the benefit. It is one of the roles of government to manage common pool resources. See Healy 1994 for a discussion of common property resources and tourism.

society.[48]

When Smith wrote in 1790 the world seemed a lot less finite than it is today. We now realise that precious commodities are in increasingly short supply. John Beddington, the UK government's chief scientific adviser, has identified the 'perfect storm' of food shortages, scarce water and insufficient energy resources, which threatens, in around 2030, to unleash public unrest, cross-border conflicts and mass migration as people flee from the worst-affected regions.[49] Tourism contributes towards this, and will not be immune to the consequences.

This is not a new problem. Hardin was writing about an issue which also concerned Aristotle: 'What is common to the greatest number has the least care bestowed upon it. Everyone thinks chiefly of his own, hardly at all of the common interest';[50] and William Foster Lloyd who, writing in the wake of the enclosure movement in England in 1833, developed a theory of the commons as a critique of Adam Smith, suggesting that improvident use of property owned in common was likely to lead to overgrazing, as individuals pursued their own short-term interest. We have known about the tragedy for a long time but continue to fail to take responsibility for it.

The tragedy of the commons is at the heart of Lord Marshall's[51] description of the tourism and travel industry as '…essentially the renting out for short-term lets of other people's environments, whether this is a coastline, a city, a mountain range, or a rainforest'.[52] These are all commons in the sense that they are open-access or common-pool resources, even though parts are sometimes privatised for tourism use. Tourism makes extensive use of common pool resources:[53] public and merit priced[54] spaces, streets, public squares, parks,

---

48   Smith (1759 6th edition 1790): 350

49   John Beddington. Speech to UK Sustainable Development 2009 conference, 18 March 2009. BBC: http://news.bbc.co.uk/1/hi/uk/7951838.stm. The Guardian: http://www.guardian.co.uk/science/2009/mar/18/perfect-storm-john-beddington-energy-food-climate

50   Aristotle: Book II Chap 3

51   Chair of British Airways speaking at the first Tourism for Tomorrow Awards in 1994

52   Quoted in Goodwin (2002): 17. The next sentence, the enlightened self-interest case for business engagement with the sustainability of tourism is more often quoted: 'These "products" must be kept fresh and unsullied not just for the next day, but for every tomorrow.'

53   See Briassoulis (2002) who concludes that 'tourism commons… the collection of all tangible and intangible resources … are identical to the tourist product.' (pp. 1081–1082)

54   Merit goods are those that a society judges should be available on the basis of need or in the public interest made freely available and which are priced, for social reasons, below cost or market value.

museums and galleries and yet pays no user fees for that public space. As Galbraith pointed out in *The Affluent Society*, first published in 1958, in communities where public services fail to 'keep abreast of private consumption', an 'atmosphere of private opulence and public squalor results...'.[55] Freeloading contributes to the destruction of public space and environment, an issue which we focus on in Chapter 4 when we look at destinations.

Dawes demonstrated how difficult it is for rational individuals to co-operate, and developed the theory of the 'Prisoner's Dilemma', which explores the difficulties that prevented prisoners trusting each other enough to co-operate in the common interest.[56] In *The Logic of Collective Action*, Mancur Olson Jr challenged the presumption that the potential benefit of collective action would naturally lead individuals to co-operate. He wrote: '...unless the number of individuals is quite small, or unless there is coercion or some other special device to make individuals act in their common interest, *rational, self-interested individuals will not act to achieve their common or group interests*'[57] (emphasis in original).

At the heart of the tragedy of the commons, the Prisoner's Dilemma and the logic of collective action is the free-rider or freeloader problem. 'Whenever one person cannot be excluded from the benefits that others provide, each person is motivated not to contribute to the joint effort, but to free ride on the efforts of others.'[58]

There are broadly three approaches to managing the tragedy of the commons: Leviathan, privatisation or collective belief systems. In traditional pre-capitalist systems tribal custom dictated who could hunt, where and in what season; and often dictated that the kill would be shared by the whole community. This form of regulation largely relied on a shared value system enforced by the chief. These 'collective belief' systems worked when populations were small and there was local governance, and before there was a market for ivory and bush meat, and the ready availability of the AK47. The conditions necessary for this form of control are rare today.[59] The Leviathan approach takes its name from Thomas Hobbes' *Leviathan,*and looks to a regulatory framework

---

55 Galbraith (1958): 191, this is most often quoted as 'private affluence and public squalor'

56 The Prisoner's Dilemma was originally framed in 1950 by Merrill Flood and Melvin Dresher, then working at RAND.

57 Olson (1965): 2

58 Ostrom (1990): 6

59 Ostrom(1990): 19 documents one such example in a fishery in Alanya, Turkey drawing on Berkes.

enforced by a strong ruler. The privatisation approach assumes that private ownership will ensure the conservation of what is no longer a common good. It relies on Leviathan for the creation and maintenance of property rights: 'the institution of private property coupled with legal inheritance'.[60] Private ownership of resources enables their allocation through the market; access is controlled and rationed through user fees, and the sale of resources and reinvestment in the resource to maintain its value. There are positive examples, such as the purchasing of large blocks of land in Africa, habitat restoration and species reintroduction and the maintenance of the resource through tourism.[61] Yet sustainability does not necessarily result. The obvious degeneration of seaside resorts in Britain and Spain and the felling of Brazilian rainforest to create palm oil plantations are examples of failure.

How does this apply to tourism? As Lord Marshall tacitly acknowledged and Holden argued in 2005, tourism is dependent upon resources – natural resources and public places in particular – which share the characteristics of open-access, common pool[62] or common property resources.[63] Healy has argued that the inability to control the use of common property resources and the absence of resource protection undermines any incentive to reinvest in the nature reserve or public space, because of the free-rider problem. Tourism landscapes are, Healy argues, subject to over-use, and to the 'investment incentive' problems: why invest in maintaining the environment if you cannot ensure that the free-riders do not gain the advantage of your investment?[64]

The most intractable open access challenge confronting the travel and tourism industry is greenhouse gas emissions. As the world's population and the international economy grow, so does the demand for aviation, one of the principal contributors. On a prosaic level, we have all experienced the tragedy of the commons, often as farce, at the luggage carousel in the arrivals hall, where individuals seek advantage by crossing the yellow line, crowding the carousel to grab their bags – at the expense of the group and their own ability to get their bags on to a trolley. Tour operators continue to organise trips, and tourists continue to visit, destinations like Venice, Prague, Machu Picchu

---

60   Hardin (1968): 1247

61   By companies like &Beyond, formerly CC Africa, and Great Plains Conservation.

62   Common pool resources are very similar to common property resources and here I am using common pool to include both.

63   Holden (2005): 340

64   Healy (1994): 597 There is little or no motive for investment if the benefit goes to all and the investor gains no advantage from it.

and the Peak District despite the congestion. The individual benefit to them of visiting outweighs any discomfort they may experience from congestion. Congestion is always caused by others.

In Peru, the Cuzco Chamber of Commerce claims that 90% of Peru's tourism revenue comes from the region, its magnet being Machu Picchu.[65] Hoteliers understandably seek to develop properties there, capturing individual benefit to the detriment of the group, just as we saw in Greece. But in Cuzco there is a further twist. Cuzco dominates the industry to such an extent that the hoteliers and tour operators are able to persuade government to continue to invest in marketing tourism to the south of Peru to the detriment of the development of tourism in the north. The north has a greater diversity of archaeological sites, including the potentially iconic treasures of Chachapoyas and Kuelap. The national tourism development strategy is being distorted by pressure on government to assist in remedying a tragedy of the commons – with a marketing campaign which only encourages more investment in hotel beds. The tragedy deepens, or turns into farce, depending on your point of view. In the Galapagos, as at Cuzco, individual self-interest in increasing visitor numbers is reinforced by government policy that seeks to promote the same and relies on existing honey pots to achieve this.[66]

How then to address the tragedy of the commons? How is tourism to be made more sustainable? Whose responsibility is it?

Krippendorf's legacy

Jost Krippendorf, more than anyone else, has promoted the ethic of responsibility in tourism. His work informed the approach taken in the UK to developing Responsible Tourism, and his influence is also evident in the South African national policy. Krippendorf was motivated by the negative cultural and environmental damage that the post-war tourism boom had inflicted on his native Switzerland in the 1950s and 1960s: right from its inception, Responsible Tourism has not solely been concerned with the developing world. In 1975 Krippendorf published, *Die Landschaftsfresser: Tourismus und Erholungslandschaft, Verderben oder Segen?* [*The Landscape Eaters*]. In 1982 he argued: 'ecology should be placed before economy in tourism, not least for the sake of the economy itself and all who participate in it.' This was an early

---

65 http://news.bbc.co.uk/1/hi/world/americas/8598154.stm accessed 3 April 2010
66 Fennell (2006): 205

assertion of the importance of business taking responsibility for the sustainability of tourism.[67]

Krippendorf was a professor of the theory and politics of tourism; he placed tourism in the broader context of consumer aspirations and of leisure in modern societies. His most influential work was first published in German as *Die Ferienmenschen: Fur ein neues Verständnis von Freizeit und Reisen* in 1984, and as *The Holiday Makers* in English in 1987.[68] Krippendorf's articulation of the importance of the ethic of responsibility set him apart from others who articulated the case for sustainable tourism. He was controversial and he was often attacked. His standard reply, according to Bernard Lane, was: 'We are damned to have the duty to be far-sighted, critical and unpopular.' However, in Lane's words too, by 2003: 'Krippendorf's vision of more sustainable and fair forms of tourism [are] now a worldwide and established paradigm'.[69] This is an optimistic assessment, but it is certainly the case that Krippendorf established a new paradigm; yet there is a long way to go to see it widely implemented.

Krippendorf understood that the holidaymaker is at the core of tourism, essential to its sustainability. A quote from the Roman philosopher Seneca prefaces *The Holiday Makers*, to reminding us that when we travel we take our selves with us: 'You need a change of soul rather than a change of climate. You must lay aside the burdens of the mind; until you do this, no place will satisfy you.'[70] Krippendorf puts this more pointedly '… when we go away we don't really leave our everyday lives behind, but take them with us rather like a passenger on the pillion seat.'[71] This is borne out by personal experience. As a tour leader I tired of hearing people discussing their garden, or the progress of their grandchildren in school, apparently oblivious to the Great Wall of China, the Hermitage or the Taj Mahal.

Krippendorf dedicates *The Holiday Makers* to 'all those who would like to think about their role as holidaymakers or about their task in the leisure and travel world of tomorrow'.[72] He dismisses those who see mass tourism as a plague[73] and makes clear that it is not his intention to abolish holidays

---

67 Krippendorf (1982): 148 he concluded with ten propositions for defensive tourism.

68 Reprinted in 1989, 1990, 1991,1992,1994, 1997, 1999 and 2002, it is now available as an e-book on Science Direct.

69 Lane, obituary in The Guardian.

70 Krippendorf (1987): xiii; Seneca, Epistle XXVIII, On Travel as a Cure for Discontent

71 Krippendorf (1987): 31

72 Krippendorf (1987): x–xi

73 Krippendorf (1987): xviii

and travel. He seeks rather to 'bring all of those involved as much benefit as possible, but not at the expense of other people or of the environment'.[74] Krippendorf is not anti-tourism.

The *Holiday Makers* begins with an analysis of life in modern industrialised societies and the role of leisure and travel. Part II looks at the holiday machine, the recreation cycle and contains reflections on travel as: recuperation and recreation; compensation and social integration; escape; communication; freedom and self-determination; self-realisation; and happiness. 'King Guest' wants 'to get the best of things, have fun, be pampered. Perhaps even play a role that would be impossible in everyday life.'[75] The holidaymaker engages in conspicuous consumption, displaying their relative wealth.[76] Holidaymaking has been commercialised as part of the recreation industry. In an echo of the tragedy of the commons, Krippendorf asserts that the 'primary interest' of the tour operator 'is the short term growth of their own business and not the long-term development of a well-balanced tourist trade'.[77]

He is also perceptive about the tourists themselves. As holidaymakers, they regard themselves as free to do as they please, to have a fling, to let off steam. 'Regardless of what other people may think about it. After all, we have paid for it. ... Responsibility is rejected, egoism rules.'[78] Yet he also points out that nobody had ever explained to tourists the consequences of their actions, or that the responsibility that is theirs. He argues that although tourists are the main protagonists they have been left out of the discussion about their tourism. 'To lay all blame at their door would be as wrong as denying their responsibility.'[79]

Among many other insights, Krippendorf identified the growth of adventure and experiential travel[80] and saw the opportunity which it presented. Applying Maslow's hierarchy of needs to tourism he argues that tourists are becoming more demanding and he foresaw the 'birth of a new travel culture', one in which tourists seek 'the satisfaction of social needs: contact with other people and self-realization through creative activities, knowledge and exploration'.

---

74 Krippendorf (1987): xxi

75 Krippendorf (1987): 29

76 A term originating in the work of Thorstein Veblen (1899) *The Theory of the Leisure Class* – a similar, more colloquial term, is 'keeping up with the Joneses' popularised in an eponymous comic strip originating in 1913.

77 Krippendorf (1987): 20

78 Krippendorf (1987): 33

79 Krippendorf (1987): 43

80 Krippendorf (1987): 38

No longer manipulated, tourists were increasingly critical consumers, 'informed and experienced', and moving towards being 'emancipated and independent' – though he accepted that 'passive and uncritical tourists' still outnumbered 'active and enlightened ones'. He concluded: 'the readiness and desire for a different tourism is becoming more widespread day by day'. [81] The growth of the experience economy has played a significant role in reshaping tourism.

Pushing the responsible agenda, Krippendorf called for a new form of tourism, one that 'will bring the greatest possible benefit to all the partici-pants – travellers, the host population and the tourist business, without caus-ing intolerable ecological and social damage'.[82] The needs of people, hosts and guests, would be at the core of this new tourism. To create it he argued, we need 'rebellious tourists and rebellious locals'. The new form of tourism must make life more 'fulfilling and enjoyable'[83] It also had to be based, he argued, on a partnership between promoters and developers and the destina-tions, and progress would be measured in higher incomes, more satisfying jobs, improved social and cultural facilities and better housing. Priority had be given to 'investment and facilities which equally benefit travellers and locals and can be used by both sides'.[84] Krippendorf called for the avoidance of dependency, the maintenance of a diversified economy and emphasis to be placed on 'cultivating what is typically local' and on local authorities to maintain control over the use of land.[85]

Particularly prescient was Krippendorf's recognition of the desirability of 'artificial holiday worlds in the form of large holiday centres' – today's all-inclusives. He argued that 'cultural protection' and 'host population protection' sometimes required tourism '...in reservations in "ghetto-like" centres'. This was a 'more "hygienic" solution, because the destination area could benefit from all the economic advantages while restricting contact to a limited area and a small circle of people and thus protect itself from the overwhelming ecological and, even more importantly, cultural "infection".'[86]

Krippendorf recognised that proposals for change needed to be 'infec-tious'. Codes and advice about improving the quality of travel must not

---

81 Krippendorf (1987): 74; Krippendorf develops his argument in Chapter 11 Changing values: opportunities for a new society.

82 Krippendorf (1987): 106, he called this soft or adapted tourism (p. 107)

83 Krippendorf (1987): 107–109

84 See below the reference to creating 'better place to live in and for people to visit'

85 Krippendorf (1987): 114,115, 119, 122

86 Krippendorf (1987): 124

'degenerate into rules for regimentation and manipulation. They must make the experience of freedom possible.' '[E]very individual tourist builds up or destroys human values while travelling.' 'Orders and prohibitions will not do the job – because it is not a bad conscience that we need to make progress but positive experience, not the feeling of compulsion but that of responsibility'.[87] Krippendorf was not content with research; he was impatient for change.[88] He was passionate about the imperative for a sustainability that would benefit holidaymakers, and communities and businesses in destinations. He also understood the changes in consumer expectations and the opportunity for a new form of tourism. Perhaps his biggest contribution was to understand the power of the feeling of responsibility.

The development of Responsible Tourism

Krippendorf authored the most powerful case for Responsible Tourism but he was not alone in articulating it. The Manila Conference on World Tourism was convened in 1980 to 'consider the responsibility of states for the development and enhancement of tourism'.[89] It expressed similar sentiments, and had also asserted that in 'the practice of tourism, spiritual elements must take precedence over technical and material elements'. Participants in the Manila conference went on to call for 'a spirit of respect for [man's] identity and dignity' and recognition of the 'originality of cultures and respect for the moral heritage of people'.[90]

The Hague Declaration, which resulted from an Inter-Parliamentary Union and World Tourism Organization Conference on Tourism in April 1989, recognised the contribution which tourism could make to peace, referring to the Universal Declaration of Human Rights and its aspiration that there should be a right to travel, and to rest, leisure and holidays with pay. It affirmed that an 'unspoilt natural, cultural and human environment' was fundamental to tourism development and that tourism could contribute to the protection and development of natural and cultural heritage and to 'improving the quality of life'. The importance of promoting the 'integrated planning of tourism development on the basis of the concept of 'sustainable development' was

---

87   Krippendorf (1987): 108–110

88   Krippendorf (1987): 148. He is a challenging read but it more than repays the effort.

89   WTO and representatives of 107 states met to 'consider the responsibility of States for the development and enhancement of tourism'

90   WTO (1980): 21 d and e

asserted along with encouragement to develop 'alternative forms of tourism which favour closer contact and understanding between tourists and receiving populations, preserve cultural identity and offer distinctive and original tourists products and facilities'. [91]

The first International Conference on Responsible Tourism in Destinations was held in Cape Town in 2002. The discussions involved delegates from 20 countries, the WTO and the United Nations Environment Programme (UNEP). The concepts of responsibility and respect played a central role in the formation of the founding principles of Responsible Tourism. The UNWTO Global Code of Ethics makes several references to 'responsible and sustainable tourism' and affirms in Article 1: '… an attitude of tolerance and respect for the diversity of religious, philosophical and moral beliefs, are both the foundation and the consequence of Responsible Tourism…'[92]

The Cape Town Declaration on Responsible Tourism identified seven areas of focus. Responsible Tourism seeks, as locally appropriate, to:

- Minimise negative economic, environmental, and social impacts and to maximise positive ones.
- Generate greater economic benefits for local people and enhance the well-being of host communities, improve working conditions and access to the industry.
- Engage local people, alongside other stakeholders, in decisions that affect their lives and life chances.
- Ensure that tourism, the industry and the consumers, makes positive contributions to the conservation of natural and cultural heritage and to the maintenance of the world's diversity.
- Provide more enjoyable, authentic, experiences for tourists through more meaningful connections with local people, and ensure that they gain a greater understanding of local cultural, social and environmental issues.
- Provide access for people with disabilities and the disadvantaged.
- Ensure that tourism is culturally sensitive, mutually rewarding, engenders respect between tourists and hosts, and builds local pride and confidence.

All solutions are ultimately local, although some address national, regional or international issues.

---

91 WTO (1989) Principle III: 1, 2b and e

92 Article I 1

Following the 'triple bottom line' model, the Cape Town Declaration provided some guiding principles, indicative of what needs to be developed for any destination (Box 1.2).

Box 1.2: Guiding Principles for Economic, Social and Environmental Responsibility

1   Guiding Principles for Economic Responsibility

♦ Assess economic impacts before developing tourism and exercise preference for those forms of development that benefit local communities and minimise negative impacts on local livelihoods (for example through loss of access to resources), recognising that tourism may not always be the most appropriate form of local economic development

♦ Maximise local economic benefits by increasing linkages and reducing leakages, by ensuring that communities are involved in, and benefit from, tourism. Wherever possible use tourism to assist in poverty reduction by adopting pro-poor strategies

♦ Develop quality products that reflect, complement, and enhance the destination

♦ Market tourism in ways which reflect the natural, cultural and social integrity of the destination, and which encourage appropriate forms of tourism

♦ Adopt equitable business practices, pay and charge fair prices, and build partnerships in ways in which risk is minimised and shared, and recruit and employ staff recognising international labour standards

♦ Provide appropriate and sufficient support to small, medium and micro enterprises to ensure tourism-related enterprises thrive and are sustainable

2   Guiding Principles for Social Responsibility

♦ Actively involve the local community in planning and decision-making and provide capacity building to make this a reality

♦ Assess social impacts throughout the life cycle of the operation – including the planning and design phases of projects – in order to minimise negative impacts and maximise positive ones

♦ Endeavour to make tourism an inclusive social experience and to ensure that there is access for all, in particular vulnerable and disadvantaged communities and individuals

♦ Combat the sexual exploitation of human beings, particularly of children

♦ Be sensitive to the host culture, maintaining and encouraging social and cultural diversity

♦ Endeavour to ensure that tourism contributes to improvements in health and education

3   Guiding Principles for Environmental Responsibility

♦ Assess environmental impacts throughout the life cycle of tourist establishments and operations – including the planning and design phase – and ensure that negative impacts are reduced to the minimum and maximising positive ones

♦ Use resources sustainably, and reduce waste and over-consumption

♦ Manage natural diversity sustainably, and where appropriate restore it; consider the volume and type of tourism that the environment can support, and respect the integrity of vulnerable ecosystems and protected areas

♦ Promote education and awareness for sustainable development – for all stakeholders

♦ Raise the capacity of all stakeholders and ensure that best practice is followed, for this purpose consult with environmental and conservation experts

Source: Cape Town Declaration (2002)[93]

Whose responsibility is it? Focusing on outcomes

As we saw earlier, the sustainability agenda is broad and complex. Sustainability, sustainable development and sustainable tourism are too abstract, too overwhelming to move people to take action: they lack meaning. Responsible Tourism is about encouraging and motivating people, individuals alone and in groups, to take responsibility for making tourism more sustainable. General concepts like sustainability, sustainable development and sustainable tourism assume that the issues and solutions are the same everywhere: they are not.

Responsible Tourism relishes the diversity of the world's environments and cultures, and accepts that responsible and sustainable tourism will be achieved in different ways in different places; issues vary from place to place. It is in destinations that tourists (domestic, international and from a range of cultures), meet with local communities in their environments. It is in destinations that tourism needs to be managed, and responsibility needs to be exercised, to make it more sustainable. One thing, however, unites the diversity of

93   www.responsibletourismpartnership.org/CapeTown.html

destinations and challenges: the need, if tourism is truly to be responsible, to measure the sustainability outcomes of the industry.

It follows from this that there is no blueprint for sustainable tourism. The issues and priorities vary from place to place; the solutions too, reflect the culture and structure of the society within which the tourism is taking place, and from whence the holidaymakers arrive. The stakeholders have different, albeit interdependent, responsibilities: tourism can only be managed for sustainability at the destination level, but much can be done in the originating markets to affect what happens in the destination, and on the journey. Responsible Tourism requires that producers and consumers identify sustainability issues which they can address, that they take responsibility for doing so and demonstrate the outcomes. At the core of Responsible Tourism is the ethic of responsibility, the willingness and capacity to respond, to exercise responsibility. In *Letters and Papers from Prison*, Bonheoffer wrote: 'We have learnt, rather too late, that action comes, not from thought, but from a readiness for responsibility.'[94] Responsible Tourism is about everyone involved taking responsibility for making tourism more sustainable. The problem is that when something is everyone's responsibility it can end up being nobody's. The Responsible Tourism agenda addresses the sustainability issues – economic, social and environmental – that arise in the tourism sector and which are exacerbated by its growth. These issues arise in originating markets and in destinations. The challenge is to ensure that tourism contributes to the sustainable development of communities.

The Responsible Tourism movement owes a good deal to its predecessors,[95] writers who asserted the importance of empathy, community engagement and ethics;[96] and the integrated conservation and development projects

---

94 Bonhoeffer (2001):103; Dietrich Bonhoeffer (1906–1945) was a leader in the German Lutheran Confessing Church who opposed anti-Semitism. Arrested in 1943 he was hanged by the Nazis on 6 April 1945.

95 Google returns links to a Centre for Responsible Tourism in Goa in 1982 and California in 1984

96 In a World Council of Churches publication in 1981, O'Grady, challenged tourists to respect the religious differences between themselves and others, and sought to establish empathy as an important element in Responsible Tourism. Haywood in 1988 argued that tourism is a community industry and that there needed to be a broader and more participatory approach to tourism planning. He called for a responsible and responsive approach to tourism planning in the community. The importance of empathy and the sophisticated social skills required in challenging tourists to respect the differences between the everyday life of Mennonites and that of tourists is picked up by Ryan (1991): 156. In 1993, Lea traced the origins of ethical concern about tourism development and located them in literature on development and environment. Lea discussed the anti-tourism campaigns in Goa and concluded with a discussion of personal travel ethics, tourism industry ethics and development ethics.

(ICDPs) of the early 1990s, as well as the ecotourism and community-based tourism that are often held up as ethical alternatives to mass tourism. Indeed, mass tourism was presented as the antithesis to responsible forms of tourism like ecotourism and community-based tourism.[97] However, whether they are responsible or not depends not on their intent or their form, but rather on their outcomes. No form of tourism is by definition responsible: all forms of tourism can be more responsible, responsibility needs to be one element in the consumer proposition, the particular brand needs to define what it takes responsibility for and deliver it.

However, Responsible Tourism is not a brand; it is a dimension of the product, of the travel experience, of the holiday. All forms of tourism can be more responsible, the tourism is what we make it whether as producers or consumers. Responsible Tourism is not a niche market, it is about making all forms of travel and tourism more responsible, it is about changing the nature of tourism.[98] The debate about ethical tourism is not focused solely on the consumer: it is also an issue for companies.[99] Companies, along with the destinations, manage the products that travellers and holidaymakers purchase and consume.[100] To a significant extent, Responsible Tourism has become the corporate social responsibility (CSR) strategy of the UK outbound industry. It is less corporate than mainstream CSR, a broader and more diverse movement.

There are three aspects of the concept of responsibility that are particularly relevant to tourism. While these elements are closely related, the differences are important.

1   **Accountability**. The liability to be called to account for actions, and omissions, where the consequences can be attributed to individuals, or legal entities that can be held accountable, and for some acts of commission or omission there may be legal liability.[101] Determining

---

97   See for example Harrison and Husbands (1996): 5, 'encompasses a framework and a set of practices that chart a sensible course between the fuzziness of ecotourism and the well-known negative externalities associated with conventional mass tourism.'

98   Goodwin and Riverpath Associates (1999)

99   cf Tribe (2009): 253

100 Harrison and Husbands (1996) in Practicing Responsible Tourism, argue that Responsible Tourism does not 'refer to a brand or type of tourism'. They argue that 'well-conceived ecotourism products' can be responsible and that 'drawing on experience, foresight, and new techniques, mass tourism itself can be practiced in ways that minimise and mitigate its obvious disbenefits' (p. 5)

101 The OED traces this usage to 1643

and revealing the consequences of actions or inactions can also be used to raise awareness and elicit a response.

2   **Capability or capacity**. Responsibility is shouldered because there is something that can be done, and the individual or organisation has the capability to act, to make a difference. With the opportunity comes the impetus to responsibility.[102] Capability assumes capacity – responsibility is attributed or accepted because the individual or group had both the opportunity and the capacity to act. Individuals and organisations are expected to respond because they can make a difference – they have 'respons-ability' because they have both capacity and opportunity. They have also to be willing and feel themselves able to react, to take the initiative and to act. The individual's peer group plays an important role in encouraging and supporting the shouldering of responsibility.

3   **Responding, to be responsive**.[103] Individuals and organisations are expected to respond and to make a difference. Respons-ability involves entering a dialogue. Dialogue opens opportunities for authentic experiences for the traveller and enables stakeholders to create solutions which deliver.

Responsible Tourism arises both from accountability, through legislation, regulation and contracts of supply and employment and from the willingness of individuals and organisations to respond. Both these forms of responsibility assume capacity. Accountability may result from legal liability and/or from social norms and peer pressure. Accountability helps progress through regulation, and through raising awareness of the responsibility to act – by holding individuals and companies to account for the consequences of their actions or inactions. Willingness and capacity to respond are also important and they are often linked: capacity, the ability to make a difference, encourages responsibility; a sense of responsibility coupled with incapacity often motivates individuals and organisations to seek capacity.

As we shall see in Part II, capacity is not necessarily sufficient. To make tourism more sustainable generally requires partnerships, a plurality of relationships between individuals and groups of individuals, learning, praxis,

---

102 The OED traces this usage to 1691

103 The OED traces this usage to 1726 – to answer by some responsive act; to act in response to some influence.

and critical reflection. People who exercise respons-ability have empathy; they have a strong sense of the 'other'. They recognise interdependence and the responsibility it implies and requires. They have or seek roles where they can exert agency, requiring what Aristotle called *phronesis*, or practical wisdom.[104] *Phronesis* is the ability to determine ends and to act in particular contexts. This requires prudence and a degree of maturity. In the *Nicomachean Ethics*, Aristotle usefully distinguishes between *phronesis* which is practical and effectively deals with particulars and *sophia*, which is concerned with deliberation about universal truths. Responsible Tourism draws on *phronesis*. It requires the determination of desirable ends and the ability to determine how to achieve them.

It is not sufficient to criticise or to understand. We must all play our part and to act responsibly – to determine appropriate ends and means in particular circumstances and to form partnerships to achieve change, to encourage, prioritise and implement Responsible Tourism principles. Fennell points out that there are 'two widely regarded conditions that free an individual of his or her responsibility: ignorance and inability.'[105] In making the case for Responsible Tourism, an essential stage is the raising of the issues – of ensuring that no one in the industry can claim ignorance. Then, we must focus on demanding action from those who have the ability to make a difference. To understand and act, producers and consumers need to be engaged: the issue must have meaning for them and they must see that they have the opportunity and capacity to make a difference. Finally, we must monitor and report outcomes. It is not enough to claim to be behaving responsibly: responsibility needs to be documented in practice, and the efficacy of the actions taken measured and reported in a transparent way. There is a role for research in identifying approaches and methods which deliver and in evaluating interventions and strategies.[106]

From 1997, the UNWTO developed a Global Code of Ethics, which was approved by the UN General Assembly in December 2001.[107] The Global Code of Ethics built on a number of other codes and documents. It pledges to:

---

104 In Nicomachean Ethics 1142, Aristotle distinguishes between two intellectual virtues: Sophia (often translated as wisdom) and phronesis translated as practical wisdom

105 Fennell (2006): 109

106 As Jeffrey Sachs (2008) has argued 'the dichotomy between research and practice is miscast', sustainable development requires the solving of complex problems: 'Engagement in actual problem solving is vital in order to construct a sound theoretical explanation of complex problems' (p. 329)

107 Adopted 21 December 2001 United Nations General Assembly resolution A/RES/56/212,

1   Increase 'mutual understanding and respect between peoples and societies'[108]

2   To provide 'a vehicle for individual and collective fulfilment

3   Provide an opportunity for 'sustainable development'

4   Designate tourists and tourism as 'a user of the cultural heritage of mankind and contributor to its enhancement'[109]

5   Make tourism 'a beneficial activity for host countries and communities'

6   Highlight the 'obligations of stakeholders in tourism development'

7   Safeguard the 'right to tourism'

8   Protect the 'liberty of tourism movements'

9   Protect the rights of 'workers and entrepreneurs in the tourism industry'.

The 10th principle deals with implementation: encouraging private and public sector stakeholders to 'cooperate in the implementation of these principles and monitor their effective application,' and to 'demonstrate their intention to refer any disputes concerning the application or interpretation of the Global Code of Ethics for Tourism for conciliation to an impartial third body known as the World Committee on Tourism Ethics'.[110] The Declaration can only be implemented through persuasion and, like all United Nations declarations, it has been agreed internationally with the necessary compromises required to secure universal acceptance.

The Global Code of Ethics is aspirational and deals more extensively with the freedom of travel and the rights of consumers rather than their responsibilities. Its principles relate to the rights of tourists, host communities, employees and entrepreneurs. In 2005 the General Assembly[111] endorsed the World Committee on Tourism Ethics' code for the Responsible Tourist and Traveller. This is a code based on the Global Code of Ethics which exhorts tourists and travellers to have an open mind, respect human rights, help to preserve natural environments, respect cultural resources, purchase local

---

108 Article 1 also deals with 'The exploitation of human beings in any form, particularly sexual, especially when applied to children, conflicts with the fundamental aims of tourism and is the negation of tourism...' (p. 4)

109 There is no mention of natural heritage the Global Code of Ethics, environment is dealt with in a number of articles, particularly in the commitment to sustainable development

110 Global Code of Ethics: 7

111 UNWTO resolution A/RES/506(XVI)

handicrafts and products to support the local economy and to learn about the destination, the health situation and the local law in order to avoid committing a crime while on holiday.[112] By emphasising buying from a local craftsperson, the Responsible Tourist and Traveller code underlines responsibility, and highlights how a holidaymaker can create a richer experience for themselves and the local person.

The financial crisis in September 2008, which resulted from irresponsible lending and borrowing, has perhaps created a more favourable environment for the Responsible Tourism approach. There has been a great deal of discussion, on both sides of the Atlantic, about the irresponsible behaviour of bankers. Politicians and other civic leaders have called for more responsible behaviour in banking and the financial services sector. There have been a number of prosecutions, and regulatory reforms proposed and implemented, designed to curb irresponsible behaviour and to hold the bankers to account. The concepts of responsibility and its converse irresponsibility littered political debates and may presage a resurgence of regulatory activity. That said, to date, market-based Responsible Tourism has been the dominant strategy: later in Chapter 4, we shall look at destinations where there has been a little more reliance on regulatory approaches.

As we shall see in Chapter 3, Responsible Tourism is not reducible to CSR. It is not merely about managing risk, philanthropy and reporting – although these may be part of it. It is about changing the way business is done, and working with a range of stakeholders, often in partnership, to make significant change. It often involves developing a more balanced relationship between hosts and guests. Responsibility, and the market advantage it may deliver, is about doing more than the minimum. It is about being transparent in demonstrating the impact of the changes made – recognising that the claims made by the business may form part of the contract between the company and the holidaymaker , and that failure to deliver on the claims or promises made may incur a successful claim for compensation.

Responsible Tourism is a diverse movement of consumers, holidaymakers and locals, making change at different speeds and with different focuses – in the next section we look at the arguments which have been raised against it. It is important to document the arguments, and learn from those who oppose the idea of Responsible Tourism.

---

112 UNWTO (2005): 1

The myths about Responsible Tourism

Responsible Tourism is not without its critics in academia, and this section will concentrate on criticisms articulated by Brian Wheeller and Jim Butcher in particular. Sometimes there is a misunderstanding of what Responsible Tourism is about; sometimes the critique is for more fundamental reasons. There is also a long-standing critique of alternative tourism, a critique which contributed to the development of Responsible Tourism. Wheeller has been a particularly articulate and trenchant critic of tourism arguing that, 'tourism will always include an element of 'exploitation'. The industry in the originating market and in the destination is seeking profit, the tourists are motivated by a 'what's in it for me?' attitude.

Similarly, the host community wants to extract something from the tourist. Assuming it's not money, it might be an opportunity to learn a foreign language, a gift, a sexual conquest – whatever. It's often a matter of 'taking'. Too cynical? Dream on. Unfortunately, this seems a far more realistic view of how things are, and will continue to be, than the wishful, wistful, whimsical, goody-two-shoes, green approach.[113]

Wheeller argues cogently in *Egotourism, Sustainable Tourism and the Environment* that ecotourism 'neatly, conveniently' sidesteps 'the critical issues of volume'.[114] Mass consumption damages cultures and environments. Alternative forms of tourism Wheeller argues are 'further fuelling the rapid spread of tourism without offering any real, lasting answers.[115]

The prescription from Wheeller's work is unclear. If the problem is mass travel and the damage that it causes, then this is a function of the increasing prosperity of ever-larger numbers of people, and it is but one aspect of the sustainability issues which arise from increasing population and a rising standard of living. The solution is presumably either to reduce population or to reduce consumption, including travel, for a growing proportion of the world's population. These are difficult management strategies to pursue. This challenge is at the heart of efforts across all consumption sectors to balance environment and development in a sustainable way.

Wheeller portrays Responsible Tourism as a 'so-called solution that keeps almost everyone happy. It appeases the guilt of the "thinking tourist"... the

---

113 Wheeller (1994): 648
114 Wheeller (1994): 653, (1992): 142
115 Wheeller (1997): 67

more discerning (and expensive) range of the market can be catered for by 'legitimately' opening up new areas of tourism...'.[116] It then allows growth to continue unabated. Responsible Tourism, he argues 'is a pleasant, agreeable, but dangerously ephemeral and inadequate escape route for the educated middle classes unable, or unwilling, to appreciate or accept their/our destructive contribution to the international tourism maelstrom.' He asserts that it might more appropriately be described as irresponsible tourism.[117]

The ambition of Responsible Tourism is to address all forms of tourism and to respond to the challenge of making tourism more sustainable. The efficacy of its approach has to be assessed against the evidence. Responsible Tourism is not – nor should it be – limited to middle-class consumers; in the UK, and increasingly elsewhere, it is the impacts of the mainstream industry and the mass tourists, that are being addressed. There is a danger that any approach which seeks to mitigate and adapt can be used as a fig leaf which legitimises unrestrained and destructive growth. The premise of this book is that the stakeholders in tourism, producers and consumers, have a responsibility to act, that it is irresponsible not to, and that tourism can be managed. Readers will form their own judgement about the extent to which Responsible Tourism provides a 'dangerously ephemeral and inadequate escape route'.[118] But the question is an important one.

Another aspect of Wheeller's critique of alternative tourism has more traction. He argues that alternative tourism is a deceptive ploy and[119] that Responsible Tourism is not the answer.[120] Wheeller is sceptical about the value and effectiveness of educating tourists. Responsible Tourism rather seeks to inspire and to offer experiences that the holidaymaker finds more rewarding. Wheeller also argues that what is 'euphemistically known as Responsible Tourism' is in fact 'an umbrella term embracing the supposedly more caring forms of tourism': alternative, appropriate, sustainable, soft, green, etc. The pace of development is slow and absorbable, decision making in the hands of the host community. He concedes that 'there are many examples of small-scale alternative successes.'[121] But the 'sensitive traveller is the perpetrator of global

---

116 Wheeller (1997): 66
117 Wheeller (1997): 66–67
118 Wheeller (1997): 67
119 Wheeller (1992): 140
120 Wheeller (1997): 61
121 Wheeller (1997): 62

spread'[122], they use the same infrastructure[123] and are just as much tourists as the packaged tourists from whom they seek to differentiate themselves. Quite so, but Responsible Tourism is not about the alternative: the ambition is bigger, much bigger than that. The goal is to change mainstream tourism. That is why one of the principles of Responsible Tourism is that all forms of tourism can, and should, be managed and consumed more responsibly.

Anna Spenceley[124] similarly reduces Responsible Tourism to ecotourism, national parks, pro-poor tourism and community-based tourism, when in South Africa responsibility has been at the core of national policy for all forms of tourism since 1996.[125] SNV, the Netherlands Development Organisation would also confine Responsible Tourism to a limited number of market segments for a limited number of products.[126] It assumes the product segments are responsible and that they are purchased by responsible tourists. The reality is that not all products in the segment are responsible, and that there is demonstrably demand for Responsible Tourism experiences from mainstream tourists who are not travelling with the 110 companies in Europe, North America and Australia the researchers identified as responsible.[127] With such limited vision and awareness of the industry as a whole, tourism cannot have a significant impact for good, or bad.

Issues of responsibility also emerged in popular culture. Alex Garland's *The Beach* was published in 1996, drawing on his experience as a backpacker, and quickly became a cult novel and subsequently a movie.[128] William Sutcliffe's *Are you Experienced?*, published in 1998, dealt in a similar vein unsympathetically with characters who escape to the Third World. Both books were critical of selfish and self-indulgent travellers, who as Wheeller argues are self-interested, taking what's in it for them.

In 2002, the year of the Cape Town Declaration, the World Summit on Sustainable Development and the United Nations International Year of

---

122 Wheeller (1997): 63

123 Wheeller (1992). Some travellers do use local services, tavernas, solar powered water, public transport but they also use the infrastructure used by mainstream tourists – if only to get a cold beer.

124 Spenceley (2008); its narrow vision is given away in the title *Responsible Tourism: Critical Issues for Conservation and Development*

125 SNV Netherlands Development Organisation (2010)

126 SNV(2010): 14

127 SNV(2010): 15

128 The movie was released in 2000.

Ecotourism, the Institute of Ideas in London published a Debating Matters text on ethical tourism edited by Tiffany Jenkins. In this text, the terms 'ethical' and 'responsible' tended to be used interchangeably.[129] Jenkins selected primarily critical contributors. One of these, Dea Birkett, the writer and broadcaster, argues that the tourist is being re-branded, that 'un-tourists go to the very same places from which many would have tourists banned'. 'Un-tourists travel as adventurers, fieldwork assistants, exploraholics, volunteers and travellers. They are not holidaymakers: they go on expeditions, cultural experiences, projects and missions. Un-tourists hold the moral high ground'.[130] Responsible Tourism explicitly recognises that tourism is what needs to be addressed; its focus is tourists and tourism. All forms of tourism – including un-tourism – can be more responsible.

Birkett uses the example of visiting New York. In New York, what might be termed 'cultural contact' is 'restricted to trading exchanges with store assist-ants, hotel porters, waiters and tickets booth salespeople… [whereas] in the developing world, we have to seek out more meaningful contact'.[131] This can result in tourists wanting to arrest the development of communities preferring that they remain undeveloped for the continued enjoyment of tourists. Paul Goldstein argues that the 'worst example of this is where tourism takes upon itself the mission to "protect" native communities while actually hindering their progression.'[132] This has been described as 'nothing more then enforcing primitivism.'[133]

The aspiration of Responsible Tourism is for more meaningful contact based on mutual respect when travelling to or from the developed and developing world. Respect does not mean 'temporarily abandoning your own principles and beliefs'.[134] Nor does it provide licence to abandon one's moral compass and to behave less well abroad. Responsible Tourism is about recognising the diversity of the world and thinking about the consequences of how and where you travel.

Jim Butcher's critique of Responsible Tourism takes the shape of a defence of the 'average tourist' and the 'carefree relaxation, adventure and hedon-

---

129 Jenkins (2002): xi
130 Birkett (2002): 6, 4 and 8
131 Birkett (2002): 9
132 Goldstein (2002): 39
133 Leech (2002): 94
134 Birkett (2002): 11

ism' that characterises a holiday.[135] '[F]un is frowned upon and a sense of adventure reined in by the ethical advocates.' Meanwhile, Butcher goes on to argue, 'ethical tourism is a barely concealed slight on the "unethical" package holidaymaker.'[136] He asserts that ethical tourism has an essentially conservative, preservationist outlook'[137] and asks 'why not leave tourists to be the judge of what makes a good holiday for them?'[138] This is undeniable: it is not tourism until it is sold, and, to be successful, Responsible Tourism has to find a market – the customer will determine whether or not an initiative is successful. If consumers do not want it they will not buy it.

Butcher's second concern is that the ethical 'advice assumes that tourists and hosts cannot get on. It ends up reinforcing differences and creating misunderstanding.'[139] He argues that cultural difference is assumed whilst shared humanity, 'common aspirations and desires shared by host and tourist are rarely considered.'[140] He concludes that '[o]ver sensitivity to otherness blinds us to common humanity'.[141] The point is well made. No doubt, some of those who argue for various forms of ethical and alternative tourism make this mistake as do some who subscribe to Responsible Tourism in name.[142] Yet Responsible Tourism encourages tourists to make their own informed choices, to engage and to respond to experiences and issues they encounter while holidaying: not to do so would be irresponsible.

Butcher also argues that 'ethical tourism encourages us all to deconstruct our experiences, to dwell on our actions, to self-consciously audit our cultural and environmental impact – and to pass judgment on others who don't.'[143] My personal concerns about the impacts of tourism preceded my engagement in its deconstruction. They arose intuitively from what I was experiencing, and led to my academic engagement and discovery of Responsible Tourism. The tendency to deconstruct can be a curse; it is difficult to shut down critical faculties, but is it desirable? In my experience, human beings do not need to ethically deconstruct their experience in order to pass judgement (often

135 Butcher (2002): 59
136 ibid.
137 Butcher (2002): 61
138 Butcher (2002): 63
139 Butcher (2002): 59
140 Butcher (2002): 70
141 Butcher (2002): 73
142 We return to this issue in Chapter 5
143 Butcher (2002): 63

negative) on others. Our prejudices are a part of our humanity. We need to recognise them, to control them and to enhance our critical faculties. Responsible Tourism is not limited to those forms of tourism we like; it is not only a matter of aesthetics. Ecotourism is good, less good or bad not because of the label attached to it or the aspiration which may drive it. Good or bad are determined by the outcomes which result from the activity. Ecotourism, voluntourism and community-based tourism should be judged not by the labels and implied intent but by the consequences of the activity.

References

Aristotle (2006) *Politics: A Treatise on Government*, Charleston, SC: BiblioBazaar.

Aristotle (2009) *The Nicomachean Ethics*, edited by L. Brown, Oxford: Oxford University Press.

Beddington, J. (2009) 'Food, energy, water and the climate: a perfect storm of global events?', Speech at Sustainable Development UK Conference, London, 19 March 2009.

Bell, A. (2009) *Peak Water*, Edinburgh: Luath.

Birkett D, (2002), *Re-Branding the Tourist* in Jenkins op.cit. 1-14, Hodder and Stoughton, London

Bonheoffer, D. (2001) *Letters and Papers from Prison*, London: SCM Press.

Briassoulis, H. (2002) 'Sustainable tourism and the question of the Commons', *Annals of Tourism Research*, **29** (4), 1065–1085.

Butcher, J. (2002) 'Weighed down by ethical baggage', in T. Jenkins (ed.) *Ethical Tourism: Who Benefits*, London: Hodder & Stoughton.

Eber, S. (1992) *Beyond the Green Horizon*, Godalming, Surrey: WWF.

Fennell, D. (2006) *Tourism Ethics*, Clevedon, Somerset: Channel View Publications.

Galbraith, J.K. (1958) *The Affluent Society*, New York: Mariner Books.

Goldstein, P. (2002) 'Can we care enough?', in T. Jenkins (ed.) *Ethical Tourism: Who Benefits*, London: Hodder & Stoughton, pp. 35–57.

Goodwin, H. (2002) 'The case for responsible tourism', in T. Jenkins (ed.) *Ethical Tourism: Who Benefits*, London: Hodder & Stoughton, pp. 15–33.

Goodwin, H. and Riverpath Associates (1999) *Changing the Nature of Tourism: Developing an Agenda for Action*, London: Department for International Development.

Gordon, H.S. (1954) 'The economic theory of a common property resource: the fishery', *Journal of Political Economy*, **6**, 231–238.

Hardin, G. (1968) 'The tragedy of the Commons', *Science*, **121**, (3859), 1243–1248.

Harris, N. (1971) *Beliefs in Society*, London and Madrid: Pelican.

Harrison, L.C. and Husbands, W. (1996) *Practising Responsible Tourism*, New York: Wiley.

Healy, R. (1994) 'The "common pool" problem in tourism landscapes', *Annals of Tourism Research*, **21** (3), 596–911.

Holden, A. (2005) 'Achieving a sustainable relationship between common pool resources and tourism: the role of environmental ethics', *Journal of Sustainable Tourism*, **13** (4), 339–352.

Hubbert, M. King (1956) 'Nuclear energy and the fossil fuels' paper at the Spring Meeting of the Southern District, American Petroleum Institute, San Antonio, Texas, 7–9 March, http://www.hubbertpeak.com/hubbert/1956/1956.pdf

Jenkins, T. (ed.) (2002) *Ethical Tourism: Who Benefits*, London: Hodder & Stoughton.

Krippendorf, J. (1975) *Die Landschaftsfresser: Tourismus und Erholungslandschaft, Verderben oder Segen?*, Schönbühl, Switzerland: Hallwag

Krippendorf, J. (1982) 'Towards new tourism policies', *Tourism Management*, **3** (3), 135-148

Krippendorf, J. (1987) *The Holiday Makers*, Oxford: Butterworth Heinemann.

Leech, K. (2002) 'Enforced primitivism', in T. Jenkins (ed.), *Ethical Tourism: Who Benefits*, London: Hodder & Stoughton, pp. 75–94.

Meadows, D.H., Meadows, D.L., Randers, J. and Behrens III, W.W. (1972) *The Limits to Growth: A Report for the Club of Rome's Project on the Predicament of Mankind*, New York: Universe Books.

Olson, M. (1965) *The Logic of Collective Action: Public Goods and the Theory of Groups*, Cambridge, MA: Harvard University Press.

Ostrom, E. (1990) *Governing the Commons*, Cambridge: Cambridge University Press.

Sachs, J. (2008) *Common Wealth: Economics for a Crowded Planet*, London: Penguin.

Sharpley, R. (2000) 'Tourism and sustainable development: exploring the theoretical divide', *Journal of Sustainable Tourism*, **8** (1), 1–19.

SNV (Netherlands Development Organisation) (2009) *The Market for Responsible Tourism Products*, The Hague: SNV.

Spenceley, A. (2008) *Responsible Tourism: Critical Issues for Conservation and Development*, London: Earthscan.

Stivers, R. (1976) *The Sustainable Society: Ethics and Economic Growth*, Philadelphia: Westminster Press.

Strong, M.F. (1972) Statement to the Conference on the Human Environment at its 1st Plenary Meeting, 5 June, United Nations, Paris, available at www.unep.org/Documents.Multilingual/Default.asp?DocumentID=97&ArticleID=1497&l=en

Sutcliffe, W. (1998) *Are You Experienced?*, London: Penguin.

Tribe, J. (2009) *Philosophical Issues in Tourism*, Bristol: Channel View Publications.

Leadership, Crawley: TUI Travel.

TUI Travel (2011) *We're On a Journey: Focused on Delivery*, annual report and accounts year ending 30 September 2010, Crawley: TUI Travel.

TUI Travel Adventure Brands (2010) *Passport to Adventure Industry Trend Report 2010*, Crawley: TUI Travel.

UNWTO (United Nations World Tourism Organization) (2005) *The Responsible Tourist and Traveller*

Wheeller, B. (1992) 'Alternative tourism – a deceptive ploy', in C. Cooper and A. Lockwood (ed.) *Progress in Tourism, Recreation and Hospitality Management*, **4**, 140-146.

Wheeller, B. (1994) 'Egotourism, sustainable tourism and the environment', in A.V. Seaton, C.L. Jenkins, R.C. Wood, P.U.C. Dieke, M.M.Bennett, L.R. MacLellan and R. Smith (eds) *Tourism: The State of the Art*, Chichester, Wiley, pp. 647–654.

Wheeller, B. (1997) 'Tourism's troubled times: responsible tourism is not the answer', in L. France (ed.), *Sustainable Tourism*, London: Earthscan, pp. 61–57.

Withey, L. (1997) *Grand Tours and Cook's Tours: A History of Leisure Travel from 1750 to 1915*, New York: Morrow.

WCED (World Commission on Environment and Development) (1983) *Our Common Future*, Oxford: Oxford University Press.

WTO (1980) *The Manila Declaration*, Madrid: WTO.

WTO/WTTC (1995) *Agenda 21 for the Travel and Tourism Industry – Towards Environmental Sustainable Development*, London and Madrid: WTO/WTTC.

2 Responsible Tourism and the UK Marketplace

This chapter focuses on the ways in which Responsible Tourism has emerged as a significant force in the UK, a consequence of campaigning for change in tourism and of changes in the broader UK consumer market, of which travel and tourism are but a part. As Krippendorf concluded, the 'great turning point will come when informed tourists take to the road and simply demand a re-orientation of commercial policies'.[1] That reorientation has gathered pace in the UK in the first decade of the 21st century and Responsible Tourism has become a part of the operations of ABTA, the UK's major travel trade association, and major companies like TUI and Thomas Cook. It is no long a niche as it was in 2001 when Justin Francis and I launched ResponsibleTravel.com.[2] This is not a history of the development of sustainable and responsible tourism in the UK; it is rather an outline of the major elements of the process through which Responsible Tourism secured a following across significant parts of the tourism outbound sector in Britain. Campaigning in the market among consumers played a prominent role in making the case for Responsible Tourism. This approach has not been consistently applied in other originating markets; internationally great emphasis has been placed on a variety of certification schemes, which have not engaged consumers.[3]

It may be objected that the UK outbound market is a narrow focus. It is. The relative importance of the UK as an outbound market is declining and will continue to do so, the influence of UK operators in destinations, and their share of the outbound market, is declining. The importance of the approach adopted in the UK is the focus on campaigning for change with consumers and the industry and recognising that this campaign will be most successful if it builds on broader trends in the particular society and on the work of others. In the UK the concept of a real holiday has traction because of a campaign about beer and

---

1   Krippendorf, 1987: 148
2   I have subsequently sold my shares.
3   See below p. 231–234

the way in which the term 'real' has for more than a generation been attached in popular usage to good holidays… we shall return to this root shortly.

Cultures of consumption

There is an emerging body of literature which explores consumerism and the importance of the cultural context in which it occurs, emphasising the persistence of social and collective aspects of consumption practices and identities[4] Much of the success of the Responsible Tourism movement in the UK is attributable to broader cultural changes; Responsible Tourism has been grafted on to, and in turn contributed to, changes in the culture of consumption. The processes used in the UK, and described here, cannot simply be replicated elsewhere, but the story may be useful for those wishing to understand why Responsible Tourism has emerged so powerfully in this originating market, or wanting to consider how a similar process might be achieved in a different consuming culture, a different originating market. Too often the cultural differences between originating markets are ignored; there is no global market for tourism.

This is not a chapter about marketing; rather it is about the process of creating change in an originating market, about how, by working to raise the issues with consumers, the industry can be encouraged to respond. The first section of this chapter describes the consumer campaign, launched by VSO and taken on by Tearfund, which built on the work of others and took the issue to the mainstream commercial companies, and which launched Responsible Tourism in the UK. Subsequent sections look at the emergence of ethical consumerism, the experience economy and authenticity, before focusing on the informed and empowered tourist. The empowered tourist takes responsibility for sustainability, and is able and willing to make 'better' choices – choices which are better for the traveller, the local communities and their environment.

Tourism is unusual in that the purchase and consumption of travel and tourism services often taken place in different jurisdictions. The British government has, in common with other states, sought to extend consumer protection beyond its borders.

That said, originating countries governments can provide only limited assistance to their citizens abroad. This has been clear for centuries. The 17th-

---

4   See for example Trentmann (2004), and Brewer and Trentmann (2006): even Coca-Cola is indigenised in consumption, Howes (1996): 6

century political philosopher John Locke put it most eloquently:

> every man, that hath any possessions, or enjoyment, of any part of the dominions of any government, doth thereby give his tacit consent, and is ... obliged to [obey] ... the laws of that government, during such enjoyment, as anyone under it; whether ... lodging only for a week; or whether it be barely travelling freely on the highway.[5]

The UK, like a number of other countries, has sought to control the worst excesses of behaviour by its citizens abroad with legislation on paedophilia and football hooliganism. Thus, through legislation, a small measure of protection – both of and from the traveller – is embedded in the UK culture.

The UK Foreign and Commonwealth Office (FCO) also recognises that neither travellers or destinations are homogenous, and that responsibility concerns vary from place to place and from traveller to traveller. It provides a 'Know Before You Go' (KBYG)[6] section on its travel advice website. It also gives limited advice on Responsible Tourism.[7] The KBYG campaign was launched in 2001 to promote a series of key messages from 'get adequate travel insurance' to 'research the destination before departure'. The FCO works with 400 travel industry partners[8] and provides advice by country and by particular groups – for example gap-year travellers, hen and stag parties, package holidaymakers and sports travellers.

Tourism is very diverse but discussion of tourism, and in particular the impacts of tourism, tends to be generic. We talk about tourists and tourism, most of the time, in an undifferentiated way. It is difficult to do otherwise given the aggregated data sources that we rely upon. It is important to enter the caveat that the argument presented here relies on data from just one originating market and that the focus is on outbound tourism, although it applies domestically too. In the UK, as in other countries with a part of their population wealthy enough in leisure and money to take holidays abroad, domestic tourism is less studied by academics.[9]

---

5   Locke: §219.

6   www.fco.gov.uk/en/travel-and-living-abroad/about-kbyg-campaign/ accessed 24 May 2010

7   www.fco.gov.uk/en/travel-and-living-abroad/be-a-responsible-tourist/ accessed 24 May 2010

8   Under the EU package Travel Directive operators have some responsibility to provide assistance to their clients in the destination

9   It was Krishna Ghimire a social scientist, not a tourism specialist, working at the UNRISD who edited the first major text on domestic tourism documenting its significance in Brazil, China, India, Mexico, Nigeria and South Africa.

Too often tourism is discussed as though it occupies a silo, with decisions being made about holidays in isolation from broader consumer trends. But, I believe, broader consumer trends in the UK have contributed to shaping decision making about holidays, by consumers and producers. Unfortunately there are very limited examples of campaigns for different forms of tourism in other originating markets; too much reliance has been placed on technical fixes like certification.[10] Research conducted by the Canadian Tourism Commission included for the first time in 2009 a standard question in large surveys of its 10 major source markets. They asked whether or not the interviewee agreed with the statement 'I always take environmentally friendly tourism considerations into account when making a decision about where to travel to.' Accepting that this only records self-ascribed aspiration there are significant differences between representative samples in Canadian source markets – 88% of Mexicans, 68% of Chinese, 60% of Koreans and 56% of the French ascribe to this view of their decision making about holidays, compared with 33% of the Germans and Japanese, 31% of Americans, 30% of Canadians and 28% of Australians. The British came bottom, only 23% responded that they always take environmentally friendly characteristics into account when making destination choices. Responsible Tourism has been successful in the originating markets which, amongst these eight markets, is the least predisposed to choose environmentally friendly options. Many will be tempted to dismiss the British experience as unrepresentative, but on the Canadian evidence there are originating markets which look significantly more propitious for this approach.[11]

As was argued in Chapter 1, Responsible Tourism is an approach which can be applied to any form of tourism. Similarly travellers and holidaymakers may use Responsible Tourism accommodation, attractions or destinations without having chosen them for that reason. They may enjoy them without having experienced the difference or been aware of the difference or they may look for all or some of the responsible elements again. The interest of the consumer in a responsible product is as likely, perhaps more likely, to be stimulated by their experience and enjoyment of it as by a certification scheme or admonition to save the planet. Justin Francis of ResponsibleTravel. com reports:

---

10 See below pp. 231–234
11 Canadian Tourism Commission (2009): 23

We often convert people to responsible tourism by stealth. They book a more interesting trip than a standard package holiday through ResponsibleTravel.com. In the destination they discover the magic of encounters and experiences with local people, cultures and ways of life. They understand the benefits their holiday creates locally. Then they are converted to a new way to travel and there is no way back.[12]

The imperative to 'think globally, act locally'[13] certainly applies to the activity of making tourism more sustainable. In the UK in the 1990s, when regulation was abhorred, the best opportunity to advance the sustainable tourism agenda was through an originating market campaign focused on the outbound industry and its consumers – a strategy of principled opportunism.

Above all, we should not forget that it is consumers that drive the industry. They are the main beneficiaries of the competition that ensures small margins for most wholesalers and retailers. In 1990s Britain, consumerism was dominant, the economy was being liberalised and regulation was not on the agenda. To create progressive change it was necessary to use market forces. The movement for Responsible Tourism commenced with a campaign that sought to raise consumer awareness, and business awareness of consumer demands, rather than to sell a particular technical fix. First establish that there is growing concern among consumers about the impacts of tourism, and a preference for a better holiday; then suggest ways of addressing that concern which make business sense. Responsible Tourism is now mainstream in the UK, and the Green Tourism Business Scheme has more than 2100 members; it is a credible sustainability certification scheme in a receptive market place.[14]

Raising the issue

By the late 1980s, concern was being expressed both about the impacts of tourism on destinations and the industrialisation of the holiday product. The *Lonely Planet* and *Rough Guide* books were carrying increasing amounts of information about how to avoid negative impacts and to increase positive ones (by 1998, they were 'devot[ing] increasing space' to 'environment, human rights and local cultures, as well as the impact of tourism'[15]). In 1988, Alison

---

12   Personal communication
13   The first coinage is disputed it has been in use since at least the 1970s.
14   www.green-business.co.uk
15   Neale (1998): xxi

Stancliffe established Tourism Concern; within a year the informal network had become a membership organisation. Its long-running campaign pointed out that we take 'Our Holiday in Their Homes' and suggested that tourists could make a significant difference through the choices they make, picking up Krippendorf's point that 'every individual tourist builds up or destroys human values while travelling'.[16]

In 1989 Frank Barrett, then travel editor at the *Independent* newspaper, wrote the first of a series of annual guides to real holidays that Andreas Whittam Smith, the paper's editor saw as part of the 'Campaign for Real Holidays'. This was an echo of the very successful Campaign for Real Ale (CAMRA). Founded in 1971, CAMRA has been remarkably successful at making the case for the quality of the Real Ale experience. In the 1970s CAMRA successfully fought the efforts of the big brewers to replace traditional ales with tasteless keg beers, near-enough creating the very concept of Real Ale and ensuring its survival. This was arguably the first major campaign for authenticity in the UK consumer market.[17] As Barrett pointed out, the idea of a real holiday was nothing new: 'What I need is a real holiday', 'a real break', to 'really get away from it all'.[18]

In the 1950s, a foreign holiday was a rare luxury. In the space of a generation, by the late 1980s, travelling to the continent had become commonplace.[19] Barrett commented that the 'rise and rise of the package holiday has imposed on travel the same problems that mass production has inflicted on beer, bread, ice-cream and many other things.'[20] He also recognised that the UK industry was competitive on price but argued that this had caused a reduction in choice. In a market dominated by volume retailers, travel agents were offering a highly restricted range of brochures. Before the emergence of the Internet (which, since the late 1990s, has made life for small independent operators much easier), the *Independent Guide to Real Holidays* sought to fill the information gap by offering a list of the smaller independent companies offering real holidays.

In 1991 Wood and House published *The Good Tourist*, which was described by Magnus Magnusson as a 'timely handbook for the sensitive tourist'.[21] As

16 Krippendorf (1987): 109

17 There have also been campaigns for real bread, real cheese and real ice-cream.

18 Barrett (1989): 1

19 The 'continent' is a reference to Europe; there are many reports of the (probably?) apocryphal British newspaper headline, 'Fog in the Channel, Europe cut off.'

20 Barrett (1989): 1

21 Quoted on the cover

with Barrett's guide to real holidays, *The Good Tourist* was consumer-oriented. The authors explained that the book was intended to help travellers and tourists make up their own minds, and to convince them there were things they can do to ensure that their holiday was a positive experience for all concerned. They argued that 'a sharpened sense of balance' was 'the essential ingredient needed for a good tourist philosophy'. Central to that 'good tourist philosophy' is the ethic of responsibility.

It must always be remembered that tourists are guests in the country in which they are staying and that as such they have a responsibility to act with tact and diplomacy, though not at the cost of limiting their freedom of choice on specific issues and from pointing out firmly but politely that they do not agree with a particular action or custom.[22]

Wood and House drew their examples from Europe: Spanish bullfights, the killing and eating of song birds in Southern Europe and the use of animals to entertain and transport tourists. But they balanced this by pointing out that hunting, shooting and fishing are the 'mainstays of much of the rural economy in Scotland'. In Scotland, these activities heavily influence the conservation of the countryside. So, they argue, it is all about balance: '… as a visitor we should seek to make informed decisions as to the impact of our behaviour and act accordingly, realising that there is not one thing in isolation that makes us good tourists, but an amalgam of many'.[23]

In 1992 Elkington and Hailes published *Holiday's That Don't Cost the Earth*, part of the emerging green consumer movement. By the time Greg Neale – the *Sunday Telegraph*'s environment editor, not a travel journalist – published *The Green Travel Guide* in 1998, the British Airways Tourism for Tomorrow Awards[24] were well established and Neale was able to feature a host of organisations, albeit mostly environmental ones, including: the World Tourism Organization, the World Travel and Tourism Council, Green Globe, Green Flag and ECoNETT, European Community Network for Environmental Travel, Campaign for Environmentally Responsible Tourism (CERT), TRAFFIC,[25] Friends of Conservation and Earthwatch. Conservation and tourism-related programmes were also being undertaken by WWF. There were also human

---

22 Wood and House (1991): 90. Krippendorf is cited in the guide to further reading

23 Wood and House (1991): 90

24 Launched in 1990 by the UK's Federation of Tour Operators and the British Tourism Authority and aimed at 'promoting environmental awareness in tourism and encouraging an environmentally responsible approach to tourism management', three years later it was taken over by British Airways.

25 Campaigning to enforce the Convention on International Trade in Endangered Species (CITES)

rights watchdogs, Tourism Concern, Survival International and End Child Prostitution and Tourism (ECPAT).

By the mid-1990s, the issues which surround the impact of tourism in destinations were being raised by academics and campaigning journalists, such as Polly Patullo[26] – although not, yet, by travel journalists. In the UK it was not until 2007 that a journalist, Leo Hickman (not a travel journalist), produced a book-length critique of the true cost of our holiday, travel journalists were slow to address the issues.

Academics had also begun to critique the emerging alternatives to mass tourism. In 1994, Richard Butler wrote a prescient piece in a collection of papers on tourism alternatives, arguing that there were always 'problems and costs' associated with the alternatives, and that these were ignored by their proponents. He concluded that alternative tourism was too often proposed as a 'snake-oil panacea' – as though all tourism should be replaced by an alternative. Alternative tourism cannot, Butler argued, replace traditional mass tourism in economic, logistical or personal preference terms.[27] Butler made the obvious but often-overlooked point that alternative tourism is 'not effective if there are no tourists'.[28] Generally 'alternative tourists' stay in the same accommodation, use the same transport and visit the same attractions. In the destination it is difficult to tell the ecotourists,[29] one form of alternative tourism, from the mainstream tourists; rarely do ecotourists make a larger financial contribution in the destination, though they may have paid more for their trip. An apocryphal (I hope) tale exists about the operator asked the difference between an ecotourism and mainstream wildlife experience: '20%' was his reply.[30] The ecotourism alternative, promoted by NGOs, conservationists and niche businesses was exaggerated as the fastest growing sector. There was no evidence for this and it was, in any case, a tiny niche – it was no alternative to mainstream tourism. It turned out to be a blind alley. Research for the World Tourism Organization conducted in the UK reported that only 12% of nature-based tourism operators surveyed in 2001 reported using 'ecotourism' in their marketing; the word was used in only 3.5% of those companies' brochures. By contrast, 7.5% of nature-based operators were using 'responsible tourism' and

---

26 Polly Pattullo wrote about the impacts of tourism in the Caribbean in *Last Resorts* in 1996
27 Butler (1994): 31–32, 43–46
28 Butler, (1994): 45
29 See Chapter 7 for a critique of ecotourism.
30 Mowforth, Charlton and Munt (2008): ix

11% 'sustainable tourism' in their brochures.[31] By 2001 'ecotourism' had lost its marketing value in the UK.[32]

Ecotourism was a diversion and left an unfortunate legacy. First, because the case made to businesses about why they should adopt ecotourism was the premium price it was claimed to attract. While some operators were able to increase their margins because of the exclusive access to wildlife or the quality of the guiding they offered, the majority were not. Advocates of ecotourism firmly established the idea that tourists would pay more for a sustainable experience, but it is now understood that the large majority of tourists will not pay a significant premium for sustainable tourism.[33] The prevalence of this erroneous idea was a significant barrier to progress as it took time to establish that consumers expected operators to address sustainability but did not expect to pay more for it. Second, other non-nature based businesses, after being pressed to be more environmentally benign would often reply that they were not ecotourism companies. The idea of sustainable tourism was so firmly niched as 'alternative' that it lost all traction within the mainstream industry. It took a long time to reverse the damage caused by the ecotourism diversion and to establish that there was a case for sustainable tourism which did not rely on being able to increase the margin. There were other reasons to take responsibility.

In the mid-1990s, Voluntary Service Overseas (VSO), a British international development charity placing volunteers abroad since 1958, established an advocacy programme. They undertook a survey of VSO volunteers working in communities in the developing world to determine what issues were currently confronting those communities. Had the survey taken place a year or two later the dominant concern in local communities reported by VSO volunteers would probably have been HIV/AIDS, but in 1996 it was tourism. They were not the first NGO to take up the issue of tourism: as we have seen Tourism Concern ran a long campaign pointing out that we take our holidays in their homes, and Action for Southern Africa ran a 'people first' campaign calling on British companies operating to South Africa to commit to a living

---

31 WTO (2001b) The British Ecotourism Market: 13

32 If you are a student reading this you may find that your lecturer attaches more significance to ecotourism than I do. There are still may papers in the journals about ecotourism, ask what the evidence is for its significance in the marketplace.

33 In 1999 Tearfund asked about willingness to pay a premium for responsible components – as we shall see below, while respondents aspired to have more responsible holidays they were resistant to paying more for them.

wage, and gender and racial equality.[34]

The VSO WorldWise campaign, launched in July 1998, asked British holidaymakers whether they ever met any local people, and by so doing pointed out that many travelled to the most distant locations on earth and never ate, drank or shopped outside the hotel. It challenged them to get more out of their holiday and asked whether they would go shopping at home dressed only in a swimsuit. Its promotional literature advised, for example, finding a local market: 'you can buy direct from the craftspeople and see local traditions come alive. An experience for you. A livelihood for local people – just ask.'[35] The campaign carried positive messages about how to have a better holiday: 'a few words of the language and a basic understanding of the culture can make a big difference in how people relate to you and how much you gain from your experience.' It was intended to be empowering, to enable the holidaymaker or traveller to get more out of their holiday. The leaflet, entitled 'Every holiday has hidden extras below the surface' echoed the concerns that so many holidaymakers have, and directly addressed their expectations:

> Fantastic, you're going on holiday. A chance to get away, to meet new people. But think for a moment. Who will you meet? A nice couple from Birmingham? Every travel brochure says 'meet our friendly local people. They are the warmth of our welcome.' But will you actually meet any? Will you go beyond just ordering a meal or a drink?

The VSO campaign, recognised that many of us want better holidays, and that, if that is our aspiration, we need to be inspired and encouraged to get it. We[36] deliberately left the questions unanswered, to encourage behavioural change. The leaflet neither preached nor prohibited, if the question was unimportant to the reader it could safely be ignored.

Another part of the VSO WorldWise campaign, 'Travelling to a fairer world', used data collected for VSO by NOP, a commercial polling company, in their random UK omnibus survey[37] on the responses of UK residents to

---

34 Goodwin and Francis (2003): 273. This paper presents a fuller account of the campaign than that presented here.

35 VSO (1997)

36 The campaign was run by Dan Rees and Ian Munt of VSO, with advice from Robert Cleverdon, Harold Goodwin, Alison Stancliffe and Richard Tapper. The campaign was launched on 2 July by Jonathan Dimbleby at Westminster Central Hall. There was a campaign film and 30,000 postcards were distributed for holidaymakers to send to their travel companies.

37 Adults aged 18–60, 17–23 June 1998

tourism impacts. 'Imagine if the roles were reversed, and rich foreign tourists continually visited your local area,' it suggested – 87% of respondents said they would object to having tourists parked outside their home every day, 'wanting to use [their] home and resources'; 83% would object to groups of tourists lining up to 'take photographs of [their] family and home without asking permission first'; and 75% objected to tourists expecting them to 'dress up as City stockbrokers or Morris dancers'. By contrast the same research found that 'rich foreign tourists' would be welcome if: they respected their culture (89%); if the money they spent on holiday stayed with local people (86%); if some of the money they spent on holiday was used to build better roads and public transport for local people (85%); and if they took time to learn about local places of interest (82%).

This commercial opinion poll research was important in establishing that dual standards existed: UK residents did not like to be treated the way some UK holidaymakers treated people in developing countries – 72% of respondents said that they 'would welcome a campaign that dealt with the impact that tourists can have on the developing world,' legitimating VSO's WorldWise action to raise awareness about tourism's impact on local people in the developing world.

The next stage of VSO's campaign was to look at UK tour operators and how well they met demands of tourists for information. *Travelling in the Dark* reported in 1999 on the performance of those tour operators sending tourists to the places where VSO had volunteers in the developing world. VSO surveyed 50 operators. Recognising that many tourists rely on their tour operator for information and guidance on all aspects of their holiday, the 50 companies were asked for copies of the information and advice they provided to their clients about local people, local customs, local goods and services and conserving the environment. The information sent was then scored[38] to determine how good it was, and league tables were constructed. The research was not undertaken by academics and the results were not published other than as a VSO campaign report.

Two-thirds of operators, reported VSO, failed to meet even a minimum standard, and many had failed to provide anything at all. It was not a clear-cut case of small specialists performing well and large multi-destination companies performing badly. British Airways Holidays came sixth and Kuoni 11th; Himalayan Kingdoms came top. The media like league tables and tour

---

38   Scored by number of items of information provided.

operators do not, unless they are near the top. The findings motivated some of the companies which had performed poorly to improve the information which they sent out to their customers. The campaign raised the profile of the issue. Subsequently, the managing director of Thomson Holidays declared: 'Our customers trust Thomson to provide them with enjoyable trouble-free holidays. We believe that providing good information and advice is essential to keeping that confidence.'[39] Unijet's marketing manager was quoted as saying: 'We're here to give customers what they want, or they'll go to other people. And our customers want to interact more, they want to get out of the resort, go out and see more.'[40] Finally, mainstream tour operators were recognising their customers were demanding more, and that they needed to deliver for good commercial reasons.

That there were good performers among the large mainstream operators, and awareness at senior levels of changing consumer tastes, was big news to many of us engaged in the campaign, including me. And we had demonstrated that by revealing good and bad practice it was possible to encourage everyone to perform better. The report concluded that good travel advice is 'a right not a luxury', and that: 'Those companies that fail to give adequate information are depriving their customers of the opportunity to get the most from their holiday. They are also depriving local people of the chance to maximise the benefits visitors can bring and to protect indigenous culture... With just a little effort and imagination all tour operators are capable of providing the quality travel advice already offered by some.'[41]

Overall, the WorldWise campaign encouraged consumers to demand more useful information about their destination, and about how they could have a better more engaged experience. They learnt how to increase their positive and reduce their negative impacts. Some operators were very annoyed by their position in the league tables, but the VSO campaign was not negative. It was provided a checklist of easy improvements that could help tour operators would enable them to improve their customer service, their product and their competitiveness. Perhaps most significantly, it had demonstrated that a qualitative, responsible approach could be a good value proposition for the mainstream travel business.

It was the start of the campaign for Responsible Tourism – albeit at this

---

39   Richard Bowden-Doyle, in VSO (1999): 1
40   Owen Whitehead, in (VSO) 1999: 2
41   VSO (1999): 5

stage focused on developing countries – and established Responsible Tourism's 'critical friend' approach. VSO concluded its *Travelling in the Dark* report by declaring that it was 'keen to work with tour operators to ensure that everyone travelling to the developing world is provided with the advice and information they deserve.'[42] The next stage of VSO's engagement was working directly, and more quietly, with the Association of Independent Tour Operators.[43]

By 2000, VSO was disengaging from work on tourism to work on other issues. The campaign was taken up by Tearfund, one of the UK's leading Christian relief and development agencies. Tearfund consciously built on the work of VSO and added the broader and more explicit language of ethical tourism. In November 2002 Tearfund published a report on *Improving tour operator performance: the role of corporate social responsibility and reporting,*[44] jointly with the Association of British Travel Agents (ABTA) and the Tour Operators Initiative,[45] which included major UK holiday companies BA Holidays and First Choice. This joint report asserted the importance of the triple bottom line and stated that companies increasingly recognised 'the need to preserve the environment, to look after their workforce and to give something back to communities.' All of which needed to be done 'while running a profitable business.' The report connected corporate social responsibility (CSR) and customer satisfaction – and made the business case for CSR,[46] The business case articulated by VSO and Tearfund for engaging with these ethical issues was founded on responding to consumer trends.

In preparation for the World Summit on Sustainable Development, ten years on from Rio, in Johannesburg in 2002, the Prime Minister Tony Blair challenged a number of industries to develop initiatives which would contribute to sustainable development in developing countries and which could be announced at the summit. The UK government[47] initiated the Sustainable Tourism Initiative (STI), a multi-stakeholder process engaging NGOs and the industry. The Prime Minister assisted by encouraging the UK's leading tour

---

42   VSO (1999): 5

43   We will return to this in the next chapter when we look at the business case for Responsible Tourism.

44   Tearfund (2002b)

45   Tour Operators Initiative www.toinitiative.org launched by UNEP in 2000

46   Tearfund (2002b): 1

47   Foreign and Commonwealth Office working with the Royal Institute of International Affairs in London

operators to support the initiative by hosting a meeting at Downing Street. He subsequently launched it at the World Summit on Sustainable Development in 2002. The STI resulted in the creation of the Travel Foundation in 2003, a registered UK charity,[48] and the Responsible Tourism Unit in the Federation of Tour Operators and now in ABTA. ABTA's work on Responsible Tourism is funded by the industry; the work of the Travel Foundation[49] is funded by donations from member companies and from individual holidaymakers too. The STI multi-stakeholder process provided a forum in which industry representatives, consultants, academics and NGOs met regularly and contributed to developing awareness of the responsible agenda. In 2004 ResponsibleTravel. com launched the First Choice Responsible Tourism awards (since 2007 the Virgin Holidays Responsible Tourism Awards). Designed to engage the public, nominations are sought from tourists. The awards seek out responsible tourism ventures that deserve to be celebrated: the Responsible Tourism Awards contribute to making the change they reward.[50]

Emerging ethical consumers

Like VSO, Tearfund engaged with tourism because it recognised its potential to contribute to development. However, it sought to engage with all UK outbound tourism, and late in 1999 it commissioned commercial market research from Ipsos-RSL about the holiday choices of the over-15s, on a national and regional level. The 27% of respondents who had never been on an overseas holiday were excluded. The results of the survey are shown in Table 2.1.

It is not surprising that a good hotel, an affordable price and good weather (this was a survey of British holidaymakers) were of the highest importance. However, the surprise was that the provision of good local information, a significant opportunity for interaction with local people and a trip was designed to cause limited environmental damage, were all rated as more important than whether the respondent had travelled with the company before. This group of holidaymakers is particularly important to a tour operator since the recruitment cost is low. Moreover, less than 5% of respondents reported in each case that these issues were of no importance to them.

---

48 www.thetravelfoundation.org.uk

49 An attempt to create a sister organisation in the Netherlands was unsuccessful.

50 www.responsibletourismawards.com

Table 2.1: For the last overseas holiday that you booked (whether via a tour company or independently), how important were the following criteria in determining your choice?

	High %	Medium %	Low %	None %
Affordable cost	82	12	3	3
Good weather	78	14	5	3
Guaranteed a good hotel with facilities	71	15	8	4
Good information is available on the social, economic and political situation of the country and local area to be visited	42	30	23	3
There is a significant opportunity for interaction with the local people	37	37	23	3
Trip has been specifically designed to cause as little damage as possible to the environment	32	34	27	5
Company has ethical policies	27	34	30	7
Used the company before	26	30	38	5

Source: Tearfund/Ipsos-RSL November 1999[51]

A majority of consumers felt that it was the industry's responsibility to provide them with more information about the people and places they were going to visit. Clearly they saw the local people and their place as part of the experience they were purchasing. Perhaps most remarkably, 61% responded that it was important to them that the company had 'ethical policies'; 27% of the sample said that it was of high importance to them. This was commercially sensitive market research: the point was not lost on the operators.

It may be objected that this market research measures and reports aspiration – upon which the respondents may not act. However, aspiration is a major element in most purchases. Most decisions about travel and the purchase of travel services are based on motivation (activity, destination or experience), opportunity (a function of available leisure time and cost) and a range of other factors which will include quality, safety, experience of and confidence in the provider and what might broadly be considered as ethical considerations. These are evident in the Tearfund research. The primary factors are motivation and opportunity, but, given the range of providers offering similar products at similar prices, the tie-breaker may be one of the ethical considerations, and particularly if these affect the quality and depth of the tourist experience.

---

51 Ipsos-RSL undertook the research of a nationally and regionally representative sample of 2032 adults (weighted to 2043) aged 15+. Interviews were conducted in the period 26–30 November 1999; dataset accurate to +/- 3% at 95% confidence level.

Influenced by the ecotourism proposition that tourists would pay more for an eco-product, the Tearfund/Ipsos-RSL research also asked about their willingness to pay a premium for a holiday which:

- contributed towards preserving the local environment or to reversing some of the negative environmental impacts of tourism (35% said they were)
- guaranteed good wages and working conditions in destination (29%)
- supported a local charity (21%).

The legacy of the excitement about ecotourism in the 1980s and 1990s is the idea that travellers and holidaymakers will pay more for the eco, ethical, sustainable or responsible elements of a holiday. It is very difficult for a consumer to attach a 'price' to any particular part of a holiday: they buy a product, an experience, comprising many elements, some of which will be essential others part of the mix of things which result in the choice. The Ipsos-RSL research asked some questions about the willingness of consumers to pay more for the ethical elements – 59% of respondents said they were willing to pay more, 41% said that they were not – 43% said they were willing to pay up to £25 more on a £500 holiday, 45% said they were prepared to pay nothing more.[52] The figure of 59% of respondents who answered that they were prepared to pay more fell to 45% when the respondents were confronted by indicative price increases. There is no data which enables analysis by destination intention or experience; we do not know whether views are different amongst travellers who had only experienced developed world rather than those who had travelled to developing countries. This research reports aspiration: only sales data records outcomes. It is likely that over time increasing numbers of consumers will simply expect these elements to be addressed already by the person selling them the product.

Unsurprisingly the Tearfund/Ipsos-RSL research suggested that those respondents who reported that they 'regularly buy fairly traded goods or use an ethical bank or investment fund', 'are a member of an environmental, development or human rights group' or travel to developing countries, were most likely to place a high importance on the four ethical dimensions of their holidays. It is also unsurprising that 47% said that they prefer just to switch off on holiday. The consumer may reasonably expect their supplier to have addressed these issues for them. In the consumer market place rarely is the

---

52 Tearfund (2000a): Tables 4 and 5 – 22% said that they were prepared to pay £10 more on a holiday costing £500 and 21% were prepared to pay £25 more on a holiday costing £500.

price premium for an ethical product obvious: rather it is wrapped up in the general proposition, often in a way that suggests a higher quality product or experience to justify the higher price. Consider for example the Union Hand-Roasted Coffee business which retails premium coffee under the Fairtrade label and attaches 'organic natural spirit' and rich clarity to the brand proposition. The focus is on the consumer experience proposition. The ethical component is only a part of that quality experience proposition, arguably adding credibility to the value proposition.[53]

In September 2000, the Association of British Travel Agents (ABTA) undertook some market research to explore this emerging agenda.[54] Their research found that the reputation of the holiday company on environmental issues was important to 70% of respondents[55] and that the provision of social and environmental information in tour operator's brochures was important to 78%.[56] They also asked about how important it was that their holiday should benefit the people in the destination through jobs and business opportunities: 71% said that it was important to them[57] – 85% said that it was important to them that their holiday should not damage the environment.[58] Aside from the questions about economic and environmental benefits, ABTA also included an experiential question asking how important it was that the respondent's holiday should 'include visits to experience local culture and foods': 77% said that it was important.[59] The aspirational trend to experience the local has grown in tandem with the trend to expect the experiences to be produced more responsibly.

The Tearfund/Ipsos-RSL research, in 1999 included the question 'Would you be more likely to book a holiday with a company if they had a written code to guarantee good working conditions, protect the environment and support local charities in destinations?' – 45% said yes, 13% said no and 42% said that it would make no difference. In 2001, the research was repeated, with the identical question asked by the same company, to a similar sample – 52%

53   www.unionroasted.com accessed 6 May 2010
54   Unpublished top line results 963 face-to-face street interviews conducted at 107 constituency-based sampling points, weighted to reflect the profile of British holidaymakers.
55   Very Important 29%, Fairly Important 41%
56   Very Important 33%, Fairly Important 45%
57   Very Important 27%, Fairly Important 44%
58   Very Important 40%, Fairly Important 45%
59   Very Important 36%, Fairly Important 41%

replied positively, an increase of 7% in two years.[60] The research has not been repeated because it has become unnecessary.

The industry's own research has confirmed the trend. A consumer survey commissioned by ABTA in October 2002 found similar results: the reputation of a travel company on environmental issues was important to 65% of respondents. The inclusion of social and environmental information in tour operator brochures was important to 75% of potential holidaymakers – 76% felt that it was important that their holiday benefited local people and 87% felt that it was important that their holiday should not damage the environment – 59% of respondents said that they would be interested in finding out more about local environmental and social issues.[61] And attitudes were changing. Jane Ashton, head of corporate social responsibility at the major UK holiday company First Choice, said in 2006: 'The product we sell is the people and environment – so we have an obvious interest in protecting them.' First Choice, she said, would be working on diverse projects, including environmental and educational schemes. She added: 'We're not experiencing a huge demand from the average consumer, but we do believe that awareness is increasing, and in a few years' time we will have needed to have integrated these principles into our supply chain.'[62]

In the UK, as everywhere else, tour operators and travel agents sell in a market place alongside a wide variety of retailers. Consumer expectations are set by developments in other retail sectors. Marks & Spencer, the major UK high-street retailer launched its 'Plan A .... Because there is no Plan B' sustainability campaign in January 2007. The five pillars of Plan A are: climate change, waste, natural resources, fair partnership, and health and wellbeing. The campaign set out 100 commitments to be achieved in five years, and has now been extended to 180 commitments to be achieved by 2018. Its objective is to become the world's most sustainable retailer.[63] Plan A was part of Marks & Spencer's strategy to reinvigorate its retailing position on the high street, the sustainability commitment, part of its brand positioning. In the past it has used the strapline 'Quality worth every penny', and has pointed out that:

---

60 Ipsos-RSL asked a regionally and nationally representative sample of 927 adults between 30 November and 10 December 2001. Tearfund (2002a):7 Tearfund also asked about the demand for more information up 2%, similar numbers of people as previously thought that it was the responsibility of travel agents (55%) and tour operators (48%) to provide the information.

61 ABTA funded MORI survey undertaken in October 2002, press released in January 2002

62 Jane Ashton of First Choice, quoted by Esther Addley in 'Boom in green holidays as ethical travel takes off' The Guardian 17 July 2006

63 See http://plana.marksandspencer.com/about

'For some retailers, green went out of fashion as quickly as it came in'. It has maintained its focus on sustainability: its 'Doing the Right Thing' campaign in 2009 explained: 'Above all, doing the right thing is doing it today, because our planet can't wait until tomorrow'. Marks & Spencer have sought to enter into a partnership with their customers and suppliers. 'Doing the Right Thing' contributes to the brand values: quality, value, service, innovation and trust. There is a marketing case, one which engages customers, and a business case, as Sir Stuart Rose, Chairman of Marks & Spencer, wrote in the *How We do Business Report in 2009*:

> Plan A isn't only important to us, it matters to our customers too. They've told us that despite the impact of the recession, our commitment to Plan A remains important to them. They value the difference between us and other retailers, they understand the commitment we've made and they trust us to stick to it. We've listened to them, and also made it easier for them to play their part in Plan A … We believe that for our business to deliver long-term value for its shareholders, it must be environmentally and socially sustainable. Over the past two years, we've found out that leading on sustainability issues not only differentiates our business and drives sales, but also makes us more efficient. In January 2007 we were prepared to invest £200m over five years in Plan A – two years on it has already become cost positive. Not only is this the right thing to do, it also makes complete business sense.[64]

When a retailer of the scale and significance of Marks & Spencer adopts this approach, for sound business reasons, spending millions of pounds on promoting the sustainability message, engaging its customers in the process and raising their expectations, it begins to reshape consumer expectations. Every year, the retailer tracks the views of its consumers on green issues, classifying them according to their activism. Between 2008 and 2009 the 'Green Crusaders' dropped to 9% (down 1 point), the 'If it's easy' group increased 8 points to 35% and the 'What's the point' and 'Not my problem' groups both declined, by 2 and 5 points respectively.[65] A business the size of Marks and Spencer both follows and makes the market.

The Co-operative Bank has been tracking the growth of ethical consumerism in the UK since 1999. The changes in the self-reported behaviour of UK consumers are striking (Table 2.2).

---

64 Marks and Spencer 2009: 1
65 Marks and Spencer 2009: 42

Table 2.2: Percentage of people undertaking the following at least once during the year

	1999 (%)	2009 (%)
Bought to support local shops/suppliers	61	87
Talked to friends/family about a company's behaviour	58	68
Avoided a product or service on a company's behaviour	44	64
Chosen a product or service on a company's behaviour	51	60
Recommended a company because of its responsible reputation	52	59
Bought primarily for ethical reasons	29	52
Felt guilt about an unethical purchase	17	43
Actively sought information on a company's behaviour/policies	24	38
Actively campaigned about and environmental/social issue	15	28

Source: Co-operative Bank Ethical Shopping Survey, annual surveys of 1000+ weighted to be representative of UK population 18+

This is self-reported behaviour and is indicative of a change in aspiration rather than an accurate report of behaviour, but, as was argued earlier, marketing measures and responds to consumer aspirations. Between the two dates, there is a marked rise in the aspiration to support local shops and in consumers reporting that they have considered, discussed, chosen or avoided a product or service on ethical grounds. The ethical reputation and behaviour of a company has become significantly more important to consumers over the last ten years. It is striking that there has been a 20% increase, to 64%, in the number of people reporting that they have avoided a product or service because of a company's behaviour and 59% reporting that they had recommended a company based on its responsible reputation. This has particular importance for an industry that relies so heavily on repeats and referrals. But most striking is the increase from 17% to 43% in the number of people saying that they had felt guilty about an unethical purchase. This is less likely to be inflated by aspiration; it may under report the numbers of UK consumers who have felt guilty. Either way it is not good news for companies selling treats and indulgences to consumers who travel. Feelings of guilt undermine holidays as they do the enjoyment of coffee and chocolate. Assuaging guilt is one of the reasons for the success of the Fairtrade labels. People argue that people on holiday are indulging themselves, taking a break. There is some truth in this, but it should not be forgotten that the large majority prefer their indulgences to be guilt free.

In 2005 First Choice commissioned Mintel[66] to survey people who had recently taken a holiday abroad. Only 21% said that they had never heard of 'the term "responsible tourism"'; an online survey of Thomson and First Choice holidaymakers in 2010 found that 51% of respondents claimed to understand Responsible Tourism and that 66% said they understood environmental and social responsibility.[67] Surprisingly in 2005 only around a fifth felt 'tourism does more good than harm to most local communities where I have taken a holiday'.[68] Of course that does not mean that 80% of recent holidaymakers would necessarily agree with the converse – that in their experience tourism does more harm, than good – but it is safe to assume that a significant proportion would, which should concern operators and retailers. Only 17% of respondents agreed with the statement, 'When on holiday I don't want to have to think about the environmental consequences of my holiday.' That may mean that they do not care, or it may mean that they expect someone else to have thought about the environmental impacts – the holiday company perhaps – and dealt with it. First Choice's research identified three segments of consumers. The lackadaisicals (30% of their sample) were unconcerned and not likely to pay attention to the ethical credentials of the company. Concerned tourists amounted to 35% of respondents and frequent flyers about 40%, defined as those taking two or more holidays a year by plane. The frequent flyers expressed higher than average interest in tackling environmental issues, but not in reducing the number of holidays they enjoy[69] – 54% said they were willing to use public transport to explore the destination; only 20% were willing to accept a smaller range of food in the buffet to reduce wastage.[70]

The Mintel/First Choice survey also found that 80% of respondents reported they recycle at home,[71] only 50% were prepared to recycle when on holiday. This can be interpreted as meaning that holidaymakers care less when they are abroad or it may mean that they did not see themselves driving to the local recycling centre with their rubbish. The problem is often that tourists do

---

66 Market Intelligence International Mintel interviewed a nationally representative sample of 2000 adults in early October 2005 about their holiday patterns, their general concern about a range of environmental issues and what they would personally be prepared to contribute to addressing some of the problems while on holiday. The main focus of the research was on people who had taken a holiday abroad since the start of 2004.

67 Unpublished on line survey of current travellers 2009/10, n=830

68 First Choice (2005): 05

69 First Choice (2005): 07

70 First Choice (2005): 08

71 First Choice (2005): 05, 08

not get the necessary information. In the Gambia if guests leave their empty water bottles in their room the person who cleans the room will get additional income by selling the bottles to be reused – an empty bottle should never be crushed.

First Choice concluded that the travelling public are 'not that concerned about the impact they have when they go on holiday and many are not that interested in wasting precious holiday time or paying extra to help the communities that they visit.' In my view, the evidence from broad consumer and travel industry research is that there is increasing concern, that holidaymakers expect the operator to address the issues on their behalf and that they do not expect to have to pay extra for it. They increasingly expect to be sold experiences, real holidays, about which they do not need to feel guilty. First Choice was more positive in the understanding it took away from this research in 2005 it concluded that: 'the industry can't pay lip service to responsible tourism... [It is] the travel industry's duty to give customers responsible tourism information in a way that will engage them, rather than preach to them in a way that will turn them off.'[72] Quite so.

Five years later, holidaymakers' awareness of Responsible Tourism issues had increased. The 2010 First Choice/Thomson survey of current travellers they found that 73% of their holiday makers wanted to be able to 'easily identify' a greener holiday [73] and 82% agreed with the proposition that 'I want to be able to choose my holiday knowing the tour operator has done the hard work in making it environmentally and socially responsible.'[74] This research also suggested that more than 80% of holidaymakers always turn off lights when they leave the room, and do not keep the room unnecessarily cool. Over 70% say they always take a shower rather than a bath, even though they are more likely to take a bath at home.[75]

In the UK the major operators conduct their own market research in house[76] and through commercial market research companies like Mintel and Ipsos. Tearfund's decision to use a commercial market research company was based on the recognition that tourism companies were more likely to give credence to research conducted by the companies which they use to guide their marketing.

---

72   First Choice (2005): 10

73   Unpublished on line survey of current travellers 2009/10, n=748

74   n=750

75   Unpublished on line survey of current travellers 2009/10, n=825

76   TUI stated that in 2008/09, 49% of their businesses carried out market or customer research related to sustainable development issues, TUI (2010): 31

Tourism companies are more interested in the shifts in market preferences, and changing preferences amongst their consumer in particular than they are in the mechanics driving the change. They are responding to changes in the market place, the changes in consumer aspirations and expectations, which shape consumer choices.

In 2007, the UK's Department for the Environment and Rural Affairs, DEFRA, commissioned focus group research into the public understanding of sustainable leisure and tourism.[77] One of the most interesting questions asked respondents who they held to be responsible for taking action to address the problems associated with large-scale leisure and tourism.[78] The researchers concluded that participants 'wanted to know that their pro-environmental choices were part of a wider movement' and that politicians and other public figures were leading the way.[79] As The report states: 'DEFRA has identified a number of pro-environmental behaviours that it would like to encourage among consumers.'[80] In the Annals paper based on their research, the authors reflected on the respondents' resistance to changing their behaviour 'unless other people and developing countries changed.' They concluded respondents 'seem to place greater responsibility on government than any other group, including themselves, while politicians needed to set an example through their own behaviour and show leadership, instead of hypocrisy.'[81] Governments, just like consumers and producers, prefer others to take responsibility rather than to take action themselves. Consumers are not being irrational when they articulate their expectation that other consumers, leaders, government and developing countries do their bit too. It is difficult, when new coal-fired power stations are still being built in Britain and elsewhere, to see how personally making fewer flights will reduce the risk of global warming. Some 'tragedy of the commons' problems require government to deal with free-riders, rather than to be free-riders themselves.

By 2010 the UK economy was in recession and the travel and tourism sector was experiencing reduced demand, and reducing its staffing accordingly. But there was no slackening in the industry leaders' commitment to making progress on Responsible Tourism. Populus, a market intelligence company,

---

77 Miller et al. (2007)

78 See DEFRA website http://randd.defra.gov.uk/Default.aspx?Menu=Menu&Module=More&Location=None&ProjectID=14639&FromSearch=Y&Publisher=1&SearchText=EV02047%20&SortString=ProjectCode&SortOrder=Asc&Paging=10 accessed 26 August 2010

79 Miller et al. (2007): 61

80 Miller et al. (2007): 75

81 Miller et al. (2010): 642

has published a monthly *Concerned Consumer Index* since before the economic crisis. In March 2007 they identified 48% of their respondents as concerned consumers.[82] They ask their representative sample of all British adults whether they aspire to 'buy the most ethical and environmentally-friendly products' they can 'even if it means paying a little extra'.[83] The proportion saying that this was their aspiration varied between 35% and 45% between November 2008 and November 2009. The economic downturn has clearly dampened the aspirations of concerned consumers but they have remained a significant part of the UK market.

Thomas Cook[84] used the Populus survey to benchmark their performance on the issues which Populus has identified as the priory issues for consumers, indexed on a scale of 1 to 5. Not surprisingly personal safety comes top (4.25), customer service (4.09) followed by those 'ethical' issues again, first identified in the late nineties 'good relations with local people' (3.84), 'welfare of captive animals' (3.75), 'impact on local communities' (3.61), 'local employee welfare' (3.60) followed by 'environmental impact of holiday destination' (3.38) and 'environmental impact of travel' (3.29). The impact of tourism on 'the availability of water for tourists and local communities at a holiday destination' was indexed at 3.98, economic benefits for the local community and the promotion of knowledge about the history and culture of the destination both scored more than 3.9. Thomas Cook concluded from their research that whilst consumers are scaling back their spending, they have not stopped caring and are looking for ways to realise their values in the holiday choices they make. They concluded by noting that over 60% of consumers have a higher opinion of those companies that stick to their ethical and environmental course in spite of difficult economic conditions. It is not surprising then that in the recession the Responsible Tourism agenda has continued to be addressed.

The evidence suggests that consumer expectations are changing and that tourism businesses cannot ignore this market trend. Back in 1999, Noel Josephides[85] argued in the *Travel Trade Gazette* against the Tearfund research

---

82 They poll online a representative sample of just over 1000 British adults. The results are published in The Times and online at www.populus.co.uk. Populus November 2009 Concerned Consumers Survey November 2009 n=452

83 For concerned consumers it varied between 55% and 60%

84 Unpublished research commissioned by Thomas Cook from Populus.

85 I quote this only to indicate how much knowledge and attitudes have changed. I am reminded of Keynes's question 'When the facts change, I change my mind. What do you change? Noel is one of the main supporters of the Travel Foundation and has contributed significantly to change in the industry.

saying that British tourists have 'absolutely no interest in supporting a host country's economy, respecting local customs or acting responsibly while on holiday.' In the same article he reported that 8% of Sunvil clients said that Sunvil's environmental initiative encouraged them to book with the company.[86] No operator in an industry as competitive as UK outbound package holidays and needing to operate with high occupancy levels can ignore one in 12 potential clients. The business case is strong for most market segments.

In response, many tour operators and others working with the UK outbound market have started to develop codes of conduct, often expressing what is special about the experience they offer, and seeking to build their relationship with their clients. Others are developed by civil society organisations in originating markets, in destinations and internationally. Box 2.1 contains an example; there are hundreds, perhaps thousands, more. It is desirable that there are many, as the issues and the places vary.

Tour operators are not alone: others have responsibility too. Guidebooks increasingly contain information to help travellers engage harmoniously with the people and places they visit. A few – too few – travel journalists weave the responsible consumption elements into their stories about the experience.[87] There are a few guides to ethical, green or low-impact travel, all of which connect ethical with great holidays.[88] And there are an increasing number of websites which provide a market place for holidays and tourism businesses which communicate to the consumer about the experience and the responsible elements.[89]

The year 2007 was something of a watershed for Responsible Tourism. Commercial market research data had established the increasing importance of the issues to consumers and major companies like TUI and Thomas Cook were addressing the issues. It was in 2007 that World Travel Market launched World Responsible Tourism Day,[90] with support from the UNWTO. Responsible Tourism was becoming part of the mainstream, and we shall see more of the reasons for this in the next chapter.

---

86 Quoted in Goodwin and Francis (2003): 282–283

87 See for example Catherine Mack at www.ethicaltraveller.co.uk and Richard Hammond at www.greentraveller.co.uk

88 For example Katz (2009); Hammond and Smith (2009) and Patullo and Minelli (2009).

89 The first and leading example is www.responsibletravel.com

90 www.wtmwrtd.com. The first World Responsible Tourism Day was 12 November 2008

Box 2.1 Tearfund's suggested code for tourists

Make the Most of Your Holidays......................

1. Find out about your destination – take some time before you go to read about the cultural, social and political background of the place and people you are visiting.

2. Go equipped with basic words and phrases in the local language – this may open up opportunities for you to meet people who live there.

3. Buy locally made goods and use locally provided services wherever possible – your support is often vital to local people.

4. Pay a fair price for the goods or services you buy – if you haggle for the lowest price your bargain may be at someone else's expense.

5. Be sensitive to the local culture – dress and act in a way that respects local beliefs and customs, particularly at religious sites.

6. Ask permission before taking photographs of individuals or of people's homes – and remember that you may be expected to pay for the privilege.

7. Avoid conspicuous displays of wealth – this can accentuate the gap between rich and poor and distance you from the cultures you came to experience.

8. Make no promises to local people that you can't keep – be realistic about what you will do when you return home.

9. Minimize your environmental impact – keep to footpaths and marked routes, don't remove any of the natural habitat and reduce the packaging you bring.

10. Slow down to enjoy the differences – you'll be back with the familiar soon enough.

...............And ensure that others can too. www.tearfund.org

Source: Tearfund 2002a:21

The demand for experience and authenticity

The idea of a 'real' holiday is ever-changing; what we want from a holiday and the language we use reflect changes in society, and particularly in consumerism. In the UK market consumers' expectations of the responsible elements of their holidays, and the authenticity and quality of their experience have risen – and there is a clear synergy between the two. Consumer aspirations for real holidays have real effects on consumer choice. The aspirations affect what sells and what does not, and most decisions about purchases are now multi-faceted: price is still important but it is not the only determinant. Destination and activity, availability, price, perceptions of quality and authenticity, and the trustworthiness of the supplier are all important. Responsible Tourism contributes to brand and experience, and consumers want to know that the holiday has been put together with due diligence, that the business has done it right. As a result the goods and services we buy are less commodified – a trend that means increasing margins for many producers and retailers of goods and services.

It is only necessary to cursorily compare contemporary brochures with those of the 1970s to see the shift from 'flop in the sun' holidays to more active and engaged experiences, often in the same destinations. It is not necessary to subscribe wholeheartedly to Maslow's hierarchy of needs to recognise that the demands of holidaymakers have changed. The need for accommodation and food, to travel safely and, for many from northern climes, the physiological need for sun, was met by brochures which featured shots of swimming pools, food, bars and restaurants, and fellow tourists having a good time. These days, there are fewer bars and swimming pools in brochures than in their predecessors and more pictures of local people and tourists engaged in activities together, though there are still market segments which emphasise bars and licentious behaviour.

TUI Travel reported in 2011 that activity holidays are amongst the most rapidly growing product ranges.[91] There is no doubt there has been an increase in activity holidays, and holidaymakers are pursuing their interests in bird watching, art or music, some in pursuit of greater personal satisfaction or wanting to give back are volunteering. John King, a tourism and marketing development consultant previously with the Australian Tourist Commission,

---

91 This trend is widely recognised in the industry. TUI Travel (2010): 12. In TUI Travel Passport to Adventure 2010 survey evidence is cited that 3 in 4 adults claim to have taken some type of activity holiday in the past three years.

wrote that travel is increasingly 'about experiences, fulfilment and rejuvenation' rather than about 'places and things' and that the lifestyle market is of increasing importance. He argued that the emphasis was shifting towards the experience rather than the place, and 'successful destination marketers will need to engage the customer as never before, to be able to provide them with the type of information and experience they are increasingly able to demand.' They need to work at 'creating holiday experiences and connecting them with the customer.' King is using the language of lifestyle marketing, which 'tends to focus and confirm more of what the customer would like to see in and of themselves'.[92] In so doing, we might hear an echo of Krippendorf's self-actualisation, and see mounting evidence of the pursuit of 'self-realization and fulfilment in all spheres of life,' including holidays.[93]

Krippendorf foresaw the emergence of a 'new travel culture' with 'informed and experienced', 'emancipated and independent' tourists seeking'... 'emotional recreation' through activities and experiences which are not possible in everyday life.' He argued that this would lead to demand from holiday makers for 'contact with other people and self-realization through creative activities, knowledge and exploration'.[94]

Authentic experience, however, is also a contested area. Some, for example Cohen,[95] have taken a contrary view, arguing that there has been a shift from the natural and authentic to the artificial and contrived. This reminds us that generalisation is fraught with difficulty. Lowenthal has argued that 'the cult of authenticity pervades modern life',[96] and Grayson and Martinec look at authenticity and the market. They distinguish between two kinds of consumer perceptions of authenticity: indexical and iconic, which, however, are not mutually exclusive.[97] Indexical authenticity, is used where the object or experience is the original or the real thing. For example to:

> determine whether a cultural dance performance is indexically authentic, a consumer must have some confidence (e.g., via additional information about the performers or cues offered during the performance) that the dancers are being true to their selves and/or cultural

---

92   King (2002): 105–108

93   Krippendorf (1987): 105. The Thomas Cook research found that 43% or holidaymakers said that they were motivated by wanting to create family memories and 84% to spend time together as a family.

94   Krippendorf (1987): 74

95   Cohen (1995)

96   Lowenthal (1992): 184

97   Grayson and Martinec (2004): 298

identity and not simply going through motions that are unrelated to their personality or heritage.[98]

Iconic authenticity is used to refer to authentic reproductions or recreations. To assess whether a cultural dance performance 'is iconically authentic, a consumer must have some sense … however sketchy or detailed—of how dances from this culture tend to look and sound'.[99] In either case authenticity is measured against the consumers' particular expectations.

Grayson and Martinec conclude from their review of the consumer literature that 'most scholars who study authenticity agree that authenticity is not an attribute inherent in an object and is better understood as an assessment made by a particular evaluator in a particular context'.[100] Authenticity is in the eye of the beholder. Their research at two sites in the UK, Shakespeare's birthplace and the Sherlock Holmes Museum, supports the view that there is a porous boundary between consumer fantasy and subjectivity and consumer perceptions of reality and objectivity and that the distinction between the authentic and inauthentic is subjective.[101] Views of authenticity will be determined by a range of originating market factors, including culture. For example, the UK market places far more emphasis on the age of the bricks and timber than do the cultures of China, India and Japan, where form matters more in determining authenticity.

The experiences sought by travellers, and the decisions which they make about their itinerary, are in large part determined by their prior knowledge of the country.[102] I was asked in the early 1990s by a group of Polish apple growers to arrange a series of study visits for them to orchards in Kent. When I asked what they would like to see in London I was stunned by their reply: the Trocadero Centre (an entertainment and shopping centre); a meal in Gerrard Street (the heart of China Town); and a performance of Buddy Holly (a musical about the American musician). I did persuade them to take a ride on an open-topped bus to see something of the city. When I asked them why these were their 'must dos', they answered that they would be ridiculed at home if they had not seen these icons. The quality of their experience of London was being framed by friends' and relatives' expectations.

---

98 Grayson and Martinec (2004): 298

99 Grayson and Martinec (2004): 298

100 Grayson and Martinec (2004): 299

101 Grayson and Martinec (2004): 306

102 Their level of satisfaction is in large part determined by the extent to which the experience matches their expectation.

It goes to prove, as Cohen argued, in *Sociology* in 1979, that there is a continuum in the tourism experience between the spurious and the superficial and a serious search for authenticity, for the real. And it follows that more care should be taken with the subtleties. The tourist experience is after all only one part of the travellers' or holidaymakers' experience: they carry with them other experiences and the culture of the society from which they originate.[103] Most adults know that Disney is not 'real' but like Father Christmas, it is more-or-less authentic.

In Yorkshire, tourists and day visitors seek out the locations where their favourite television programmes and films have been shot – *Last of the Summer Wine* at Holmfirth; James Herriot in the Dales. This is also a global phenomenon: just think of the *Lord of the Rings* in New Zealand, Burgundy, the setting for *Chocolat*, or Manhattan, in that most cinematic of cities, New York. There are so many Japanese people visiting Brontë country, centred on Haworth in west Yorkshire, that signage, guidebooks and postcards are all available in Japanese. Chieko Iwashita has demonstrated, using Japanese respondents, how representations and images of tourism destinations in films, television and literature affect the choice of destinations including, in addition to Haworth, Beatrix Potter and Hill Top Farm in the Lake District, and Conan Doyle and the Sherlock Holmes Museum at 221b Baker Street. Literature, painting, film and photography, among other art forms, and the general media contribute to the ways in which people in different cultures imagine and envision places. Squire, for example, has pointed to the way in which Beatrix Potter and Hill Top are used to mediate the values of English rural life and the countryside, and that the quest for English atmosphere is important to Japanese visitors.[104] Their view of authenticity is certainly nostalgic, but these scenes match Japanese visitors' expectations, and those of many others.

The experience economy is not limited to the UK, or to travel and tourism. Alvin Toffler in *Future Shock* in 1971 wrote about his expectation that in the future people would spend more on living amazing experiences, and the German sociologist Schulze in 1992 coined the term 'experience society'.[105] In 1999, Pine and Gilmore published *The Experience Economy, Work is Theatre and Every Business a Stage*. Their theory is largely descriptive of the shift from raw materials to manufactured goods, then services, and next, they suggest, to experiences. At places like Disneyland where consumers purchase experi-

---

103 Cohen (1979)

104 Squire (1993)

105 In Erlebnisgesellschaft – published in 1992

ences, they suggest, holidaymakers pay 'to spend time enjoying a series of memorable events that a company stages as in a theatrical play – to engage [the consumer] in a personal way.'[106] This is not dissimilar from what happens when a tourist visits St James's Park in London on a summer afternoon, a local market in The Gambia or the Trevi Fountain in Rome – except that these are public experiences, and they are free.

The point is that experiences can be highly differentiated. They can be made unique and they enable a business to charge a significantly higher price and secure a larger margin. Experiences also engage the consumer, creating opportunities for additional sales and encouraging repeats and referrals. Pine and Gilmore quote Sir Colin Marshall, Chairman of British Airways, who distinguishes between the business objective of providing an experience and that of transporting a passenger from A to B on time and at the lowest possible price. Speaking in 1995, he argued that BA's ambition was 'to go beyond the function and compete on the basis of providing an experience'.[107] Many would argue that Virgin Atlantic and a host of other airlines do the same, or do it better. But the essential is to differentiate the product or service, whether you are a destination or a tourism business. Destinations like the Gambia risk being perceived as merely 'bed factories' on the beach have to differentiate themselves from their competitors if they are to be sustainable, able to secure a bed/night price which permits reinvestment in the product. It is the strength of the social and cultural experience in the Gambia that enables it to compete, but it is a constant struggle for the Gambia to avoid being commodified. If forced to compete on price alone, in the highly competitive winter sun (for northern Europeans) market, hotels fail to secure enough margin over operating costs to reinvest, and slide towards dereliction.

In some ways, the idea of the experience economy, the demand for the real, sits awkwardly with ethical and Responsible Tourism. It has overtones (often far more than overtones) of self-indulgence and hedonism. Consider the 'last chance to see'[108] trend: Antarctic cruise numbers doubled between 2000 and 2007 – 59% of those surveyed on the cruises did not feel that their travel impacted on climate change.[109] The relationship between the increasing demand for authentic experiences and responsible tourism is complex, con-

---

106 Pine and Gilmore (1999): 2

107 Pine and Gilmore, (1999): 4

108 The title of a BBC series with Stephen Fry and Mark Carwardine searching for endangered animals on the edge of extinction.

109 Eijgelaar et al. (2010)

sumerism devours our planet. In the same year that *The Experience Economy* was published, Hawken, Lovins and Lovins published *Natural Capitalism* in 1999, which argues that the global economy is dependent on the natural resources of a finite world and that in a sustainable future natural resources would be accounted for as a finite and integrally valuable factor of production. By attaching value to finite resources, the tragedy of the commons is addressed: as we approach the limits of our finite world resource costs will increase. This is a responsible way of thinking about the future, but there is less empirical evidence of this change in thinking happening than there is of the growth of the experience economy.

On the other hand, real and authentic experiences that generate empathy and understanding contribute to creating responsible behaviour. Where businesses operate responsibly, and offer responsible products to attract responsible consumers, their other buyers are de facto consuming responsibly too. Consumers are attracted to desirable and responsible experiences for the experience alone, but they may also become educated about responsibility. Thus, businesses and attraction managers can change behaviour; conversely, when consumers complain about irresponsible elements in their holidays, they too drive change. However, more can always be done. The survey of Antarctic cruise tourists found no evidence that the trips developed greater environmental awareness, changed attitudes or encouraged more sustainable future travel choices.[110] Such tourism could potentially offer an opportunity tourists a glimpse of climate change, or of endangered species, raising awareness and encouraging behaviour change. At base camp on Everest, and in the Alps, the issue is discussed by Explore's tour groups[111] as it is no doubt amongst other tourists, travelling with other operators.

The challenge of realising value in the experience economy is shaping and meeting customer expectations – pre-formed expectations they have of what is, after all an unpredictable, real experience. Pine and Gilmore state: 'experience derives from the interaction between the staged event and the individual's prior state of mind and being.' There is a paradox in that 'the *work* of the experience stager perishes upon its performance' but 'the *value* of the experience lingers in the memory … where it remains long afterward.'[112] A meal in an expensive, themed restaurant is perhaps the best example. The product has been consumed; only the memory, good or bad, lingers. The

110 Eijgelaar et al. (2010) : 337

111 John Telfer personal communication.

112 Pine and Gilmore (1999): 12–13

restaurant is expensive largely because of the quality of the service and the experience. The message is simple: the business can capture more value if it sells product, service and an experience. Think about the grass-fed steak from a local farm, cooked and served in a gastropub overlooking the sea. Or fishing for mackerel and barbecuing them over a wood fire on the beach with local fishermen as the sun goes down. No wonder we pay more for these experiences and the producer earns more. Hawkers and costermongers, with their sing-song cries and banter, have understood the value of creating an experience for centuries.

In 2007, Pine and Gilmore published *Authenticity* subtitled *What consumers really want.* What is real is valued, and people spend 'the currency of experiences' – money and time – on what they perceive to be real. Selling experiences, 'rendering authenticity' is what an increasing part of the market demands. 'Your business offerings must get real', warn the authors, and conclude that the 'management of the customer perception of authenticity becomes the primary new source of competitive advantage'[113] Lewis and Bridger argue that authenticity was a new strain in consumer desire which develops with abundance: for consumers in a world of abundance, authenticity is of increasing importance. There is a tendency in both works to imply that this new 'consumer desire' is widespread, although there is no survey evidence to suggest that this is the case.[114] There is an intrinsic difficulty with this focus on authenticity in that it is relative, very relative. Recently, when walking down London's Regent Street, I was accosted by a small group of young male Lithuanian tourists, asking with some anxiety where they could find Abercrombie and Fitch. Lithuanians on holiday in London looking for an authentic American store: globalisation.[115]

The growing demand for experience-based products, is good news for the commercial viability of UK outbound tour operators – and for the inbound operators, hotels and attractions who can sell experiences to the UK public. However, a large part of the holiday experience takes place in public space. In China in 1983, long before mass tourism took off, I was extremely disappointed by the experience of the Great Wall, it was crowded, surrounded by tacky souvenir stores and had nothing of the anticipated grandeur better captured

---

113 Pine and Gilmore (2007): 1,3

114 Pine and Gilmore (2007): 4 quote Boyle's assertion that these 'New Realists' constitute 'a little less than half the British population and just under a quarter of the American population'

115 I had no idea, having looked them up I now discover that their history is in New York, their strapline is 'Genuine for over 100 years'.

by the photographs. Originating market operators have to work with inbound operators and local authorities to address these issues.

Many UK companies, including TUI, are addressing this. It is reporting growing demand for 'genuine travel experiences' and consequently anticipating 40% growth in the employment of local guides over the next three years [116] Andulela Experience[117] based in Hout Bay near Cape Town in South Africa is one example of the many new companies which are offering 'unique encounters with unique people', offering an insider's experience. Jazz, cookery and garden tours provide an opportunity to connect with South African culture. Andulela claims to provide personal enrichment, opening 'doors to a truly authentic South African experience' and offering 'real people, real places, real experience' to 'send you home with much more than a snapshot-perspective to show for your time here'. In the UK, the Ludlow Marches Food and Drink Festival attracts locals, day excursionists and tourists by providing an opportunity for people to meet the producers and enjoy the provenance of the produce.

UK tourism businesses are adapting their products to meet the expectations of its clients for real experiences, and are hoping by so doing to build loyalty among the travelling public. Our changing demand for 'real' experiences is being driven by our increasing experience of travel, but also by wider trends in consumerism in the UK. The real, authentic, holiday experiences enjoyed by holidaymakers can build a tour company's relationship with its clients, clients who are then more likely to repeat and refer others encouraging them to buy the experience. Like CAMRA did with its real ale campaign, many holiday companies have tapped into this desire for the real and turned it into a sustainable, viable business model, which (though 'realness' changes) shows no sign of abating.

The original VSO campaign encouraged people to find out about local culture, history and language and encouraged holidaymakers to have a better, more enjoyable, holiday by preparing themselves to engage and deepen the experience. This may in turn change their expectation of what makes a good holiday, a real holiday, and about who can provide it, building consumer loyalty. Pine and Gilmore argue that experiences are 'memorable, transformations and effectual'. These experiences transform people and have consequences, the consumers become aspirational. Pine and Gilmore note that experiences

---

116 TUI Travel Adventure Brands (2010): 16

117 www.andulela.com accessed 3 May 2010

too can be commodified if they are created or managed badly, the phrase, 'Been there, done that, got the T-shirt' suggests that the experience has been commodified and that it is not worth repeating.

New tourists?

It has probably always been possible to place travellers on an ethical continuum from the concerned to the could-not-care-less and from those seeking the real and authentic to those seeking the opposite. However, there is evidence that these trends toward more ethical awareness and a greater willingness to take responsibility for the impacts of tourists and the industry, and the pursuit of real authentic experiences, are affecting travel in particular. The trends are not unrelated. The desire to engage, to be part of the place and to meet the people who live there through proximity raises awareness of impacts and issues. In the UK, these broad consumer trends and targeted campaigning, increased awareness of the issues resulted in better, more responsible behaviour from travel and tourism businesses.

Consumers in the UK now expect tourism businesses to take responsibility. We shall see in the next chapter just how tourism businesses have responded to these changes.

References

Barrett, F. (1989) *The Independent Guide to Real Holidays*, London: Newspaper Publishing.

Brewer, J. and Trentmann, F. (eds) (2006) *Consuming Cultures, Global Perspectives, Historical Trajectories, Transnational Exchanges*, Oxford: Berg.

Butler, R.W. (1980) 'The concept of a tourist area cycle of evolution: implications for management of resources', *Canadian Geographer*, **24** (1), 5–10.

Butler, R.W. (1994) 'Alternative tourism: the thin edge of the wedge', in V.L. Smith and W.R. Eadington (eds), *Tourism Alternatives*, Chichester: Wiley, pp. 31–46.

Butler, R.W. (ed.) (2006a) *The Tourism Area Life Cycle, Vol. I: Applications and Modifications*, Clevedon, Somerset: Channel View Publications.

Butler, R.W. (2006b) 'The origins of the tourism area life cycle', in R.W. Butler (ed.), *The Tourism Area Life Cycle, Vol. I: Applications and Modifications*, Clevedon, Somerset: Channel View Publications, pp. 13–26.

Cohen, E. (1979) 'A phenomenology of tourist experiences', *Sociology*, **13** (2), 179–201.

Eijgelaar, E. Thaper, C. and Peeters, P. (2010) 'Antarctic cruise tourism: the paradoxes of ambassadorship, "last chance tourism" and greenhouse gas emissions', *Journal of Sustainable Tourism*, **18** (3), 337–354.

Elkington, J. (1997) *Cannibals with Forks: Triple Bottom Line of 21st Century Business*, Oxford: Capstone.

Elkington, J. and Hailes, J. (1992) *Holidays that Don't Cost the Earth*, London: Victor Gollancz.

First Choice (2005) *Responsible Tourism – Who Cares?*, Crawley: First Choice.

Goodwin, H. and Francis, J. (2003) 'Ethical and responsible tourism: consumer trends in the UK', *Journal of Vacation Marketing*, **9** (3), 271–284.

Grayson, K. and Martinec, R. (2004) 'Consumer perceptions of iconicity and indexicality and their influence on assessments of authentic market offerings', *Journal of Consumer Research*, **31**, 296–312.

Hammond, R. and Smith, J. (2009) *Clean Breaks*, London: Rough Guides.

Howes, D. (ed.) (1996) *Cross-cultural Consumption: Global Market, Local Realities*, London: Routledge.

Katz, L. (ed.) (2009) *The Guardian Green Travel Guide*, London: Guardian Books.

Krippendorf, J. (1987) *The Holiday Makers*, Oxford: Butterworth Heinemann.

Locke, J. (1946 [1690]) *The Second Treatise of Civil Government*, Oxford: Blackwell.

Lowenthal, D. (1992) 'Authenticity? The dogma of self-delusion', in M. Jones (ed.) *Why Fakes Matter: Essays on Problems of Authenticity*, London: British Museum, pp. 184–192.

Marks & Spencer (2009) *Your M&S: How We Do Business Report 2009: Doing the Right Thing*, London: Marks & Spencer.

Miller, G., Rathouse, K., Scarles, C., Holmes, K. and Tribe, J. (2007) *Public Understanding of Sustainable Leisure and Tourism: A Report to the Department for Environment, Food and Rural Affairs*, University of Surrey. DEFRA

Miller, G., Rathouse, K., Scarles, C., Holmes, K. and Tribe, J. (2010) 'Public understanding of sustainable tourism', *Annals of Tourism Research*, **37** (3), 627–645.

Mowforth, M., Charlton, C. and Munt, I. (2008) *Tourism and Responsibility Perspectives from Latin America and the Caribbean*, London: Routledge.

Neale, G. (1998) *The Green Travel Guide*, London: Earthscan.

Pattullo, P. and Minelli, O. (2009) *The Ethical Travel Guide: Your Passport to Exciting Alternative Holidays*, London: Tourism Concern.

Pine II, B.J. and Gilmore, J.H. (1999) *The Experience Economy: Work is Theatre and Every Business a Stage*, Boston, MA: Harvard Business School Press.

Pine II, B.J. and Gilmore, J.H. (2007) *Authenticity: What Consumers Really Want*, Boston, MA: Harvard Business School Press.

Schulze, G. (2003) *The Experience Society*, London: Sage.

Squire, S.J. (1998) 'Rewriting languages of geography and tourism', in G. Ringer (ed.), *Destinations: Cultural Landscapes of Tourism*, London and New York: Routledge, pp. 80–100.

Tearfund (2000a) *Tourism – an Ethical Issue Market Research Report*, London: Tearfund.

Tearfund (2000b) *A Tearfund Guide to Tourism – Don't Forget Your Ethics*, London: Tearfund.

Toffler, A. (1970) *Future Shock*, New York: Random House.

Trentman, F. (2004) 'Beyond consumerism: new historical perspectives on consumption', *Journal of Contemporary History*, **39** (3), 373–401.

TUI Travel (2010) *Sustainable Development Report 2009: Taking on Responsible Leadership*, Crawley: TUI Travel.

VSO (Voluntary Service Overseas) (1997) *Every Holiday has Hidden Extras Below the Surface*, London: VSO.

VSO (Voluntary Service Overseas) (1999) *Travelling in the Dark*, London: VSO.

WTO (2001a) *Global Code of Ethics*, Madrid: WTO.

WTO (2001b) *The British Ecotourism Market*, Madrid: WTO.

3 The Business Case for Responsibility

Doing well is the result of doing good. That's what capitalism is all about.

Ralph Waldo Emerson

Two young women, friends, meet on the concourse at a London station, late in a long, wet British summer. The story quickly told: anticipation of a great holiday, poor hotel, the food, the beach – none of it as she had hoped, and the tears, at Victoria, in the rush hour. The young woman had saved all year for a holiday that had not come close to her expectations, and told her friend it would take her another year to save enough to have the holiday that she deserved. I know because I watched, embarrassed, as she blurted out her story amidst the commuters. For many British people their summer holiday is their most expensive annual purchase, something they save for all year; precious holiday entitlement and money put aside for the annual indulgence. They need to be able to trust the company to deliver what they purchase.

As we have seen, the changes in the UK and other originating markets over the last fifteen years have raised people's expectations. They aspire for more, a richer experience and one about which they need not feel guilty. No longer are people automatically satisfied with a clean room, cheap booze and access to a crowded beach – although some do still want only that. Increasing numbers of holidaymakers are defining a real holiday as an authentic experience of somewhere exotic. They want and expect the operator, the person who puts together and sells them the package, to ensure that it meets their expectations and that they get the most out of their annual indulgence.

More is expected of tourism businesses, and in the UK more is expected of the tour operators in particular. This expectation results from the broad changes in consumerism and from the continued campaigning that we looked at in the last chapter. In this chapter, we shall look first at how tourism businesses have responded to changing expectations among consumers, and the opportunities and challenges presented. Then we shall turn to corporate social responsibility (CSR) and how that relates to Responsible Tourism;

and finally at the business case for facing up to responsibility. The chapter concludes with some reflections on opportunities and pitfalls, at the case for green or sustainable tourism business certification and the limitations of that approach from a business perspective.

The travel industry has had to shoulder increasing responsibility for ensuring the delivery of holidays that meet the purchasers' expectations. This has extended from financial security and contractual obligations to health and safety and, more recently, to the broader experience of the destination and its sustainability. The Association of British Travel Agents (ABTA) is the trade association that has for sixty years represented the interests of its members. From the outset, ABTA has taken responsibility for ensuring that its member tour operators and travel agents adhere to minimum standards of trading – ensuring that British holidaymakers get what they pay for. ABTA enforces compliance through fines and expulsion, and provides an arbitration service for holidaymakers who have complaints against operators and agents.

In August 1974, in a time of recession and three-day weeks, caused by the first oil shock and the miners' strike respectively, package holiday bookings were down 30%. Court Line, a major UK tourism business went bankrupt. The cost of repatriating 49,000 holidaymakers 'marooned at holiday destinations' was put at £1.5m, and hotel and other bills were estimated at a further £0.5m.[1] Those stranded abroad were repatriated, but there were insufficient funds in the bond to provide financial protection for all customers, and those who had paid but not travelled lost out. Consequently, the bonding system was strengthened; UK travellers and holidaymakers who book though ABTA were subsequently protected against the financial insolvency of the business through which they have booked and ABTA enforces a code of conduct on its members which goes well beyond the statutory minimum.[2]

Consumers purchase package holidays long before departure, and consumer legislation has developed to provide for their protection in these circumstances. The EU Package Travel Directive requires that all packages – any combination of transport, accommodation or other services purchased on a pre-arranged basis at a single price – comply with minimum requirements on the provision of accurate information, consumer remedies where failure to deliver occurs, and refund and repatriation in the event of financial failure.

---

1   Flight International, 22 August 1974, pp. 197–198
2   Details of the decisions of the Code of Conduct Committee and the Appeal Board, and the fines imposed, are published on the ABTA website.

Originating market legislation on health and safety also applies to products sold to consumers in one country and consumed in another. In order to protect the consumer rights of holidaymakers travelling beyond national borders, governments and trade associations have effectively enforced legislation, regulations and codes of conduct in other states. Developed country consumer regulations are enforced in developing countries. For example, in the Gambia, hotels have had to raise their balcony barriers and food hygiene standards to comply with European legislation. For commercial and legal reasons, the tour operators, as wholesalers and major retailers, have put the onus on their suppliers to comply with source-market developed-country contract law, regulations and health and safety. Compensation paid to UK consumers (sometimes without the destination country supplier being part of the decision-making about the validity of the claim or appropriate amount of compensation), is charged to the supplier and deducted from invoices before payment.

The Responsible Tourism agenda has been pursued within the context of the regulatory framework and the broader expectations of consumers. Outbound tourism businesses are recognising and accepting a much broad definition of responsibility: the agenda now extends well beyond legal compliance. In 2004 the major UK operators signed a statement of commitment to the sustainable development and management of tourism. They recognised that 'tourism can contribute to the viability of local economies' and also that 'tourism can have negative impacts on the economy, environment, nature, social structures and local cultures.' The ABTA operators who signed the declaration – and all the large ones did – committed to 'prevent or minimise' these negative impacts: they accepted their responsibility. In 2004 this was a major step forward: the operators moved beyond denial.[3] In 2010 the larger tour-operator ABTA members, using the language of the Cape Town Declaration, recommitted to tourism that 'creates better places for people to live in and better places to visit'.[4] They affirmed that as 'responsible tourism operators we are committed to the development, operation and marketing of sustainable tourism'.[5]

---

3   The FTO Responsible Tourism Committee, Statement of Commitment was signed in January 2004 by all those businesses which were members of the Federation of Tour Operators. The operators committed to 'adopt, as appropriate, the steps and procedures of the FTO Integrated Responsible Tourism Programme' and to encourage their partners, suppliers and sub-contractors to improve their contribution to sustainable development.

4   They recognised that whilst the 'industry can be a powerful force for positive change' it also has 'the potential to cause negative impacts on host-destination environments, economies and communities'.

5   FTO/ABTA Responsible Tourism Committee – Tour Operator Statement of Commitment 2010. The FTO merged with ABTA in July 2008

Individuals in the tourism industry adopt a responsible approach for a wide variety of reasons, ranging from an ethical commitment to straightforward commercial advantage. In companies, which are after all comprised of many individuals, there is unlikely to be one reason. It is also erroneous to assume that the idea of social responsibility in business is entirely new. Quakers were pursuing socially responsible investments from the early years of the Industrial Revolution in the 1750s: they respected wider social values, including good employment practices, customer and supplier relationships and philanthropic engagement with the community which their business was a part.[6]

Facing up to responsibility

Many will contest the quote from Ralph Waldo Emerson at the head of this chapter. It is used to justify the operation of the hidden hand of the market. The objective of 'doing well by doing good' is not restricted to individuals or groups working for profit-making companies. Social entrepreneurs often use the same phrase as do business people more generally, when they are explaining their enlightened self-interest, taking a longer-term perspective and having objectives that include more than short-term commercial gain through maximising profit or shareholder value. There are many examples of the damage that can result from irresponsible business practices, where people have done well by doing bad, and tourism is clearly not a pollution-free industry.

The VSO campaign, discussed in the previous chapter, was an opportunity to undertake research[7] with the Association of Independent Tour Operators (AITO) into the activities and attitudes of its members towards ethical tourism. The research undertaken in the summer of 1999 revealed that 40% of respondents felt that their company's ethical commitment meant very little to their travellers; 30% felt that it meant something; 12% felt that it meant a great deal. We asked AITO members the open question: 'What motivates you, or might motivate you, to follow an ethical trading policy?' The answers were then clustered, each reply being placed in only one cluster according to the balance of their response (Box 3.1).

---

6   Adkins (1999): 144

7   The research was conducted by Harold Goodwin and Caroline Warburton. Covered by confidentiality clauses, the research has not been published.

> ## Box 3.1: Ethical motivations reported by AITO Members, Summer 1999
>
> ♦ Moral imperative/personal values/common decency/conscience/guilt   22%
>
> ♦ Desire to preserve destination/maintain quality of the product
>   (culture/environment/facilities)   17%
>
> ♦ Personal interest in ethical issues/local politics/concern for
>   environment/culture   14%
>
> ♦ Desire for partnership with locals/ treat people fairly -benefits communities
>   and also enhances supplier/staff loyalty   7%
>
> Unpublished data[8]

It is striking that none of the individual owners or managers surveyed identified a commercial or market advantage. There is arguably an enlightened self-interest in the benefits of partnership, and enhancing supplier and staff loyalty. However, the AITO owners and managers reported to their trade association that their motivation was largely personal or ethical (36%). One in six was concerned for the quality of the destination and the product. One in 14 saw it as part of their approach to doing business based on partnership and loyalty to suppliers and staff. Asked separately about how they characterised their supply chain, two-thirds saw their suppliers as like-minded partners, working with common goals.

Thirty-three members, about a fifth of the membership, reported that they were working with or investing in local projects intended to improve the situation of local people, to contribute to conservation or improve the local environment. One in three companies were making charitable donations in destinations. Half of respondents reported that they were concerned about the impact of tourism at locations featured in their brochures, and one in five reported concern about the impacts of their own company in destinations.

The final question canvassed their view on whether AITO members should share a stated commitment to ethical tour operations: 52% felt that they should, 20% sat on the fence and 27% said that they should not. The AITO sub-committee concluded that the survey revealed 'unexpectedly extensive good practice in responsible tourism', that members operating within Europe as well as further afield were engaged, and that individual AITO members were making a significant difference. AITO's Responsible Tourism Com-

---

8   The results were reported to Council and to members but they were not published. The figures do not add up to 100%, as there were non-responses to this question; the percentages are of total survey forms returned

mittee[9] concluded that by 'working together as AITO we can have a bigger impact, whether in initiatives which involve the whole membership or through members who share a common approach or a common destination working together to make change'.[10] After that survey, the AITO Responsible Tourism Committee grew from three member companies to seven.[11] However, it felt unable to commit to the word ethical, which it thought 'carried with it unacceptable implications and inferences',[12] and its recommendation to adopt a set of advisory rather than prescriptive guidelines was agreed in May 2000 (Box 3.2).

The commitment to responsibility, rather than to ethical practice, may be seen by some as a weaker proposition. However, the advantage of the concept of responsibility is that it suggests that members need to respond, to act, rather than standing, or sitting, on their principles and their ethics. Responsibility implies and requires action. AITO was the first trade association to commit to Responsible Tourism, and the recognition that sometimes harmful effects outweigh the good was important. Critical to creating change is acknowledging and owning up to problems, and taking responsibility for making changes.

The association took responsibility on behalf of its members, and the guidelines it adopted became part of its membership criteria. The AITO itself developed *Tips for Travellers*[13], a move that was followed by some members. Exodus, for example, produced advice on *Your Role*[14] to encourage their travellers to contribute; Explore, meanwhile, asked: *So that's us but what about you?*

> No lectures…we want you to relax and enjoy yourself whilst you're on holiday. No-one would want their enjoyment at the expense of others or to damage the beautiful places they are travelling to though so we've thought of a few small things you can do which will really help the people and places you are travelling to.[15]

---

9   It was originally established as the Ethical Tourism Committee, 'responsible' was favoured because it enabled AITO and members to be clear about what they were taking responsibility for.

10   Hearn and Goodwin unpublished sub-committee report, September 2001

11   The member of the Responsible Tourism sub-committee then were Annabel Lawson, Andante Travels; Mark Leaney, Arctic Experience; Mike Sykes, Dragoman, David Gillespie, Exodus; Martin Garland, Expressions; Richard Hearn (Chair), Inntravel; Jonathan Vernon-Powell, Nomadic Thoughts. It subsequently introduced a basic rating system and in 2003 announced its first Responsible Tourism awards.

12   Hearn and Goodwin, unpublished sub-committee report, September 2001

13   www.aito.co.uk/corporate_TipsForTravellers.asp accessed 2 June 2010

14   www.exodus.co.uk/responsible-travel/your-role? accessed 2 June 2010

15   www.explore.co.uk/responsible-travel accessed 2 June 2010

Box 3.2: AITO Responsible Tourism Commitment, 2000

As members of AITO we recognise that in carrying out our work as Tour Operators we have a responsibility to respect other people's places and ways of life. We acknowledge that wherever a Tour Operator does business or sends clients it has a potential to do both good and harm, and we are aware that all too often in the past the harm has outweighed the good.

All tourism potentially has an Environmental, Social and Economic impact on the destination involved. We accept, therefore, that we as Tour Operators should aim to be responsible in all our dealings on each of these three levels. To help us to do so we have proposed a set of guidelines intended to help companies, customers and local suppliers recognise their common responsibilities to:

- Protect the Environment – its flora, fauna and landscapes
- Respect local cultures – traditions, religions and built heritage
- Benefit local communities – both economically and socially
- Conserve natural resources – from office to destination
- Minimise pollution – through noise, waste disposal and congestion

We are an Association of individual, independent companies, each with our own distinctive style and field of operation. As such, we each have our own ways of fulfilling the details of these responsibilities by:

- Establishing our own policies and involving our staff
- Informing our clients about Responsible Tourism and, where appropriate,
- Encouraging them to participate
- Working with our suppliers and partners to achieve responsible goals and practices
- Publicising good practice to encourage and spread Responsible Tourism

Source: AITO Council Minutes 2000

Each company explained its engagement with Responsible Tourism in different ways, and smaller, often owner-managed companies, were able to respond to changes in the market and implement new policies more quickly.

Responsible Tourism developed most rapidly in the adventure and activity sector of the UK outbound market, followed by the nature-based and cultural tourism operators. The stronger experiential dimensions of these products raise the ethical and responsibility issues in the minds of both operators and travellers, and the increased proximity to communities and their environ-ments heightens awareness of the issues.[16] Explore was, and remains, one of the leaders, and continues to evolve its strategy. In 2010 it advertised its approach as: 'Looking after the planet … with added adventure'. Explore states that its approach to Responsible Tourism is: ' doing business well, and travelling with a mind to how it affects the places we are going'. This means:

- We work to ensure people who work for Explore are treated fairly and paid a fair wage

- We learn about and respect the customs and culture of the country we are visiting so that we do not offend local people

- We ensure that local people benefit economically from tourism by employing them as leaders and guides, eating out in local restaurants and using family-run hotels where possible

- We minimise our impact on the environment by travelling in small groups, offsetting our carbon emissions, reducing waste and support-ing conservation projects.

And it explains why:

> We've worked hard at these things to ensure we are welcomed in the places we all love to visit, meaning local people benefit and you get a better trip. It could be through some of our great community based tourism experiences, meeting local people or experiencing the pristine wilderness and leaving it untouched.[17]

This is highly developed enlightened self-interest – for operator and traveller alike. ResponsibleTravel.com,[18] the UK's leading responsible travel agency, established as a founding principle that each property, experience or trip had to be explicit about the ways in which it was responsible. The information provided about 'How this holiday makes a difference' is as much a part of the contract with the purchaser as are the price and the itinerary.

Among tour operators, in 2001 there was little recognition of any market advantage. Tearfund reviewed good practice amongst 65 UK outbound operators and reported on benefits to local communities, charitable giving in

---

16 For those interested in exploring the different approaches, take a look at the policies of the many companies and properties which market themselves on ResponsibleTravel.com

17 www.explore.co.uk/responsible-travel accessed 2 June 2010

18 I co-founded www.responsiberavel.com with Justin Francis. I subsequently sold my shares.

destinations, the development of local partnerships, and the policies of companies. Only 30% of the companies surveyed reported that clients were asking more about the social, economic and environmental issues. Those companies, which had adopted a Responsible Tourism policy, said that they had done so because the principles were integral to the company (78%) or to educate their travellers (72%) – only 12% mentioned market advantage.[19]

In the first decade of the 21st century the broad changes in consumer expectations, and the increasing demand for authentic experiences and more responsible products, chronicled in the last chapter, combined with the impact of the development of the Responsible Tourism marketplace to bring about change. ResponsibleTravel.com, the Responsible Tourism Awards (which they launched in 2004 with First Choice Holidays and then with Virgin Holidays), and the increasingly evident engagement of UK outbound operators with the issue, all contributed to growing consumer awareness and to raising expectations. A market has emerged, one in which consumers favour companies with clear social and environmental objectives.

What of Corporate Social Responsibility?

Corporate Social Responsibility (CSR) originated in the 1930s and gained prominence in the 1950s.[20] It focused first on the role of business leaders and then, from the 1970s, on companies. CSR is about companies voluntarily embracing responsibility for the impact of its activities on the environment, consumers, employees and communities. CSR implies that the company needs to consider the interests of other stakeholders when deciding how it operates. It is voluntary corporate activity which exceeds what is normally expected by society of business: holding to legal minimum standards, not engaging in corruption and trading legally is not CSR: it is compliance. Companies may do more than the minimum for altruistic, do-gooding reasons but also for commercial advantage and to contribute to the creation of a more prosperous and sustainable society.[21] Many businesses recognise that they trade and make profits within a society: that they too are dependent on a sustainable environment, recognising that it is in their interest and their responsibility to contribute to the maintenance of the environment in which they do business

---

19   Tearfund (2001) The majority of the companies were independent and owner-managed.

20   Bowen (1953); Carroll (1999) There is a useful graphic showing the evolution of the concept in Blowfield and Murray (2008): 57

21   See for example Falck and Heblich (2007)

across the triple bottom line – economic, social and environmental. CSR is not without its critics. Milton Friedman, of the Chicago School of Economics, told the New York Times in 1970: 'the social responsibility of business is to increase its profits'.[22] But by the end of the century Lazlo, among others, was arguing that the world's leading companies were doing well by doing good.[23]

CSR activity is diverse. For example, in 2005 Ashridge Business School surveyed businesses in Denmark and identified 147 species of CSR in seven areas of activity: leadership, vision and values; market place activities; workforce activities; supply chain activities; stakeholder engagement; community activities; and environmental activities.[24] The issues which companies address depend upon the activities in which the businesses engages, the prominence of different issues and the capacity of the company to make a difference. In the UK, animal rights have had particular salience; Blowfield and Murray identified these concerns as a stimulus to CSR in the 1980s, and an issue for business since at least the 1960s The English have historically had a particular concern for animal welfare. When the tour operators in the UK addressed responsibility through the Responsible Tourism Unit of the Federation of Tour Operators, animal welfare was one of the first policy areas they addressed. Needless to say, local and international priorities may differ. Western corporate priorities for Africa often include combating corruption, improving governance, transparency and infrastructure, whereas local priorities may be technology transfer of technology, creating good jobs and improving the terms of trade.[25] These objectives are not necessarily entirely mutually exclusive but they are different, and the differences often need to be negotiated. This is a particular issue in travel and tourism when originating market companies seek to address their issues, and those of their travellers, in someone else's place.

The deep banking and financial crisis in 2008 caused considerable rethinking about the purpose of business. General Electric's long-time CEO and leading business thinker, Jack Welch expressed the point forcefully in March 2009: 'Shareholder value is the dumbest idea in the world ... Your main constituencies are your employees, your customers and your products'.[26] Stephen Green, Chairman of HSBC, argued at length in 2009 that the core question for

---

22   Quoted in Seldon (2009): 102.
23   Lazlo (2008), Sustainable Value, How the World's Leading Companies are Doing Well by Doing Good
24   Reported in Blowfield and Murray (2008): 15–16
25   Blowfield and Murray (2008): 178
26   Quoted in Seldon (2009): 100

banks and the corporates is 'How does the business we do contribute to the common good?' However, anxieties, even among big business, pre-date the latest crash. In January 2005, *The Economist* occasioned debate by presenting corporate responsibility as a threat to the effective functioning of capitalism, free markets and global prosperity. In reply, Geoffrey Chandler of Amnesty International pointed out that CSR does not stem from a belief that capitalism fails to serve the public interest but rather that 'unprincipled capitalism inflicts collateral damage on all its stakeholders, including ultimately its shareholders'.[27] The Union Carbide chemical disaster in Bhopal in 1984, Enron, British Petroleum's Gulf of Mexico oil spill in 2010 are two more examples of the damage to corporate shareholder value when things go wrong. In a study of 27 corporate events of socially irresponsible and illicit behaviour, Frooman reported that the negative effect on stock market value was so statistically significant and substantial that rationally self-interested firms would act in a socially responsible and law-abiding manner. Perhaps more relevant to the travel and tourism industry have been the series of exposures affecting leading brands of the labour conditions in their supply chains.[28] Tourists visit the factories, they travel to the place where the experience is consumed, they talk with the workers who deliver the product and have the opportunity to see and hear about the working conditions.

CSR is undoubtedly moving up the corporate agenda, but companies, even wealthy ones, have limited resources. They cannot do everything: choices have to be made. Those choices are made within a framework conditioned by the culture(s) and place(s) they operate in, the interests and preferences of their staff, customers and suppliers and the resources that can be committed. The impact on the reputation and success of the business if it fails to take responsibility will also affect its CSR decisions. It is clear that no company can do everything. Each company is likely to set different priorities and to define its responsibilities differently, reflecting the nature of its business and the needs and choices of its stakeholders: customers, staff, suppliers, local communities, and the environments to which they operate. A UK operator providing bird-watching tours in India may provide funding for hides and bird-watching opportunities for children in rural areas near reserves. A com-

---

27 Quoted in Blowfield and Murray (2008): 343

28 The Ethical Trading Initiative Base Code published in 2001 defines minimum standards and makes clear that companies must also comply with national and other applicable law, and apply whichever standard provides the greater protection. The ETI does not deal with services. www.ethicaltrade.org

pany offering walking tours in rural Italy may help with footpath restoration and the conservation of churches.

As already mentioned, many UK tour operators have been concerned for some years about the impacts of their business and of tourism in destinations. In 2003, when the Responsible Tourism Unit was established in the Federation of Tour Operators, the unit recognised that acting responsibly made long-term business sense because environmental and social issues were becoming more important to holidaymakers' decisions. There was recognition that they needed to work together, and with other European operators, to 'deliver the right balance' in a destination. The sustainability guidelines now recognise that:

> **To deliver the right balance we must work together.** Suppliers are at the sharp end of the holiday experience. What happens in the destination matters most; from the warm welcome and the quality of the local environment to the services available. In other words, the balance between the local economy, nature and the community.[29]

The mergers which resulted in the Thomas Cook Group[30] and TUI Travel[31] in 2007 accelerated the development of Responsible Tourism in the UK and, since both are multinationals, created favourable conditions to extend the ideas across European outbound travel. Both companies are stock-market listed and now produce CSR reports. Thomas Cook reports on CSR and greenhouse gas emissions within the Group Annual Report and Accounts and produces an Annual Group Sustainability Report. It also reports for the Carbon Disclosure Project, the EU Emissions Trading Scheme, the Dow Jones Sustainability Index, the FTSE4 GOOD, the Carbon Reduction Energy Efficiency Scheme and a number of other survey and reporting initiatives. The demand from investors and others has resulted in significant resources being deployed to reporting.

The Thomas Cook Group's CSR commitment to responsibility has some basis in its history. Thomas Cook, a former preacher, devised the first package holiday in 1841 and founded a business which, claims the company's 2007 Corporate Social Responsibility Report, 'has helped millions of people to relax, unwind – and broaden their horizons'. But more than that: 'Thomas Cook didn't just want people to have fun. He believed affordable travel could

29 www.fto.co.uk/responsible-tourism/sustainability-guidelines/#c2868 accessed 4 June 2010

30 My Travel Group and Thomas Cook merged to form the Thomas Cook Group

31 TUI, which owned Thomson, merged with First Choice to form TUI Travel

change working people's lives for the better. His company was inspired by a strong sense of social justice and moral responsibility'. The group asserts its belief that its founder's values 'make a world of difference – not only to our customers, but to all the people whose lives we touch. Our mission is to perfect the personal leisure experience. And that includes managing our activities in a morally and socially responsible manner'.[32] These are the aspirations against which consumers, employees, shareholders and the communities they touch will judge them. In 2009, Thomas Cook shifted its focus to sustainability, although, the 'team's main focus remains ensuring the long-term success of the business through the integration of principles of sustainability into the heart of the business'.[33]The sustainability team has responsibility for the development and implementation of the Group's corporate responsibility strategy, reporting on performance, sharing best practice and identifying targets for improvement. Thomas Cook's 2009 Sustainability Report addresses the Group's impacts on customers, employees, the environment and its home (originating market) and destination communities.

Before First Choice Holidays' 2007 merger to form TUI Travel, the company had purchased a significant number of adventure and activity companies, many of them leading examples of Responsible Tourism practice and winners of the Responsible Tourism Awards. Within First Choice and subsequently TUI Travel there was a melding of a Responsible Tourism-led approach to communities, places and the customer experience and the corporate need for risk management, brand value and the investor perspective. TUI recognises 'that the environment, communities and cultures within which [we] operate are vital to the success of [our] business'. The company links the product experience with sustainability to: 'make travel experiences special by providing holidays that cause minimal environmental impact, respect the culture and people of destinations and offer real economic benefit to local communities'.[34] Responsible leadership is one of the company's core values. It has work-streams addressing climate change, destinations, staff and customers. TUI's chief executive, Peter Long, reported in 2009 that TUI had 'already experienced a range of business benefits from sustainability management, including cost efficiencies, quality improvement and the enhanced engagement of customers, colleagues and suppliers'.[35] Sustainability management is

---

32   Thomas Cook Group (2008): 1
33   CEO writing in the Thomas Cook 2009 Annual Report and Accounts: 30
34   TUI Travel 2008: 12
35   TUI Travel 2010: 3

becoming a mainstream part of TUI's company management.

Although both the companies in the examples given are subject to the same pressures as any to maintain and enhance stakeholder value, their CSR agendas are broad, extending well beyond short-term profitability. Tour operators are not alone in the tourism sector in reporting on their CSR performance. The Intercontinental Hotels Group, for example, recognises that with 4000 hotels globally it has 'a big responsibility and a big opportunity to make a positive difference'. In the tension between tourism and environment they identify an opportunity for innovation and they are focusing on 'better ways to design, build and run' their hotels, seeking to lessen negative impacts while 'enhancing the guests' hotel experience'. An easy example is that being responsible reduces energy costs.[36] The large international hotel groups have particular problems in that the brand owner does not necessarily own the property and, as with tour operators, they are often operating in other peoples' places with local legislation and norms affecting employment conditions. As with others, their responsibility agenda is bound to reflect destination, source market and international preferences and priorities, as well as local realities. Balancing competing interests and priorities, coming to a shared understanding of what the issues are and what might be done about them, is fundamental to taking responsibility. It is easy to write a list of issues, but harder to agree it between two or more people from one culture, and far more difficult to do it across timezones and cultures. Often, in the struggle to accommodate everyone, little is achieved.

CSR developments in travel and tourism parallel those in other industries and sectors. All major listed companies are now reporting on their CSR performance and adopting national and international best practice. Both Thomas Cook and TUI Travel use the international Global Reporting Initiative (GRI)[37] Sustainable Reporting Guidelines. These provide a common set of standards for defining the content and quality of sustainability reporting and a process for setting the boundaries of what needs to be reported in order to ensure completeness. These GRI guidelines supplement national legislation and are beginning to require directors to take a broader view. Section 172 of the UK's 2006 Companies Act introduced a new 'enlightened shareholder value' duty, requiring directors to think about the longer term, and CSR factors includ-

---

36   Andrew Cosslet, CEO www.ihgplc.com/index.asp?pageid=725 accessed 4 June 2010. Their 2008 report was their third CSR Report

37   www.globalreporting.org

ing the interests of employees, suppliers, consumers and the environment. Since October 2007, all publicly listed companies in the UK have had to include information on environmental, employment, social and community issues and the main factors likely to affect the companies' future business in their annual reports. The trend is towards transparent reporting of progress on sustainability against clear targets. Although reporting does not reduce emissions, or contribute to any other change, it is an important first step. Water and biodiversity reporting are likely to be added to the growing list of requirements on companies in the next few years.

CSR, especially among the big multinational firms is a crucial boost to the Responsible Tourism movement. Yet Responsible Tourism is broader than traditional CSR. The movement is diverse encompassing action by: independent travellers; small enterprises; national parks and local authorities and many more players. Responsible Tourism involves a considered approach to adapting the way the business operates; it affects all departments of the business from office supplies to local guiding; it needs engagement by staff across the company and the participation of suppliers and customers. So-called 'green-washing' remains a threat. Where companies try something more superficial, like putting a towel card in the room and doing no more, it is quickly identified as green-wash and brand damage may result. It is generally desirable that companies concentrate on one initiative at a time, but there needs to be a consistent approach. Responsible Tourism and sustainable tourism should not be used interchangeably: Responsible Tourism refers to the willingness to take responsibility, to respond, to do something to contribute to sustainability. Sustainability is an aim which remains unreached for many: the concept remains broad and undefined, supported in word but not in action, and with no progress reported.

The business case

The diversity of Responsible Tourism is reflected in the business case for it. There is not one business case for Responsible Tourism: there are many – a number of different, but interrelated reasons for taking responsibility for sustainability. But companies do not make decisions: individuals severally and in groups within the company do. Those individuals responsible for marketing, product development, financial performance and human resources may also see the business case differently depending upon their personal ethics and business function. Product managers will generally see the case for engagement differently from the marketers and the finance director. These individuals need to be persuaded to take responsibility and make a difference. It is unlikely that any one reason for exercising responsibility will convince a company: a range of reasons generally needs to be argued to achieve change. They are, as we saw in the AITO membership survey, likely to be motivated by personal ethics and concern for the destinations and the people who live there.

Many companies are doing a great deal, but are not communicating it to their customers and stakeholders. AITO achieved its breakthrough when it realised how much its members were doing, and helped them articulate their commitment and activity with their peers. This developed the momentum necessary to act as a group. Although AITO is now less active as an association, some member companies remain leaders. When asked about why they are nervous to share what they are doing with their competitors, with other businesses, with clients and the media, senior managers and owners often reveal a degree of embarrassment and sometimes concern about 'standing out from the crowd' or 'tall poppy syndrome'.[38] They express concern about setting up the company or themselves as individuals to be shot at, and attracting 'knocking' attention: there is safety in numbers. Yet real progress would be made if companies could be convinced to see responsible action as a non-competitive area. When the Federation of Tour Operators[39] in the UK set up the Responsible Tourism Unit, they modelled it on the work the trade association had done, and continues to do, on health and safety in resorts. They saw it as a field where progress could best be made through co-operation, where taking responsibility for health and safety or for sustainability was best achieved as a group.

That said, some elements of competition are emerging as the market value of responsibility becomes more apparent. In June 2010 Thomson and First Choice launched their Holidays Forever[40] campaign, encompassing 20, targeted and time-lined, sustainable tourism pledges, from reducing carbon emissions to having all of their suppliers Travelife-awarded within five years. Travelife is a sustainable tourism certification programme. Thomson and First Choice, both TUI companies, are seeking to differentiate themselves from competitors by demonstrating their commitment to sustainable tourism.

38   This has developed wide usage in Australia, Canada and New Zealand – see Peeters (2004) for a discussion of its origin and the relationship with egalitarianism.

39   The FTO grew out of the Tour Operators Study Group

40   www.holidaysforever.co.uk

In the adventure and activity sector the value of Responsible Tourism as a differentiator was apparent from the beginning. Once some operators were sufficiently confident to risk putting their heads above the parapet, others followed and it became an area of competition and innovation that was not just about cost-cutting: a means of differentiating and enriching the travellers' experience and of engendering loyalty. Competition in this market drove the Responsible Tourism agenda for the first four or five years, and remains one of the most competitive and difficult categories to judge in the annual Virgin Holiday Responsible Tourism Awards. Research by Nicolau, into share price response one day after 26 CSR announcements by two listed Spanish hotel companies, found significant positive effects. He concluded that 'acting as a responsible 'citizen' is not incompatible with obtaining economic profits'.[41]

There are some overlaps between the different elements of the business case for Responsible Tourism identified here; they are in no particular order. There is an interconnected web of reasons for adopting Responsible Tourism which collectively constitute the business case. The elements of the business case are trust, reputation and consumer loyalty; product value, good neighbour and license to operate, marketing and PR, shareholder and investor value, the management of risk and pre-empting government regulation, cost savings, improved margins and competitiveness, and staff morale and retention. Different parts of the web have different salience and efficacy with individuals and groups of decision makers.

Trust, reputation and consumer loyalty

When travelling to somewhere that is new to them, people are purchasing products and experiences that they only know second-hand or vicariously. They trust the operator to be selling them products of a quality that will provide them with a good experience, a real break. The stories that circulate in the Gambia about people coming off the plane and being surprised that there are so many black people there may be apocryphal – one hopes that they are – but the circulation of stories like this reflect the extent to which the sun, sand and sea product is commodified, and the fact that holidaymakers buy the product from the brochure having done little or no research into the destination.

Trust has always been fundamental to successful business, particularly across international boundaries where enforcement of contract by legal process was either impossible or impracticable. 'My word is my bond' or 'My word,

---

41   Nicolau (2008): 1001

my bond' is a maritime brokers' saying which since 1801 has been the motto of the London Stock Exchange. Regulatory frameworks cover outbound travel from the UK and other major originating markets, but trust is also important in framing the choices people make. People booking holidays are purchasing complex packages. Some elements can be, and are, covered by contract, for example, a clean room, with a bed and functioning shower in a hotel with an adequate fire escape. Other aspects are not: for example, the experience at immigration or walking in public spaces. The holiday experience sold by the agent, operator or hotelier cannot be reduced only to what is contracted. Consumers expect that they will not be sold experiences that fail to meet a minimum threshold. This is acknowledged in the phrase, 'when a place gets spoilt we move on' – a sentiment often applied by tour operators, rarely said publicly, and almost never written down. Different companies will define spoilt in different ways, reflecting the clientele they serve. The company's brand – its reputation and ethos – is the 'guarantee' that people rely on for assurance that they will get what they are looking for.

Consumers are looking for companies that they can trust to deliver the experiences they seek. Whilst some elements of the holiday they aspire to enjoy can be guaranteed by bonding (financial security) and regulation (services, health and safety and some elements of quality), many elements can only be assured by the commitment of the company to deliver a quality experience and their intention to ensure that you will travel with them again and encourage others to do so. Repeats and referrals are of increasing importance to businesses. It often occurs to me when, for example, I have been deliberately overbooked in a hotel near Paddington, and displaced, or when travelling on the railways in the UK,[42] that had I booked with an ABTA agent or operator I would be having a better experience.

As Kohn has persuasively argued, trust is intimately connected with risk. Historically, people interacted with small numbers of other people over extended periods of time.[43] Travel takes us to places where we are unlikely to know people or to be in relationships of mutual obligation, and we feel vulnerable. Abroad, we are in places and with people where behaviour is

---

42 This occurs on the railways because of their monopoly. It is quite possible to find yourself on a train with all the toilets locked, because no penalty is incurred by the operator for not providing adequate toilets. At Paddington, so many people want to stay near the station in order to catch the Heathrow Express that hotels do not need to be concerned about repeat bookings, and can overbook at no penalty to themselves. In neither case does the consumer have any practical recourse.

43 Kohn (2008): 4–5

unregulated by concern for reputation and our potential need for support in the future. Failure to deliver what was promised creates mistrust and a sense of betrayal and outrage. You may be able to secure compensation for contractual failure and some recompense for a spoilt holiday, but many of the more intangible aspects of expectation cannot be recompensed, and the most precious thing of all, free time, is lost. Impotence, outrage and tears at Victoria station.

By using the services of a trusted intermediary, such as a travel agent or operator that will have ongoing relationships in the destination, the risk is reduced. If they want to secure repeat business, they have both reason and opportunity to protect our interests and ensure that our trip meets our expectations. In turn, their suppliers in the destination have reason to maintain their relationship with the operator who sends them business. The relationship chain encourages responsibility and builds trust. We may know and trust our local high-street travel agent, and we especially tend to trust a brand. But the brand is not enough; it needs to be backed up by its staff and the experience it delivers. We expect employees of the company to treat us with a degree of consistency and to care that we have a good holiday – to do their best to ensure that we get a 'real holiday', not one beset by problems. That is where the brand value lies.

In some cases, particularly with specialist or niche companies, the brand extends to creating something of a club atmosphere: the brand defines the clients, their interests and their preferences when travelling. In this case, the group has some shared values and a shared expectation about what makes for a good holiday, and travelling with likeminded companions is part of it.[44] The individuals who book have similar views about how they want to travel and expectations that the company will deliver this. Club Mediterranean, Explore, Exodus, Inntravel (who offer a particular shared activity holiday walking experience) and Martin Randall Travel which offers a very intense and learned art and architecture experience. The opportunity created by the company, to travel with a like-minded group, is a significant part of their product, and of the value they add. It is part of the guarantee of the anticipated holiday experience, since how we travel, and with whom, with are major parts of the experience we buy. 'Mutual benefit lies at the heart of trust', and it can become

---

44 'Small Group travel is forecast to increase to nearly eight million adults over the next three years. Although this includes all small group travel types, it is strongly indicative of the popularity and acceptance of holidaying with likeminded travellers.' TUI Travel Adventure Brands (2010): 10

a commercially valuable habit.[45]

Trust, like reputation, has to be worked at. It has to be maintained and the company has to demonstrate respect for the client.[46] The brand alone is no longer enough, and, where responsibility is a part of the consumer proposition – and particularly where it contributes to repeat bookings and referrals – the values need to be demonstrated and acted upon. Otherwise, an additional powerful cause of dissatisfaction has been added to the consumer's expectation. Irresponsibility like disrespect is generally non-negotiable and generates a powerful response. Demonstrating and delivering the company's Responsible Tourism policy across the brand is a major challenge for management, particularly since it includes so many intangible elements over which the company does not have direct control, including the behaviours of locals and other travellers. User-generated feedback and holiday blogs can provide invaluable independent validation of the company's values, or undermine its reputation in a market where these things matter, and the internet makes it so easy to search for comment, good or bad.

The most cost efficient way to attract clients each year is to foster repeats and referrals. Goodwill has a market, as well as marketing, value. Reputation amplifies repeats and referrals and, as we have seen, the Responsible Tourism agenda supports the development of a good reputation. At least one operator in the adventure and activities sector in the UK explicitly linked its Responsible Tourism policy to securing a 50% repeat-booking rate from one year to the next. The policy is widely seen as a way of building an expectation of a special experience which then needs to be delivered.

Explore is a UK market leader in small group adventure holidays, with 60% of their travellers having travelled with them before, some of them over 50 times. Explore plans its itineraries to enable their clients 'to get below the skin of the country or area in which we are travelling… and always with an 'Explore Twist'. Its buzz-words are 'quality', 'safety' and the 'very best tour Leaders'. It pledges to 'travel only in a responsible and sustainable way. Ensure the local people we meet and work with along the way are well looked after and that the environment is cared for and not damaged'.[47]

Exodus is a direct competitor of Explore in the same market. Its managing director, Peter Burrell, commented on the credit crunch in July 2009: it

---

45 Seldon (2009): 3, 2

46 For a discussion of respect, rights, responsibilities and duties see Seldon (2009): 37–39

47 www.explore.co.uk/about-explore/ accessed 8 June 2010

'brought into sharp focus the real value of money and how we all choose to spend it'. He argued that:

> Spontaneous purchases of the frivolous, the unnecessary, or products that simply will not last, now feels irresponsible. However I believe that our holidays can and do deliver the opposite. Discovering other cultures, giving something back to the communities you visit or challenging your fitness on a trek or cycle ride are surely meaningful.

He also stated that for 36 years:

> ...we have always believed in giving you the best experience, not the cheapest price. We ensure our overseas staff and partners are paid fairly and our long-term commitment to them helps build the passion and in-depth knowledge needed to give you the travel experiences you want and have come to expect from Exodus.

The company details the ways it claims to make a difference. 'We have many successful projects around the world that help house the homeless, educate the poor, protect the environment and wildlife and help reduce or offset carbon emissions, all designed to ensure that tourism is a force for good!'[48]

Explore and Exodus are by no means unique in taking this approach to presenting their companies; but they were amongst the first to develop a coherent Responsible Tourism approach, and they are in competition with each other and with many others using similar approaches.[49] The Responsible Tourism approach was in the DNA of both Exodus and Explore, but they only began to articulate it in their marketing as the concept of Responsible Tourism emerged in the marketplace after AITO's adoption of its Responsible Tourism policy in 2000. Both companies continue to prosper, Exodus is now part of TUI, Explore is part of Holidaybreak. They remain leaders, demonstrating how to integrate Responsible Tourism into a travel business. These are just two examples of travel businesses telling the 'back story', the narrative which explains the values and activity which underpin the product and the experience. They do this to encourage new business, repeats and referrals – explaining their ethos to help knowledge-hungry consumers make informed choices.. Tour operators are also increasingly using the internet to develop

---

48 www.exodus.co.uk/news/2007/08/whats-so-special-about-exodus accessed 8 June 2010

49 Take a look at the winners in the tour operators category in the Virgin Holidays Responsible Tourism Awards: Adventure Travel Company, Exodus, Explore, Geckos Adventures, Intrepid Travel, Tribes Travel and Village Ways. Many examples can be found at www. responsibletravel.com

online communities, using Facebook, Twitter, YouTube,[50] blogs and podcasts to experiment with user-generated content of the sort which has made Active Hotel and TripAdvisor so successful.[51] Increasingly consumers are trusting peer reviews rather brands.

By booking with a business that cares about its reputation, the consumer feels a degree of security that the experience will meet their expectations, and the business benefits from attracting clients whose expectations it is likely to be able to meet. In 2010, UK tour operators were reminding clients that their money was safe with them and to look for the consumer protection of ABTA membership or an ATOL licence.

Brand values are particularly important in travel and tourism. Holiday purchases are amongst the most expensive made regularly by consumers, and are expensive in both money and time. If holiday purchases 'go bad', or fail to meet expectations, as it did for the young woman on Victoria Station, anger and resentment will run deep.

Where clients have a relationship with the company and believe the operator or hotel to have taken responsibility – to have done what they could to remedy any defect – they are less likely to seek compensation. An established reputation provides a degree of protection when things go wrong; it is easier to get a fair hearing for the company's response when it is recognised as one of the better businesses in the sector. The volcanic ash cloud from Iceland, and the travel chaos it caused in 2010, was just one example of the various challenges – natural or man-made – that travel companies have to deal with. They provide significant opportunities to make or break reputations. By mid-May 2010, Thomas Cook was reporting that the closure of air space had cost it £70m; TUI Travel reported costs of £90m. It would have been comforting to those caught up in it that, as ABTA puts it: 'our members have been looking after British holidaymakers for the last 60 years, come rain or shine – or even the odd Icelandic volcano'.[52] Reputation is a significant part of the brand value.

Saga is one of the UK's leading holiday companies for the over-50s. The brand, built by Roger De Haan, understands the core value of customer service: that when things go wrong, what matters is how you put them right. He

50   http://www.dreamgrow.com/how-one-video-in-youtube-can-cause-millions-in-brand-damage/ accessed 28 August 2010
51   www.explore.co.uk/contact-us/community.htm accessed 8 June 2010
52   Alex Brownsell reporting in Marketing Magazine, 13 May 2010

got it very right: the reputation founded on the sustainable and responsible management of holidays has now expanded into insurance, financial services, magazine publishing and radio. It has a database of 7.6 million customers and a turnover of £382m.

Product value

Responsible Tourism can add to the quality of the tourist's experience. It can assure access for the tourist or assuage guilt; all these things help give competitive advantage. Where price, quality and availability is similar between operators for a destination or experience then one of the ethical or responsible elements may well be a tiebreaker. Moreover, non-price competition is better for margins. Responsible operators reported that where there was broad parity on the other criteria, their Responsible Tourism practices made the difference 'nearly every time'.[53]

Motivation, price and availability shape consumer choice, and the Responsible Tourism elements of a particular experience or product can only be one part of the mix that results in a particular purchasing decision. There is a 'trade-off between economics and aspirations for operators as well as tourists'.[54] Tourists look for products which provide value for money and which they can afford. Tour operators are constrained by their resources and the need to make a profit.

A visit to the local market or to the craft worker to purchase souvenirs, to a local shebeen to enjoy a beer in a township in South Africa, a walking tour with a coffee farmer and lunch at the farmstead, all these experiences enhances the product and benefit local people as well as the tourist. The Responsible Tourism product has one advantage over many other ethical products: the consumer generally experiences the difference. Where the Responsible Tourism elements either create a better experience (visiting a local market) or are necessary to it (employing a local guide), consumers are attracted to it for both experiential and responsible reasons. As Justin Francis of ResponsibleTravel. com often says, the traveller should be able to 'taste the difference'; and, he argues, they return because of this. Exodus makes a similar point 'If you've travelled [with us] you already know – if you haven't we'll show you'.[55]

The strength of the experiential difference is significantly greater than for

---

53 Francis (2000), undertaking research to develop the business case for ResponsibleTravel.com.

54 Goodwin and Francis (2003): 283

55 www.exodus.co.uk/news/2007/08/whats-so-special-about-exodus accessed 8 June 2010

example in Fairtrade tea or coffee, where you cannot taste the difference and instead must make do with a description of the loving care with which the beans are grown and prepared. The Fairtrade movement has been successful in achieving a significant price premium, but this premium is not necessarily expected in Responsible Tourism – even though, as part of the overall product, the levels of experience and service may contribute to a higher price point. Intercontinental Hotels have long sought to attract guests, and ensured that they repeat and refer, by offering a consistent quality experience in the property. In 2010, they were running film clips on the in-house channel informing guests that staff were willing 'to share their local knowledge with you, so you enjoy authentic experiences and go home with more to share … go home more inspired … go home with more to reflect on'. The high-end travel company Pure Life Experiences quotes Jean-Jacques Rousseau on its website: 'The person who has lived the most, is not the one who has lived longest, but the one who has had the richest experiences.' They may have a point.

Neighbourhood and licence to operate

Neighbourhood is important to all businesses where the clients visit the premises, or where confidence may be affected by the street address, but it is unusually important to travel and tourism businesses. The neighbourhood, the area around the hotel, and the people who live, work and play there, is generally a fundamental part of the product, and one over which the operator generally has no contractual control. Most tourism products extend into the public realm: the trail, beach, cathedral, museum or the streets of the city, the neighbourhood of the accommodation. Even where the company controls the destination – as in Disneyland, or an all-inclusive hotel – the tourist experience still includes the immigration controls at the airport and what is seen from the windows of the transfer coach or car; increasingly, too, holidaymakers expects to be able to explore independently beyond the confines of their accommodation.

Hotels are immovable assets and are particularly vulnerable to changes in the neighbourhood when crime rates rise or socio-economic or environmental degeneration occurs. Tourism businesses in the destination and those who send tourists to the destination can contribute to improving the local neighbourhood by working with local government and the police to reduce hassle, and encourage the development of craft markets, local restaurants and entertainment around hotels and resorts.[56] In the Gambia, the hotels offer a

56   Ashley et al. (2006): 3, 7

free market day to traders from local craft markets, during which they can sell inside their hotels – usually selling far more than they do in a normal day.[57]

And it's not just in far-flung or developing countries that this can work. Near London's Victoria Station, The Goring Hotel is part of the local Business Improvement District (BID) which is working to improve the quality of the public realm, regenerate business in the area and promote social and economic benefits, to make Victoria a destination of choice. The BID initiatives are funded by levies on local businesses. David Morgan-Hewitt, GM of the Goring Hotel, enthusiastically backed the proposal. 'For too long we have been a thoroughfare in peoples' minds as they travel onwards to their destination. It is a wonderful neighbourhood and it deserves more. Through the work that this extra revenue will allow us to undertake, Victoria will once again become a destination in her own right'.[58] This is an example of enlightened self-interest, with clear private costs and public and private benefits.

Marketing and PR

In addition to generating the experiences and stories which fuel repeats and referrals, the Responsible Tourism agenda can be used to generate market awareness and media attention. Carey's Manor in the New Forest offers a 10% discount for anyone arriving by public transport, and now has a much healthier mid-week conference market as a consequence.[59] Another benefit is that the experiential and Responsible Tourism elements of a holiday provide something meatier for travel journalists to write about. Catherine Mack surveyed ten national UK travel supplements over 10 weeks in 2005–06. She found that 35% of articles included Responsible Tourism issues, and one in twenty were 'wholly dedicated' to it.[60] Responsible Tourism has been used by companies as a tool to generate press releases, to provide social media news, to be remembered by customers and to encourage repeats and referrals, without having to send coarse blanket mailings. The Lancaster London Hotel has been doing all their homework in water, waste and energy management for years, yet it was their PR campaign highlighting their rooftop beehives that provided honey on the breakfast tables that attracted local and international media attention, including BBC, ITV and CNN in 2009–10.

---

57   Bah and Goodwin (2003): 32–33
58   Victoria Partnership Ltd (2009): 16
59   Visit England, Keep it Real (2010b): 17
60   Mack (2006): 18

Shareholder and investor value

When goodwill is such a significant part of the value of the company, shareholder value is necessarily heavily dependent on brand value and public reputation. Both the Thomas Cook Group and TUI Travel in the UK are actively involved in CSR reporting, as are the major hotel groups. The sustainability performance of any company is important to investors, who are looking for a return over the medium term. As an example, Lonrho, whose Fly540 regional airline operates from Angola, Ghana and Kenya, and which has hotels in Southern Africa and the Indian Ocean, has a larger CSR section on its corporate site than it is on the consumer site.[61] Fly540 has planted trees, paid for the construction of a kitchen block at a children's home, hosted the children's party and provided free flights for doctors involved in Operation Smile.[62] The Intercontinental Hotel Group (IHG) now reports to shareholders and potential investors on responsible business as one of its four 'How we win' priorities alongside the guest experience, financial returns and investing in its staff. IHG sees strategic corporate responsibility as driving innovation and collaboration.[63] Their corporate site reports on their Global Reporting Initiative performance. IHG identifies specific risks related to corporate social responsibility in 2010:

> The Group is exposed to the risk of damage to its reputation if it fails to demonstrate sufficiently responsible practices, or fails to comply with regulatory requirements, in a number of areas such as safety and security, sustainability, responsible tourism, environmental management, human rights and support for the local community. [64]

The growth in CSR reporting reflects the increasing importance of the ethical and socially responsible investment funds in share markets. Campaigning groups are able to use even small share ownerships in companies to effect change in company policies.[65] In 2006 Boston Common Asset Management and First Swedish National Pension Fund filed a shareholder resolution with Marriott after it came to light that a receptionist at the Marriott in San Jose,

---

61 www.lonrho.com and www.lonrhohotelsafrica.com respectively

62 Operation Smile provides free surgeries to repair cleft lips and palates and other facial deformities in children www.operationsmile.org

63 www.ihgplc.com/index.asp?pageid=718 accessed 11 June 2010

64 www.ihgplc.com/files/reports/ar2009/2010-risk-factors.html accessed 11 June 2010

65 SRI World Group founded in 1999 provides two websites: one focused on institutional investors www.institutionalshareowner.com; the other www.socialfunds.com addresses individual investors

Costa Rica, had been involved in providing children for sexual purposes. The resolution called on Marriott to adopt a comprehensive human rights policy to 'enhance corporate reputation, improve community and stakeholder relations and reduce risk of adverse publicity, consumer boycotts, divestment campaigns and lawsuits'.[66] In November 2006 Marriott revised its Commitment to Human Rights[67] and the resolution was withdrawn. This is an extreme case, but all publicly listed companies are vulnerable.[68] Marriott acted properly: it is the willingness and ability to respond positively that demonstrates responsibility.

Risk, of this and other kinds, is an integral part of business. Maintaining profits, protecting investments, finding shareholder value and dealing with technological change all involve risk. Managing public perceptions of firms and the risks which result from 'civil society and stakeholders' is more challenging in a complex and interconnected world. One definition of social risk is 'when an empowered stakeholder takes up a social issue area and applies pressure on a corporation (exploiting a vulnerability in the earnings drivers, e.g. reputation, corporate image) so that the company will change policies or approaches in the market place'.[69] There is no doubt that watchdogs, and the public, are becoming more vigilant. For example, the UK campaigning NGO Tourism Concern exposes companies it regards as having negative social, economic and environmental impacts, In 2009, it published a report on human rights abuses in the tourism industry [70] and a specific report on *How UK Tour Operators are Supporting Burma's Military Regime through Tourism.*[71]

Cost savings, improved margins and competitiveness

Real cost savings can be achieved through improved environmental performance, and, as resource costs increase in a finite world, the returns on investment in greener technology and environmental efficiency are increasingly significant. Hotels are being driven to improve their environmental performance by increases in the costs of fossil fuels and water, the costs of

---

66 Resolution available on line at www.socialfunds.com/pdf/1206/Marriott_Filing_Resolution. pdf and there is a report at http: //www.humantrafficking.org/updates/494

67 Available on line at www.marriott.com/Multimedia/PDF/Corporate/HumanRights.pd

68 The Third World Network based in Singapore records and supports a number of campaigns. http: //www.twnside.org.sg/title2/tourism/mega-resort.htm

69 Kytle and Ruggie (2005): 6

70 Erikkson et al. (2009)

71 Tourism Concern (2009)

dealing with waste and by consumer pressure, particularly from corporates who are pushing for better performance from their suppliers.

Taking responsibility and managing negative impacts which may damage reputation or incur liability has business value. It promotes a more efficient use of resources – the more so if likely rises in future costs are factored in – and increases the resilience of the business or destination. Pre-empting the impact of anticipated regulation also has commercial value if the business is able to adjust its operation in anticipation of regulatory change its compliance costs will probably be lower.

Increasingly there are Key Performance Indicators (KPIs) for staff and hotels are creating green teams to push innovation and change. For example, the International Hotel Group, which includes the InterContinental brand, has put nearly 1000 people through sustainability training. In addition, 900 of its hotels set up Green Engage groups in 2009 and in 2010 it planned to roll out Green Engage to all of its owned and managed hotels – achieving a reduction in energy use of between 6% and 10% in 2010–12 on the per-available-room-night basis – the same basis that hotels use to set their sales targets. The IHG has key performance objectives in place throughout the business.[72] In 2009 Accor reported a 7.8% reduction in its energy consumption for room from 2006 levels, and 79% of its owned and managed hotels now have tap and shower flow regulators. It reported average water and fuel consumption by hotel group, and detailed data by region on the deployment of different environmental management techniques.[73]

Moreover, these savings are notwithstanding the challenge, faced by all major international hotel brands of operating in diverse cultures and environments and of implementing environmental management systems in hotels which they do not own.

The major international hotel groups rarely build their own hotels and more often manage rather than own the properties, limiting what the management company can achieve. Hotels are often built for a local owner, who may not engage a management company from the outset and who in any case may be building to sell. Environmental sustainability is likely to be a higher priority if the developer is going to operate the hotel and therefore stands to recoup the environmental cost reductions. When there is no link between construction and operations, building control and regulation are an important mechanism for ensuring that hotels are built to high sustainability standards.

---

72 www.ihgplc.com/index.asp?pageid=740 accessed 12 June 2010

73 Accor (2010): 71, 110 ff

Staff morale and retention

Though perhaps relatively minor, it is at least a contributory reason for engaging with the responsibility agenda. At the AITO's first training session, one of the owners who attended explained that he had come along to find out about Responsible Tourism because, at recent interviews, his preferred candidate had asked whether or not he had a Responsible Tourism policy. There is plenty of anecdotal evidence to suggest the responsibility agenda generates pride in the business and helps to attract and retain enthusiastic and loyal staff. Reducing turnover can be a significant business benefit, reducing recruitment and training costs and training in an industry which relies heavily on the knowledge and skills of its staff.

The reasons why a particular business adopts a responsible approach will depend upon the cultural and geographical environment in which the business operates; the salience of the responsibility agenda amongst its clients, individual and corporate; and the attitudes and management decisions of the company's leaders. There are a range of reasons, which are used to explain why business takes responsibility: trust, reputation and consumer loyalty, product value, neighbourhood and license to operate, marketing and PR, shareholder and investor value, risk, cost savings, improved margins and competitiveness and staff morale. We live in a diverse world and those engaged in working with businesses to encourage responsibility also need to be aware of the personal understandings of responsibility and ethics of those they are engaging with.

Opportunities and pitfalls

There is a strong business case for engagement with sustainability. The cost-saving strategies are relatively free of risk, and are often pursued without informing customers and partners. The business reasons associated with reputation carry their own risks of green-washing and tall poppy syndrome. But, as more businesses engage with, talk about, and to derive commercial benefit from it, it becomes more difficult to be seen to do nothing. This is true in business-to-consumer relationships, and more so in business-to-business relationships where companies push responsibility for delivery on sustainability down their supply chain. For example, the Travelife[74] sustainability system is being used to improve the supply-chain performance of European tour operators: it also assists suppliers to make the change, and provides additional marketing through *The Travelife Collection*[75] brochure, which encourages travellers to make more sustainable choices.

Owners, managers and staff in tourism and hospitality businesses see issues and problems. Sometimes they respond; sometimes they do not. Sometimes they carry others with them, and the business engages. As we have seen, many tourism businesses see their opportunity to inform or suggest to guests how they can get more out of their holiday and reduce any negative impacts from their trip – and this information is generally welcomed. Tour operators and hoteliers respond: they take responsibility for providing advice and information and encourage people, without preaching, to travel more responsibly.

Opportunity creates responsibility – for example, when an operator raises money for children's charities in the UK or a returned traveller establishes a charity to assist an orphanage or neuter cats. Nurture Lakeland[76] is a Lake District charity working with visitors and tourism related businesses, fundraising to support conservation and raise awareness of environmentally sustainable practices within the tourism sector. It has 220 corporate members who, together with their customers, have raised £1.5m for projects in the Lake District ranging from red squirrel conservation and fixing the fells, to low-level footpath repair and supporting local children's wildlife education. Village Ways,[77] which offer walking tours with local communities in remote areas, was developed as a partnership between business people with the relevant market experience in the UK and local communities, initially in India and now in Ethiopia. Individuals saw the need, realised they had the relevant knowledge and skills, and responded.

Responsibility is not something separate, something bolted on as an addition, an optional extra. It has to be part of the way the company does its business. Staff throughout the company need to be engaged. The failure to deliver on the expectations generated by marketing or by previous experience of the

---

74 Travelife is supported by major European Tour Operator Associations and their members including the UK Federation of Tour Operators (FTO), the Dutch Association of Travel Agents Tour Operators ANVR and the German Forum Anders Reisen FAR.

75 http://travelifecollection.co.uk/

76 www.nurturelakeland.org

77 www.villageways.com/

company will result in disappointment, and may also result in adverse comments to friends and family, as well as online criticism in the many forums that are used by travellers to check places and businesses out. Responsibility requires transparency and credibility in a world where customers can speak directly to others about their experiences – sometimes on the provider's own site. Businesses publicly taking responsibility need to do so seriously and consistently, avoiding anything that smacks of hypocrisy, marketing hype or green-washing. Businesses need to engage seriously and think hard about the quality of their initiatives if they are to add, rather than subtract, from the experience and the brand value.

One of the simplest opportunities – and consequently one of the biggest pitfalls – for accommodation providers is the towel exchange programme, the card travellers find in so many bathrooms enjoining them to save the world by not having their towels washed. Many of us have dutifully put our towels back on the rack and returned to find that the towels have been changed – the room cleaner having correctly surmised that leaving used towels is more likely to provoke a complaint than is providing unwanted clean replacements. In these cases, the hotel has failed to support a behavioural change it asked of the guest. Often the environmental gesture is further undermined by the absence of any water flow control on the bath or shower; having the TV and lights on to welcom you to the room, the air-conditioning is turned unhealthily low and the key card switch, designed to save power when the room is unoccupied, has been over-ridden and is permanently switched on. There is generally plenty to complain about more productively. And you should: the responsibility is all yours.

Sheraton introduced a 'make a green choice'[78] option that credits guests with five euros, to spend in the hotel on food and beverages, if they forgo housekeeping for a day: participation rates are reported at between 10% and 15%. This approach is claimed to save cleaning materials, water and energy, reduces labour costs and drives additional business to the restaurants and bars in the hotels. In Winnipeg it drew press coverage of complaints from the room cleaners' union that it was costing them shifts, that extra water and chemicals were used in tackling the dirtier rooms and that guests leave the lights and TV on burning fuel.[79] Further proof, if needed, that responsibility is complicated

---

78   www.greenlodgingnews.com/content.aspx?id=3748 accessed 11 June 2010

79   www.winnipegfreepress.com/greenpage/environment/green-programs-in-some-toronto-hotels-fake-say-workers-92871659.html accessed 11 June 2010

and that it is important to take an informed holistic view, and to manage it accordingly. The Novotel Benoa in Bali has adopted a simpler approach: they invite guests to reuse their towels and bed sheets and the savings are put towards Accor's Tree for a Child programme. For every 10 reused towels or bedsheets, one tree is planted at Accor's tree planting project in Gelandung village in Central Java. In 2007 Accor Indonesia planted 7900 trees through this programme,[80] and it is now is now promoted by Accor worldwide: between 2008 and 2010, a thousand hotels have financed the planting of a million trees. The goal is to plant three million by the end of 2012.[81]

Stories such as these are important to the process of securing change and to ensuring that the exercise of responsibility generates consumer loyalty, repeats and referrals. We have seen that tourism businesses are increasingly evidencing their responsibility as part of the consumer experience, engaging their travellers and guests and reporting their sustainability targets and progress towards meeting them. Certification by contrast is less easy to effuse about. It is an opaque process: the consumer may be able to find out what the criteria are, but may not know why a particular business gained bronze, silver or gold, nor what progress, if any, was achieved in reducing water consumption or emissions. The certificate carries no story and there is consequently little or no marketing or PR value. Most certification agencies have been poor at marketing their members, although the Green Tourism Business Scheme's Green Places to Stay[82] site lists members, and the Travelife Collection[83] is being marketed both in the brochures of the major UK outbound operators and in dedicated online brochures. The certificate tells the consumer that the business is making efforts to be greener, more responsible. However, that message is largely devoid of meaning: the certificate does not permit the consumer to anticipate how the experience will be different and better. The explicit claims made on a website, for example to have local produce on the breakfast table, are part of the contract: the holidaymaker can demand recompense if the expectation is not met. If a certificate is misleading there is no contract between the traveller and the certification agency and no recompense to be had. We shall return to certification in Chapter 7.

---

80   http://www.novotelbalibenoa.com/wp-content/uploads/2010/04/NBB-Green-Globe-Certified-Press-Release.pdf accessed 11 June 2010

81   Accor Press Release, 27 May 2010

82   www.green-business.co.uk/GreenBusiness_GreenPlacesToStay.asp

83   www.travelifecollection.co.uk

Increasingly tour operators and accommodation providers are communicating their sustainability priorities to their clients, and their progress in achieving them. Their priorities reveal to the consumer a good deal about the values of the business and the experiences it provides. The next chapter looks at Responsible Tourism in destinations – a diverse world in which different issues are priorities in different places. Who should decide what the issues and priorities are in particular destinations, for businesses and for public spaces? The business case for responsibility is strong, but responsibility rests not only with business: there is a public interest too. Local authorities have a responsibility for ensuring that tourism is sustainable and for defining and communicating what the local priorities are.

References

Accor (2010) *2009 Annual Report*, Paris: Accor.

Ashley, C., Goodwin, H., McNab, D., Scott, M. and Chaves, L. (2006) *Making Tourism Count for the Local Economy in the Caribbean*, London: Pro-Poor Tourism and the Caribbean Tourism Organisation.

Bah, A. and Goodwin, H. (2003) 'Improving access for the informal sector to tourism in The Gambia', Pro-Poor Working Paper 15, Pro-Poor Tourism, London.

Blowfield, M. and Murray, A. (2008) *Corporate Responsibility: A Critical Introduction*, Oxford: Oxford University Press.

Bowen, H.R. (1953) *Social Responsibilities of the Businessman*, New York: Harper & Row.

Carroll, A.B. (1999) 'Corporate social responsibility: evolution of a definitional construct', *Business and Society*, **4** (4), 268–295.

Erikkson, J., Noble, R., Pattullo, P. and Barnett, T. (2009) *A Challenge to Human Rights Abuses in the Tourism Industry*, London: Tourism Concern.

Falck, O. and Heblich, S. (2007) 'Corporate social responsibility: doing well by doing good', *Business Horizons*, **50** (3), 247–254.

Francis, J. (2000) 'Can the Internet be used to expedite the growth of more responsible forms of tourism by creating an online marketplace of pre-screen and monitored processes/services', unpublished MSc dissertation, University of Greenwich.

Goodwin, H. and Francis, J. (2003) 'Ethical and responsible tourism: consumer trends in the UK', *Journal of Vacation Marketing*, **9** (3), 271–284.

Kohn, M. (2008) *Trust, Self–interest and the Common Good*, Oxford: Oxford University Press.

Kytle, B. and Ruggie, J.G. (2005) 'Corporate social responsibility as risk management, a model for multinationals, Corporate Social Responsibility Initiative Working Paper 10, Harvard University.

Laszlo, C. (2008) *Sustainable Value: How the World's Leading Companies are Doing Well by Doing Good*, Stanford, CA: Stanford University Press.

Mack, C. (2006) 'Context analysis of the UK travel print media and responsible tourism', Occasional Paper 4, International Centre for Responsible Tourism, Leeds.

Nicolau, J. (2008) 'Corporate social responsibility worth-creating activities, *Annals of Tourism Research*, **35** (4), 990–1006.

Seldon, A. (2009) *Trust, How We Lost It and How to Get It Back*, London: Biteback Publishing.

Tearfund (2001) *Tourism: Putting Ethics into Practice*, London: Tearfund.

Victoria Partnership (2009) *Victoria Business Improvement District Business Plan 2009*, London: Victoria Partnership.

Visit England (2010a) *England: A Strategic Framework for Tourism 2010–2020*, London: Visit England.

4 Responsible Tourism in Destinations

Take responsibility for achieving sustainable tourism, and to create better places for people to live in and for people to visit.

Cape Town Declaration

To experience a different place, to see other peoples' places and how they live there, is a major generator of travel and tourism. The celebration of, and respect for, diversity are fundamental to Responsible Tourism. Article 1 of the UN World Tourism Organization's Global Code of Ethics for Tourism asserts the importance of an 'attitude of tolerance and respect for the diversity of religious, philosophical and moral beliefs', as 'both the foundation and the consequence of responsible tourism'. It calls on stakeholders in tourism, including the tourists, to 'observe the social and cultural traditions and practises of all peoples'. The world's destinations reflect our planet's ecological and socio-cultural diversity. Responsible Tourism places importance on all three pillars of sustainable development – economic, social and environmental – and accepts that the priorities will vary from place to place. We take our holidays in other peoples' places, their places; it is for the people who live there to determine their priorities. Unfortunately there is often an imbalance of power, and the interests of the tourists and the businesses which cater to them can distort local priorities in favour of the visitors over the visited, in favour of the travel and tourism sector over other groups.

The case for tourism often, by default, assumes that more is better. For the businesses involved, this may be the case, but for local communities, their environments and our climate it is important that we debate the purpose of tourism. What is it for? Why do we want it? How much of it do we want? Tourism affects local people and their places, through a range of local organisations and government structures. Tourism, unmanaged, can easily create a tragedy of the commons; it is the locals – authorities and government, who make decisions about regulation, public spending, taxes and subsidies – who must manage it, and bear the costs of doing so. They must shape the activity of tourism and its scale. Destinations are not infinite, neither individually nor collectively. Not everywhere can be a destination, able to attract people to travel and destinations themselves cannot absorb limitless numbers of tourists.

This chapter looks first at the concept of destination and who shapes it. Then, we ask, what is the purpose of tourism? From a destination perspective, what is it for? We shall then look at national governance in Thailand, England and South Africa, then at local governance, before looking at the role that tourism marketing can play in enabling communities in destinations to use tourism and to address its sustainability.

The Responsible Tourism imperative, to 'create better places for people to live in and for people to visit', requires that priority is given to local people. Even in those places that exist entirely because of tourism, people are leading their lives, going to school, going to work, growing old. One of the fundamental inequalities of tourism is that between the visited and visitor: those for whom tourism is part of their routine life, at work or in the streets, and those who are on vacation away from their everyday experience, in someone else's place. Krippendorf argued that in 'cases of incompatibility or doubt, the interests of host populations must have precedence over those of outsiders.'[1] It follows from this principle that it is for local people to determine how they wish to use tourism and how it needs to be managed in order that it is sustainable in their place and for their community. It is for locals to define sustainability for their place, to determine the issues that need to be addressed. This is their responsibility.

Destinations can be contested spaces where the social constructs of visited and visitors collide. Eade describes London's young Bangladeshi community in Brick Lane,[2] the 'wider context of the increasing Islamisation of public space in the area' and conflict with a Jewish historian providing Jewish heritage tours of the same space.[3] Tourism is a cultural process, and a destination is a social product: the 'visible structure of a place expresses the emotional attachments held by both its residents and its visitors';[4] it also creates and forms those attachments. Tourism plays a prominent role in the social construction of a place, not only because of the activities of those who market them, but also as a consequence of the interactions which take place there, interactions

---

1   Krippendorf,(1987): 118

2   In Spitalfields in the East End of London immediately adjacent to the City of London.

3   Eade (2002): 137–138

4   Ringer (1998): 10

in which tourists and day visitors are not the only actors. As Squire points out, '... destinations are not merely a leitmotif for geographical place. Rather they are also social and cultural constructions whose meanings and values are negotiated and redefined by diverse people, and mediated only tangentially to a particular tourist setting.'[5]

People in destinations, local communities, are rarely, if ever, of one opinion about tourists and tourism, or about anything else. Different individuals, businesses and groups want to see different kinds of visitors, or none at all. In any community where tourism occurs there will be direct and indirect beneficiaries, those who are unaffected and those who are disadvantaged. Different kinds of tourism and tourists have different economic, social and environmental impacts, affecting different stakeholders. Those who are content with things as they are may argue for little engagement by national or local government, although they will probably want public money to be used for promoting the sector. Government legislates, regulates and is responsible for land use and development planning: it imposes taxation and it benefits businesses in the tourist sector by providing marketing, a benefit rarely afforded to other sectors. Businesses and the 'industry' tend to want more marketing and less regulation and taxation. It is to local government that people turn to manage the pollution caused by tourists, to remove litter from the streets and commons, to regulate coach parking or through planning to object to a change of use or the building of a hotel.

Destinations

Destinations attract tourists. Tourists and travellers have a place to go: whether they plan to go on to another or to return, they are travelling with a destination in mind. Generally a destination will have a number of attractions and provide tourism services, accommodation and hospitality. Destination implies a place which attracts non-local visitors, people who have travelled some distance from their homes. How far from home they travel is determined by the strength of the attraction(s) at the destination and the tourist's capacity to journey there – principally defined by their money and holiday time. Destinations will be attractive to different people, a function of motivation, ease of access and cost. Some will be attractive only to domestic tourists; others will have the capacity to attract from particular national and international source markets, and not only the most proximate.

---

5   Squire (1998): 82–83

The market plays an important role in shaping destinations. Locals, local tour operators and ground handlers, accommodation providers, guides, other businesses, investors, architects and planners, attractions, cultural and natural heritage managers, tourists, guide-book writers, travel writers and journalists, airlines, cruise companies, tour operators and travel agents in originating markets all have their influence on perceptions of a particular destination and can affect how tourism develops and occurs there. Tourists' perceptions and behaviour are direct results of marketing by businesses based in the destination and in originating markets, as well as by destination marketing that is funded by the destination and by the media. But the images created, the perception of the destination and the viral marketing by tourists on the internet and by word of mouth, are shaped by the product and the experience people have of it.

Tourism businesses need to find clients, whether they are airlines or hotels. The issue is who decides – who has the power to determine who arrives in the destination? What kinds of people are invited? Who issues the invitation? This is likely to be a matter for debate within the tourism sector; businesses often want particular kinds of tourists, and in the destination different businesses and attractions will have often divergent market priorities. The problem is more acute when the dominant presence of one kind of tourist displaces others. The development of new air routes can be influenced by destinations through subsidies, but traditional airlines, charters and budget carriers both respond to and create demand. They are powerful in shaping potential travellers' perceptions of destination – why they should travel there and how they might expect to behave when they get there. They create expectations and are responsible for them. The Hungarian low-cost airline Wizz Air operates to secondary airports to keep costs down, and by doing so it generates new markets for destinations like Budapest, Krakow and Warsaw. However, by encouraging thirsty people to travel for cheap beer, they cheapen these great cultural cities. One Wizz Air advertisement read: 'Beer from £0.49. Thirsty? Book a flight to Hungary and Poland from £24.99…'.

Krippendorf used the term 'hard tourism' to describe tourism which is shaped purely by economic and technical forces.[6] The concept of *sanfter Tourismus* or 'soft tourism', originated in the early 1980s in the German speaking Alpine areas of Bavaria, Austria and Switzerland, in a part of the developed world significantly affected by both summer- and winter-sports tourism.

---

6   Krippendorf (1982)

Emphasis is often placed on the environmental impacts of tourism development, but those who originated the concept of 'soft tourism' define it more broadly. The 1984 Chur[7] Declaration describes:

> ...a form of tourism which leads to mutual understanding between the local population and their guests, which does not endanger the cultural identity of the host region and which endeavours to take care of the environment as best as possible. 'Soft tourists' give priority to using infrastructure destined for the local population and do not accept substantial tourist facilities harmful to the environment.[8]

However, we should avoid the polarised, and polarising, simplicity of 'hard equals bad and soft equals good'. The world is diverse and circumstances alter cases. All forms of tourism can be more (or less) responsible.

If it is accepted that tourism is not a pollution-free industry, that it can have negative social, economic and environmental impacts, then managing tourism so as to optimise its impact in any particular destination makes sense. Large volumes of tourists present management challenges. Urry identified the 'collective tourist gaze' where 'congregation is paramount',[9] the crowd is part of the attraction at the races, a street market or on the beach. Where this occurs the tourists may predominate and become the place. In this context, a hardened 'factory', designed to manage the negative social and environmental impacts of large numbers of tourists and their hedonistic, party animal behaviour, may be the most responsible option. Sun, sand, sea and sex tourism may be better managed within hardened and contained all-inclusive resorts than in a Greek fishing village or a Baltic capital.

An interesting comparison can, and has, been made by Bramwell between tourism enterprises on the Spanish Catalan coast, which are mainly small scale, owned and managed by local entrepreneurs and where the penetration of foreign capital has been limited, and Crete, where local businesses have transferred their management to foreign multinationals and an estimated 70% of beds are controlled by foreign tour operators.[10] The oversupply of beds in destinations, generated in part by the absence of alternative land-use opportunities, is a consequence of a misreading of growth trends or of speculation

---

7   Capital of the Swiss canton of Graubünden

8   Chur Declaration of the Commission Internationale pour la Protection des Régions Alpines quoted by Broggi cited in Smith and Eadington (1992): 18

9   Urry (1995): 140

10   Bramwell (2004): 9

in real estate, and generally results in declining bed occupancy and bed night rates, and the deterioration of accommodation. In Greece in the ten years from 1983 to 1992, the official supply of hotel beds increased at an average 4.7% per annum. The average annual increase in international bed nights sold was 2.7%, and the problem of oversupply was exacerbated by illegal unregistered beds. In Faliraki on Rhodes 40% of rooms are thought to be illegal and 70% of the buildings are in violation of the law.[11] In a significant number of Greek municipalities, the failure to enforce planning regulations effectively has resulted in declining accommodation standards and oversupply. The responsibility for this tragedy of the commons rests with the investors, and the local government for its failure to manage hotel development. The dominance of market forces was not counterbalanced by regulation.

Ludlow is a small market town in Shropshire on the Welsh border. It has a strong sense of place – its rural hinterland, and the Welsh Marches, ensuring its distinctive identity. It was the first *Cittaslow* or 'Slow City' in the UK.[12] In 2004 it produced a leaflet declaring that if you visited you would be 'treated like a temporary resident' in a town determined to improve the quality of life for 'all the people who live and work there', and for visitors whose needs 'should be catered for and anticipated fully'. Ludlow's economy is buoyed by tourists and by day visitors, without whom it could not support so many shops restaurants and food businesses – and the annual food festival. Good food, good drink, a relaxed pace of life, a fine built heritage and beautiful countryside; visitors are invited to 'Come and join us – for a day, for a week or just for a weekend. Dip your toe into slow and unwind a while with us....' Good places to live make good places to visit. 'Don't be surprised if you find yourself coming back regularly, for "just another visit"!'[13] Krippendorf argued that when people become repeat visitors in a destination, they benefit from 'destination loyalty' and develop a 'true relationship' with the place and its people – and the locals benefit too.[14] This as a form of 'soft tourism': tourism that meets the needs of all stakeholders, including local people. He argues that tourism can in this way be used for the economic and social advancement of the place and its people, and that it is important to cultivate what is typically local.[15]

---

11   Bramwell (2004): 9–10

12   It is not a city – it is a town of 10,000 people on the border with Wales.

13   I go at least once a year. www.visitsouthshropshire.co.uk/ludlow.htm accessed 14 June 2010

14   Krippendorf (1987): 135

15   Krippendorf (1987): 107, 117 and 123, 119

The people who live and work in a place can, and do, use the attractions and services used by tourists. Faversham, the small market-town where I live in Kent, benefits from visitors and has much in common with Ludlow: there is a wealth of good food producers, restaurants and pubs, and the town is part of the East Kent food triangle with Whitstable and Canterbury. The Tourist Information Centre is run by volunteers in the Heritage Centre, which, along with the museum are the embodiment of years of work by local people who campaigned through the Faversham Society to maintain the town's very rich inheritance of vernacular architecture – an inheritance that needs to be given meaning for future generations if it is to be sustained. We take pride in being visited, we get satisfaction from other peoples' enjoyment of our place, we have our own trained guides and take pleasure in seeing them out and about with groups of visitors explaining about brick manufacture and gunpowder. Each year there are Secret Garden and Open House weekends when residents open their gardens and houses to be visited by locals, day-visitors and tourists, raising money for the Faversham Society. They are embodiments of local pride, an opportunity to share with neighbours and visitors. Faversham developed in this way as local residents developed resources and activities for their own enjoyment, and to share with others. None of this was developed particularly for tourism. When visitors come, they come as guests. Some stay overnight, we encounter them in the streets and in our cafes, bars and restaurants and in larger numbers at our street festivals. They are welcome, most of the time. For there is also an ambivalence about tourism. Some tourists are not so welcome – particularly those who walk around the town in large groups, with their own guide, or compete for the use of our space. They are out of place, get in our way, and sometimes appear to treat us with contempt. They peer through the windows of our houses, or arrive in the back bar of a local hostelry on a cold Sunday evening and greet a lone man with a pint and a book by the fire with: 'Is it always quiet like this in here?' It used to be – but then the brown tourist sign went up on the A2, the old Roman road from London to Dover, and people who did not know why they were coming turned up and disturbed me in my local pub on a winter Sunday evening; like weeds, the wrong people in the wrong place. There is generally a degree of ambivalence about tourism but behind the ambivalence are deeper questions about what is tourism for, what is its purpose, who benefits?

What is the purpose of tourism?

From a destination perspective, what is the purpose of tourism? It is clear what the purpose of tourism is for a business providing accommodation or an attraction: tourists are customers. For service providers, tourists and day visitors are an additional market. For locals there may be a sense of pride that their place attracts visitors from around the world and awareness that there would not be such a rich variety of restaurants, cafes, bars and shops if it were not for visitors. On the other hand, tourism may bring congestion, litter and unruly behaviour – for which read behaviour that does not fit in and imposes costs on the community. Tourism brings additional customers, but it may also displace local businesses from high streets if rents rise because of the tourism dollar.

There is a wide range of reasons why government needs to deal with tourism. These reasons range from economic development, regeneration to place-making, social inclusion and the maintenance of cultural and natural heritage. Sustainability is everyone's responsibility and therefore often nobody's. In local government, the tourism function is often limited to, or dominated by, promotion. The tourism officer is vulnerable to being seen as someone who spends public money on printing paper which attracts visitors from outside the area, increasing local authority costs: the visitors need to be managed and their litter needs to be removed. The tourism impacts need to be managed, and in this context, tourists may be seen as freeloaders who contribute nothing to the costs of their being in the public realm in the destination. This is perhaps an exaggeration, but there is truth in it. It is certainly not self-evident that ever-rising tourist numbers are in the public interest. A country's heritage and places have purposes and functions for worship, education, leisure, culture and recreation that precede, and are arguably more important than, tourism. Tourism can help to create better places for people to live in and for people to visit. However, this outcome can only be achieved if tourism is managed for that purpose.

In Venice, the local population has declined as tourism has increased. There were more than 170,000 residents in 1951: the city now has an estimated 18 million visitors per year and fewer than 60,000 inhabitants. In the eyes of some of it residents, tourism dominates the city to its detriment and, in November 2009, a mock funeral was held for the death of the city. As former inhabitants moved out to the suburbs, the urban core of the old city has been converted to tourism accommodation. Did tourism displace local residents and the traditional commercial activity of Venice, or did tourism fill the vacuum as residents left attracted to the suburbs? The answer to this is less clear than are the feelings of some residents.

A common issue in all these examples is the contested nature of public spaces. Destinations are generally composed of public and private spaces, but not always. For example, Disney's attractions are privately owned destinations, as are some all-inclusives and resorts. Yet they too are dependent on public resources such as roads, airports, customs and immigration which are funded primarily from the public purse. The public realm degenerates if local councils are unable to fund the maintenance of public space and the provision of services such as public toilets, litter collection, management and maintenance of parks and gardens, national parks and public spaces. And tourism often puts large – and sometimes unreasonable – demands on these resources.

In an influential paper in 1980, Butler originated the concept of the Tourism Area Life Cycle (TALC). Referencing much earlier work on the subject, Butler postulated that tourism areas are dynamic and that they evolve and change. The TALC hypothesis suggests that destinations are discovered and then developed, and that, as tourism peaks, consolidation and stagnation ensue. Following stagnation, the tourism area and destination may either decline or be rejuvenated. The TALC model drew on the concepts of the product life cycle and carrying capacity, an approach which draws on rangeland ecology to determine the optimal numbers which can use an area without degradation.[16] but it was not deterministic. Butler recognised that efforts by the public and private sector can rejuvenate a declining area – that it can be managed out of decline. Many English seaside resorts have declined and decayed as they have lost tourists, losing jobs and prospects for locals in the process; but others have attracted universities and student populations, or the elderly. Tourism can be used for regeneration; a decline in tourism can result in degeneration. It depends on circumstances and how tourism is managed.

What, then, are the justifications for government engagement and for spending public money on tourism? It is important to recognise that government provides and funds a range of services which are used by tourists and tourism businesses, as well as locals and non-tourism businesses, ranging from immigration to education and that tourism businesses (and tourists) benefit from these services and facilities such as transport, museums, galleries, parks

16   Butler (2006a)

and public spaces. Tourism businesses pay the same taxes as other businesses, use the same facilities and receive the same services, but the value of free public goods to tourism businesses is greater than to non-tourism businesses. What is the case for additional government activity in support of the tourism sector?

Economic development

Tourism provides an additional local market for goods and services, bringing spending power into the local economy. It provides economic opportunities for local businesses, creates employment and can have a positive effect on the economic wellbeing of local people. The additional market of the visitor economy (tourist and day-visitors) contributes to the retail, leisure, hospitality, transport, heritage and arts and culture sectors. Local government works to attract inward investment in hotels, conference centres and attractions and uses public resources to attract tourists. In urban areas there has been greater focus on the night-time economy, although this may also bring additional management costs.

Social inclusion

Social inclusion is a public policy objective recognised in the UNWTO Global Code of Ethics.[17] This asserts that the right to tourism is the corollary of the right to rest and leisure. This public policy objective is recognised and is operative or inoperative in different destinations. There are a wide range of reasons why people are excluded from being able to take a holiday, ranging from income to disability; often reasons for exclusion are cumulative. Disability awareness and access campaigns, backed by legislation in some jurisdictions, lead to improved access for people with disabilities.

Placemaking

Placemaking, the art of making places, emerged in the 1970s. Placemaking is used by architects and planners to describe and discuss the process of creating public spaces, such as waterfronts, squares and shopping malls, which attract people, residents, day excursionists and tourists, because they are interesting

---

17 Article 7 draws on Article 24 of UN's Universal Declaration of Human Rights 'Everyone has the right to rest and leisure, including reasonable limitation of working hours and periodic holidays with pay.'

and pleasurable places to be.[18] When Bluewater, the shopping mall on the outskirts of London opened in 1999, it was, claims its website, Europe's 'largest and most innovative retail and leisure destination'. It is managed as a 'day-out destination' with an average stay of three hours. 'Situated in a stunning location among towering 50 metre high cliffs', the site continues, 'Bluewater is surrounded by a tranquil landscape of lakes, parkland and trees.' Bluewater is located in a former chalk quarry. 'The Bluewater philosophy is simple: to make shopping an enjoyable, stress-free experience, to treat its customers as guests.' [19]

Placemaking is still largely the prerogative of investors, developers and the professionals they employ. Placemaking is about the design and experience offered by places, buildings, landscapes and public spaces; it is undertaken for the benefit of local people and businesses, as well as to attract visitors. Tourism and economic development are often combined in local government as the reputation and facilities of the place are used to attract inward investment and to realise competitive advantage from local distinctiveness. The Lyons Inquiry into local government in the UK concluded that if one of the roles of government is to 'manage frameworks for long-term economic, social and environmental sustainability', then local government has an important role to play in 'allowing different communities to make choices for themselves, and relating and shaping the actions of government and the public sector to the needs of the locality'.[20] This recognition of the importance of engaging local communities in decision-making about tourism echoes the Cape Town Declaration's assertion of the importance of involving local people in decisions that affect their lives and life chances. The active management of tourism is an important element in placemaking, but it should engage the people who live there and not be left to the professionals alone. [21]

Regeneration

The regeneration of declining areas and facilities through tourism is a well-established strategy: redundant docks, shipyards, railway stations, potteries,

---

18   There is a journal for this emerging field: Places: Forum of Design for the Public Realm. See also http: //places.designobserver.com and the Institute of Placemaking.

19   www.bluewater.co.uk/content/ab_history accessed 29 June 2010

20   Lyons (2007): 13. The report was subtitled Place-shaping: a shared ambition for the future of local government

21   Schneekloth and Shibley (1995) recognise that 'the appropriation of placemaking activities by professional place makers denies a fundamental human expression.' (p. 1)

mines, iron works and ports have all been converted to tourism attractions, as have castles and forts from earlier periods. In rural areas, as was revealed following the foot-and-mouth epidemic in the UK, the tourists' and day-visitors' spending provides additional livelihood opportunities for rural communities, providing jobs and helping to keep village stores and pubs open. Over the last thirty years the de-industrialisation of Britain has resulted in the redevelopment of industrial heritage sites: Coalbrookdale, Ironbridge, the Chatham Historic Dockyard, mines, mills and railway lines have been preserved and developed for heritage and tourism reasons, and this has also resulted in local economic development.[22]

Cultural and natural heritage

Both these facets of heritage are supported by tourism. The argument that tourism makes an important contribution to local and national economies, and that tourists are attracted to places by natural and cultural heritage, is used to justify investment in public assets. The UK's Tomorrow's Tourism policy asserted that tourism 'can provide an incentive and income to protect ... built and natural environment and helps to maintain local culture and diversity'.[23] Since the World Parks Congress in 1992, tourism has been explicitly recognised as one of the purposes of national parks and protected areas.[24] Rarely is the net contribution of tourism to the maintenance of natural and cultural heritage calculated – the benefit is simply assumed to be positive. Tourism is regarded as an important economic driver and most places, or at least the governments and the businesses in the sector, want more of it. Rarely are the costs accounted for when the turnover is trumpeted.

The British Museum in London attracted 5.5 million visitors in 2008–09, of which 3.2 million were from overseas.[25] Admission to the museum is free, although special exhibitions incur a fee. On the Visit London website, seven of its top 10 attractions are free, with the British Museum being at the top of their list. These attractions are major public assets: free to tourists and the tourism industry. There is a strong public argument for museums to be free for residents, for education and recreation: museums and galleries, particularly the major national collections, contain the collective heritage of humankind.

---

22   See for example Wright (1985); Hewison (1987) and Lowenthal (1998)

23   DCMS (1999): 8

24   Recommendation 9.

25   British Museum (2009): 23

However, as with all other attractions, museums need to be maintained. Each visitor imposes costs in maintaining and protecting the collection. Residents and taxpayers are entitled to ask whether London's major museums should be free to visitors. Tourists and tourism businesses benefit from free access, yet they impose costs and create congestion and overcrowding, with the attractions taking responsibility for the costs.

Destination sustainability

This is not generally seen as a responsibility of the tourism sector. One of the paradoxes of discussions about travel and tourism is that whilst the sector is widely recognised as important, and is often claimed to be the 'world's largest industry', the issue of its economic contribution to the sustainability of destinations is not an issue. The industry captures most of the rent but makes no contribution to the maintenance of the public assets upon which it depends. It is generally not seen as the sector's responsibility, and businesses in the sector do not recognise the extent to which they are dependent on public assets, the costs of which are met by the community. Destination management is often reduced to destination marketing with tourism businesses seeking public support for their marketing.

For example, the UK Tourism Alliance, which represents tourism businesses in the UK has, four highly focused goals designed to benefit their members: reducing the fiscal and regulatory burden; improving quality; improving customer service; and increasing investment. There is not a mention of sustainability, despite its declared objective 'to work with and lobby government on key issues relevant to the growth and development of tourism and its contribution to the economy.' The Alliance expects government 'to take a proactive approach to planning and regulation that fosters enterprise and investment in new and innovative products, while ensuring appropriate environmental protection'.[26] This is a very narrow view of sustainability, and one which offloads the responsibility to government. The Tourism Alliance seeks a favourable operating environment for the businesses they represent, but ignores the industry's responsibility for the management costs of tourism in the public realm.

The UK's Tourism Alliance is not alone in failing to identify any responsibility for the management of tourism in the public realm. The World Travel

---

26   Tourism Alliance (2008): 4. Established in 2001, the Tourism Alliance comprises some 50 Tourism Industry Associations that together represent almost 200,000 businesses of all sizes throughout the UK. www.tourismalliance.com

and Tourism Council (WTTC) has worked tirelessly to create awareness of the scale of the industry, which employs 235 million people and generates more than 9.2% of world GDP,[27] but the industry is discussed as though it were pollution free, with no externalities to be held responsible for. The sector generally is in denial about the polluting consequences of its activities and its responsibility to address them.

There are exceptions, as we have seen, in the practice of individual businesses and of trade associations like AITO (as detailed in Chapters 2 and 3), which acknowledged a decade ago that tourism businesses have a responsibility for negative impacts in destinations. The ABTA 2010 *Travel Matters* manifesto identified 'thriving destinations' as part of its responsibility. It clearly recognises the importance of its role in encouraging the 'travel and tourism sector to become more accountable and responsible for the impacts of UK operations, and the welfare of destinations'. ABTA accepts its responsibility to lead efforts to ensure that tourism develops in a sustainable way in a finite world and that 'real benefits' accrue to the destinations that UK travellers visit.[28] There is of course an enlightened self-interest motive that lies behind this acceptance of responsibility. If this responsible view predominated in the sector it would not be worthy of comment, but this is not the case. Many tourism businesses still expect government to deal with all of their externalities, to provide the resources, maintain them, and promote the sector. The public interest justification is assumed and is rarely questioned.

Many council officers and workers have responsibilities for destination management, although they may not realise it. The impacts of tourists and day visitors are managed, as are those of local residents and commuters, by local government staff responsible for infrastructure and facilities. The quality of the public realm and public spaces are the responsibility of many parts of local government: parks and gardens, fountains, squares and pavements, signage and information, car parks, public toilets and public transport are all central to the process of destination management. The costs of tourism – the externalities, the pollution caused by the industry – are borne by local taxpayers. Tourism in the public realm, if it is managed at all, is managed by local authorities, in national parks by park authorities and at religious and cultural sites by their custodians. Planning departments and councillors shape destinations through planning and decisions about land use and infrastructure.

---

27   www.wttc.org/eng/About_WTTC/ accessed 29 June 2010
28   ABTA (2010): 4

There has been concern in European outbound tour operating for many years about the impact of mass tourism.[29] The ECOMOST[30] study in the early 1990s looked at the sustainability of tourism on Mallorca and Rhodes. It addressed fundamental questions about preserving local prosperity and economic efficiency, cultural identity, the maintenance and modernisation of accommodation, guest and tour operator satisfaction, environmental awareness and carrying capacity, including attractions, water supply and sewage and the presentation of landscape. It was a project initiated and led by the International Federation of Tour Operators[31] and it had a remarkably enlightened-self-interest approach. Thriving destinations are important to tour operators. In 1994, when the ECOMOST study report was published, it recognised the need for 'ecologically-oriented quality standards', regional planning for the 'uncompromising enforcement of ecologically-oriented planning procedures' and public and industry engagement in the planning process.[32] With local stakeholders, the study developed action plans for Mallorca and Rhodes based on an analysis of local prosperity, the attractiveness of the tourism product, the state of the ecology and the effectiveness of the political framework.[33] For Mallorca the priorities were identified as improving the occupancy rate, using legislation to improve existing and future accommodation, and securing the public water supply.[34] Subsequently some hotels were compulsorily purchased and demolished, with one cleared site being developed as a green space. The Calvia local authority on Mallorca turned from quantity to quality in its tourism development strategy. For Rhodes the priorities identified were to improve the revenues and investment in tourist establishments, the development of modern sewage and waste schemes and to manage enterprises in a more environmentally friendly way.[35]

Collective services

Collective services for tourism often require government assistance, because of the weakness of the sector's organisation, its inability to recognise collective responsibilities and the benefits to be gained by greater co-operation

---

29   Since the 1970s. IFTO (1994): I

30   ECOMOST (1994): 8

31   Now superseded by the European Tour Operators Association www.etoa.org

32   ECOMOST (1994): 10–15

33   ECOMOST (1994): 82

34   ECOMOST (1994): 89

35   ECOMOST (1994): 97

within the sector. The issue is about the terms on which this public support is provided to the industry. *Tomorrow's Tourism*, published by the British government in 1999, identified that the domestic industry in the UK 'lacks the ability to think and act strategically' and 'suffers from a lack of market information, or the ability to interpret and respond to it'.[36] National government often funds market research, marketing and training for tourism. These collective benefits are sometimes supported by levies on the industry. Tourism information is often provided by local government and provides services about what's on for residents and visitors alike through websites and offices: increasingly these services are expected to be at least partially funded by commissions on bookings and sales of literature and souvenirs.

Tourism businesses are keen to receive public subsidies for the marketing of the sector, but are generally unwilling to contribute to the costs which arise as a result of the activities of their clients, activities upon which their businesses depend. Local councils fund heritage attractions, public spaces and facilities for coach parking. Public services and facilities as well as tourism sites and attractions cost money to maintain but tourism businesses lobby hard to avoid making any contribution to these costs. Their objection is that they already pay their taxes like any other business. Many of them do, but there are few businesses which place so much reliance on public and 'free' assets. When a tourist buys a trip to London they are not attracted by the hotel, the bus operator or the guide – the experience they are sold is largely London itself, much of which is free, from the British Library and Trafalgar Square to the Science Museum. Other businesses which provide goods and services benefit too – but neither the businesses nor the tourists pay for their use of the public realm. The tourism industry is more reliant than other industries on free access to a wide range of public goods and services and is a significant freeloader when businesses in general are facing rising charges for their use of the commons through landfill and carbon taxes.

However, in some places tourism taxes are levied and tourists pay local taxes. In France tourists pay a flat rate per night local tax, a *taxe de séjour*, of between €0.15 and €1.07 per person.[37] In Hawai'i, Transient Accommodation Tax (TAT) is levied at 8.25%. The Hawai'i Lodging and Accommodation

---

36 DCMS (1999): 9

37 The tax is levied by the Marie and there is considerable variation in the tax by location and category of accommodation; national legislation is permissive. www.francetourism.com/practicalinfo/Whileyourethere.htm accessed 20 July 2010. Germany has reduced VAT on hotels and France has reduced VAT on restaurant meals.

Association calculates that Hawai'i's hotels paid US$244.4 million in taxes in 2008, taxes which were not paid by other industries. TAT is payable in a number of cities and resort destinations in the USA, including New York City, Washington DC, San Francisco, Chicago and Seattle.[38] In the Balearics there was an attempt to introduce a €1 per night tax on international and domestic tourists staying in hotels; it was not paid by those with second homes or staying in rented accommodation.[39] The tax was to be used to pay for efforts to counter sand erosion and other environmental measures, but was withdrawn following campaigns by the source-market operators who argued that it would discourage holidaymakers; in addition, hoteliers resented being expected to collect the tax. There were also issues about the constitutional legality of the tax, which was imposed by the Government of the Autonomous Community of the Balearic Islands. The imposition of the tax in May 2002 was concurrent with a significant decline in arrivals from Germany, which was then in recession. It is difficult to determine the extent of consumer resistance: although opposition from the industry locally and in originating markets was vocal, there is some evidence that residents approved of the 'polluter pays' principle.[40] The tax was withdrawn following a change of government in 2003. The Gambia introduced a Tourism Development Levy in 2003, initially paid by all tourists as they arrived at immigration. There was no opposition from the industry and it has now been absorbed into ticket prices and paid by the charter operators directly to the government. The money has been used to fund street lighting in tourism areas, and other environmental improvements; it is now part of general taxation in the Gambia. In Belize, travellers who stay 24 hours pay a departure tax of US$15 and a levy of US$3.75 which goes to the Protected Areas Conservation Trust. Efforts to tax tourists and tourism to cover some of the costs borne by destinations have had patchy results. Yet the 'polluter pays' principle requires that they take responsibility for cleaning up after themselves.

Taxes and levies are imposed to cover airport development and security, as well as to raise revenue for destination promotion. Resort taxes and 'local option sales taxes'[41] have developed in the USA and the Caribbean to

---

38   Hawai'i Hotel and Lodging Association. 2010 Public Affairs Positions, Honolulu, Hawaii www.hawaiihotels.org

39   Children under 12 were exempt

40   See Bestard and Nadal (2007)]

41   Sometimes abbreviated to LOST, these are taxes levied in the USA at city or state level as a means of raising funds for a particular purpose. The rules under which they are imposed vary significantly from state to state.

enable local government to manage the local area without overburdening small resident populations faced with maintaining large areas used by non-resident tourist and day visitors.[42] On a local or regional level, government has generally been funded by property taxes and local income or sales taxes, and there has been resistance to the imposition of tourism or tourist taxes. In the UK, local government is funded from local rates and grants from central government. Some local authorities suggested to the UK government's Lyons Inquiry that there should be some form of tax on 'tourism pressures'. Lyons argued that it was important 'to weigh the contribution that tourists make to the local economy against the costs they impose and the likely impact on the tourist industry of any taxation proposal'. Lyons concluded that the government should consult about providing a 'permissive power for local authorities to levy taxes on tourism, including a possible tax on accommodation...'.[43] National government did not pursue the idea, but the idea of a tourist tax has now again been raised in the UK, with the aim of ensuring the responsibility for the costs imposed by the industry and tourists are met by the polluters.

Government plays a key role at national and local levels in the promotion and management of tourism, and tourism businesses campaign through their trade associations in competition with other sectors for government's time and favour. Despite their heavy reliance on public authorities to create, manage and maintain the destinations they use, they have been very successful in ensuring that households and other businesses shoulder these tourism generated costs. It may be contentious to point out that in biology hosts have parasites – but it does underline the importance of ensuring that tourists and the host communities enjoy a symbiotic relationship, one where both groups, the visited and the visitors gain, where both enjoy added value.

If tourism continues to grow at the pace it was growing before the 2008 recession, then the costs of managing its externalities will need to be addressed in many destinations around the world as a matter of some urgency. What sense does it make for a destination to attract shopping tourists and to refund consumption taxes[44] as they leave the country? It suits the interests of hoteliers and service providers, but tourism's burdens in the destination, and those which arise from the flights, fall on all of us and our shared environment. Is that responsible or sustainable? Is that in the national interest?

---

42 For further details for Montana see http://mdt.mt.gov/research/toolkit/m1/ftools/fd/rlot.shtml

43 Lyons (2007): 42

44 Sales Tax and Value Added Tax

National government perspectives

Tourism in destinations is generally managed by local government, except in small countries when national government performs the local government functions. National governments provide the legislative and administrative frameworks within which tourism is locally managed, and the work of many national ministries affects tourism – home affairs, transport, education, treasury, health, education and so on. The tourism sector is regulated and sponsored by a wide range of ministries, and businesses in the sector need to maintain relationships across government. As Elliott points out, the 'responsibility for establishing objectives and prioritisation, for policy formulation and implementation lies with government', he lists no less than fourteen offices, ministries and agencies with a responsibility for an aspect of national tourism development. [45] As he demonstrated in his review of tourism, politics and public sector management, there are a number of general principles on which public administration is founded –public interest, public service, effectiveness, efficiency and accountability – all interpreted within national cultures and political frameworks.[46] The national environments within which tourism occurs, and consequently the ways it is managed, are diverse. The 'values, characteristics and behaviour of the political and administrative system' reflect these diverse national environments.[47] The exercise of responsibility is shaped by culture.

The World Economic Forum publishes annual *Travel and Tourism Competitiveness Reports*; its index is composed of three categories of variables: regulatory framework; business environment and infrastructure; and human, cultural, and natural resources. Governments play a key role in more than half of the assessment criteria: policy rules and regulations, environmental sustainability, safety and security, health and hygiene and air, ground, tourism and ICT infrastructure.[48] One of the biggest challenges is to co-ordinate the way that national, regional and local levels exercise their responsibilities, to secure a 'whole-of-government' or 'joined-up' government strategy. Such a strategic approach is rare. Tourism ministries are often weak, with limited professional staff, and where there is a cabinet role, the post is usually

---

45   Elliott (1997): 119

46   Elliott (1997): 7

47   Elliott defines the national environment as being composed of 'geography, climate, history, culture, economics and politics' (1997): 124

48   World Economic Forum (WEF), (2009): xiii www.weforum.org

regarded as junior to be occupied briefly by a politician on the way up, or on the way down. There is rarely a co-ordinated approach and they are unable to exercise responsibility.

National governments' primary interests in tourism are export and foreign-exchange earnings, inward investment and economic growth. Development banks and other international development agencies fund master planning exercises in order to identify opportunities for loans and investments that can be repaid through foreign exchange earnings. Tourism master-planning is designed to identify bankable investment opportunities so that governments and the private sector can borrow to fund infrastructure development, which can then be funded by loans. It is tourism development's ability to attract foreign currency that makes the sector attractive to lenders. National governments also see the potential to use tax revenues and foreign-exchange earnings to pay for capital goods and other imports, as well as for health, education and defence.

In Thailand, tourism developed first as a domestic industry. International tourism arrived with the Rest and Recreation (R&R) programmes of the American military during the Vietnam War in the 1960s and 1970s. Encouraged by the World Bank and the International Monetary Fund, Thailand published in 1976 a National Plan for Tourism Development. The objectives of the plan were optimising growth, tourism planning, economic development and 'to preserve and enhance the social, cultural and historical aspects of Thailand'. In the sixth National Economic and Social Development Plan (1987 to 1991), the objectives were: domestic and international tourism; incentives for private sector investment; public investment to encourage tourism in specific areas; the preservation of the tourism environment; the maintenance of 'a high standard of tourism business and services'; and the 'enforcement of safety measures provided for tourists'.[49] Growth has been rapid and sustained. In 1967 Thailand had 336,000 foreign visitors and 54,000 military personnel on R&R. By 1998 it had 7.76 million international arrivals, and 14.48 million in 2007. Thais made 83.23 million trips in 2007. The Tourism Authority of Thailand calculates that domestic tourism was worth 69.4% of the value of international tourism in 2007 – but, of course, the international tourists paid in foreign exchange.[50] Foreign exchange is particularly valuable because it enables the repayment of debt to international banks, often borrowed to fund

---

49   Elliott (1997): 118–119

50   Tourism statistics provided by TAT, available at www2.tat.or.th/stat/web/static_index.php

airports, roads and hotels for tourism development, and to fund the purchase of capital equipment or arms from abroad.

As early as 1993, there was mounting concern in Thailand about the impact of tourism growth. A government memorandum on tourism was published by the Tourist Authority of Thailand (TAT), and with rare candour reported a 'disturbing litany of adverse impacts'.[51] TAT reported in 1993 that, although tourism was recognised as the economic activity generating the highest foreign-exchange revenues, the absence of management had resulted in the deterioration of destinations and pollution, encroachment on public land, illegally placed building, lack of regard for the environmental impacts of new infrastructure, sex commerce, increasing crime against tourists and provision of public infrastructure services to tourism areas rather than local communities. It also noted the unfair exploitation of tourists, manipulation of traditional culture, a decline in the quality of artefacts sold to tourists and occasional hostility to tourists when locals found tourist behaviour offensive.[52]   There is nothing unusual about this litany other than the government's frankness in publishing it. The same problems are found in many other destinations, although the particularities vary. It can be argued that problems like these occur where there is no effective management of tourism growth, and that such problems are not inevitable.[53] In Part II we shall look at how some of these issues can be addressed, but in each case someone has to take responsibility. If they do not, then, in the absence of management, the negative impacts of tourism will grow to the detriment of local people and their natural and cultural environment – and potentially of the destination itself.

VisitBritain is responsible for marketing tourism internationally and attracting tourists to the UK from abroad. It has a sustainability strategy that 'covers four main elements: greening VisitBritain's own operations; marketing to promote sustainable consumer activity; supporting government's sustainable development plans; and supporting businesses to help them grow sustainably'.[54] Each of the four home nations has its own national marketing organisation. In England, tourism is the responsibility of the Department of Culture, Media and Sport (DCMS), though, as in other countries, governance is complex and a large number of government departments have responsibilities which directly affect inbound and domestic tourism in the UK. In its

---

51   Bosselman, Peterson and McCarthy (1999): 8

52   Bosselman, Peterson and McCarthy (1999): 8–9

53   See, for example, Bosselman, Peterson and McCarthy (1999): 9

54   http: //www.visitbritain.org/aboutus/policy/sustainability/index.aspx accessed 5 July 2010

1999 strategy, DCMS placed emphasis on sustainability and adopted a 'wise growth strategy for tourism … which integrates the economic, social and environmental impacts of tourism and which spreads the benefits throughout society as widely as possible'.[55]

VisitEngland was established in 2009 as 'the strategic leadership body representing the public- and private-sector stakeholders of English Tourism.' It is the 'custodian of the England tourism strategy'. It defines its role as creating a national tourism strategy, optimising marketing investment and developing the customer experience. It does this by improving the perception of England, communicating the wide range of experiences and activities there available, promoting key brand characteristics and working with tourism businesses to drive excellence in the quality of England's tourism experience.[56] VisitEngland published a strategic action plan for English tourism in March 2010, one year after it was established. England's visitor economy is estimated to be worth £97bn, but the industry is operating below capacity. The VisitEngland strategy is intended to deliver 5% annual growth in the visitor economy, and to 'increase England's share of global visitor markets'.[57] The 5% equals 3% real growth in terms of visitor spend plus 2% inflation – calculated using an average prediction over 10 years.[58] VisitEngland does refer to the importance of underpinning the growth strategy with a sustainable approach:[59] growing the visitor economy and ensuring that the experiences remain appealing is recognised as a challenge faced by the industry.[60] There are references in the action plan to destination management, and taking into account both visitors' and residents' needs; and in 2011 VisitEngland is developing both Destination Management and Wise Growth action plans.[61]

Despite being the tourism authority for England, VisitEngland's responsibilities are primarily marketing and it is primarily trying to grow the industry. There is value in this approach. UK visitor numbers have been falling and Britain has a substantial balance of payment deficit on tourism estimated for

---

55 DCMS (1999): 48

56 www.enjoyengland.com/corporate/corporate-information/index.aspx

57 Visit England (2010a): 15

58 This was explained in the accompanying briefing note.

59 There is less emphasis on sustainable development in the Coalition's government's Tourism Policy – there is only one explicit reference: 'Creating a presumption in favour of any application which satisfies the criteria of being a genuinely sustainable development' DCMS (2011): 39

60 Visit England (2010a): 18

61 Visit England (2010a): 13

2008/9 at £20 billion.[62] In 2008, the UK population spent only 36% of its total tourism spend at home. Tourism is the UK's fifth biggest industry, employing an estimated 1.5 million people – an industry, moreover, which should be ripe for government investment since it cannot be offshored, and has potential for expansion. The current coalition government's target is that 50% of UK tourism spend would be in the UK, resulting in a major improvement in the balance of payments.[63] It plans to '… create a new fund, with the goal of generating £1 billion worth of PR and marketing activity in [the UK's] 20 priority markets in the years around 2012'.[64] The target is imprecise and the sources of funding even more so: it seems likely that much of it will be funding in-kind. In 2010 the government has a relatively narrow focus on growth in domestic and inbound tourism spend in order to address the balance of payments deficit, to create jobs and use surplus capacity. Responsibility for ensuring its triple-bottom-line sustainability is neither clearly articulated nor allocated to any government agency for implementation.

By contrast, South Africa was the first country explicitly to commit to Responsible Tourism in its national policies. When the African National Congress took power in South Africa in 1994, it had not developed a tourism strategy. Under apartheid the industry had been very limited, due to anti-apartheid boycotts and the security situation. It was out of the democratisation of South Africa and the need to harness tourism for economic and social development in the new South Africa that the concept of Responsible Tourism was first used in a national government policy. The 1996 White Paper was conventionally titled: *The Development and Promotion of Tourism in South Africa*.[65] However, the ANC's policy on tourism was radical in both the South African and international context. Responsible Tourism was in the graphics on the cover of the White Paper and used throughout. Responsible Tourism was defined in the White Paper as:

> tourism that promotes responsibility to the environment through its
> sustainable use; responsibility to involve local communities in the
> tourism industry; responsibility for the safety and security of visitors

---

62   House of Commons, Hansard, 12 June 2009, Column 1027W

63   This is neither a new problem nor a new approach. Winston Churchill sponsored the Come to Britain Movement in 1926 when he was Secretary of the Department of Overseas Trade, and in 1929 the government sponsored the creation of the Travel Association of Great Britain in efforts to improve the balance of payments. Elliott (1997): 25–26

64   Keynote speech by Rt Hon Jeremy Hunt MP Secretary of State for Culture, Olympics, Media and Sport

65   Department of Environmental Affairs and Tourism DEAT (1996)

and responsible government, employees, employers, unions and local communities.[66]

Tourism was identified as a missed opportunity. There had been 'limited integration of local communities and neglected groups into tourism',[67] which presented a significant opportunity for South Africa to create employment, draw on a multiplicity of skills create entrepreneurial opportunities, bring development to rural areas and generate foreign-exchange earnings. Tourism was seen as a way of establishing a taste, and therefore an export market, for South African products such as wine. The paper also stated, 'all the final touches (value) have to be added in South Africa... the value added in final stages of production is created in South Africa'.[68] This was the 'final good': one of the advantages of tourism is the opportunity to capture the final retail value to the product in the country.

The new government recognised the breadth of opportunities which tourism could offer the country and in particular the informal sector:

> The tourism industry accommodates a thriving and dynamic informal sector - from craft and fruit vendors to beach vendors, chair rentals, and others. ... there are many business opportunities to involve previously neglected groups in the tourism business: entertainment, laundry and transportation services, craft rental; arts, craft and curios sales; tour guides and walking tours of places of interest; teaching of African languages and customs to interested visitors; restaurants emphasising local cuisine; guest houses; beach manicures and pedicures; and much more.[69]

It also proposed:

> **Responsible Tourism** as the key guiding principle for tourism development. Responsible tourism implies a proactive approach by tourism industry partners to develop, market and manage the tourism industry in a responsible manner, so as to create a competitive advantage. Responsible tourism implies tourism industry responsibility to the **environment** through the promotion of balanced and sustainable tourism and focus on the development of environmentally based tourism activities (e.g. game-viewing and diving). Responsible tourism means responsibility of government and business to involve the local communities that are in close

---

66   DEAT (1996): vi

67   DEAT (1996): 4, 5

68   DEAT (1996): 14–18, 17

69   DEAT (1996): 16

proximity to the tourism plant and attractions through the development of meaningful economic linkages (e.g. the supply of agricultural produce to the lodges, out-sourcing of laundry, etc.). It implies the responsibility to **respect, invest in and develop local cultures** and protect them from over-commercialisation and over-exploitation. It also implies the responsibility of **local communities** to become actively involved in the tourism industry, to practice sustainable development and to ensure the safety and security of the visitors. Responsibility to visitors through ensuring their safety, security and health is another consequence of responsible tourism. Responsible tourism also implies the responsibility of both **employers** and **employees** in the tourism industry both to each other as well as to the customer. Responsible **trade union** practices and responsible employment practices will be the hallmarks of the new tourism in South Africa. Responsible tourism also implies responsible government as well as responsibility on the part of the tourists themselves to observe the norms and practices of South Africa, particularly with respect to the environment and culture of the country.[70]

As can be seen, the South African government took a broad and proactive view of the importance of tourism to the development of the country and its people. The vision was to develop the tourism sector as 'a national priority in a sustainable and acceptable manner, so that it will contribute significantly to the improvement of the quality of life of every South African'. Empowerment of 'previously neglected communities ... and the empowerment of women in such communities' were guiding principles.[71] Clearly, the ambition was that tourism should be an important sector for delivering sustainable development in South Africa. The paper committed the Department of Environmental Affairs and Tourism (DEAT) to a triple-bottom-line approach. The white paper also defined the consequences of failing to adopt a responsible approach, pointing out the effects of irresponsible tourism.[72] DEAT's 1996 vision was to develop

---

70   DEAT (1996): 19, emphasis in the original

71   DEAT (1996): 23

72   DEAT (1996): §3.5: 22 'If a responsible approach to tourism is not adopted and the industry is not adequately planned a number of negative impacts can occur. These include environmental degradation; skewing of job creation to prostitution and vice industries; seasonality and unemployment during the off-season; the use of seasonal and contract labour at the expense of permanent employment; leakage of foreign exchange earnings; increased urban/rural polarisation; concentration of wealth in the hands of owners of tourism plant at the expense of population as a whole; and exploitation of local cultures and community groups.'

the tourism sector to make a major contribution to the reconstruction and development efforts of the government.[73] The purpose of tourism was clear: economic development to benefit all South Africans.

DEAT produced Guidelines for Responsible Tourism in 2002, comprising 'three inter-related sets of guiding principles, objectives and indicators' and organised around the triple bottom line of social, economic and environmental responsibility. The guidelines provided a 'menu of opportunities'[74] designed to encourage the private sector to select initiatives which made social and business sense for them. The guidelines were indicative, providing ideas that could be adopted and implemented. There was no monitoring or reporting, but in 2003 the Minister designated them as the national sector guidelines to be applied in local government's Integrated Development Programmes. DEAT had a national responsibility for tourism policy until 2009, when tourism became a separate department, identifying its mission as: 'Collectively and boldly promoting responsible and sustainable tourism for the benefit of all South Africans.'[75]

DEAT was able to offer national policy direction and guidelines, but other spheres of government had more effective administrative powers for the responsible management of tourism. National government in South Africa is one of three autonomous (not hierarchical) spheres of government: national, provincial and local. They are inter-related and interdependent but distinct, operating according to the constitution and laws and policies made by national Parliament. South Africa's 1996 constitution makes clear that all three spheres have responsibility for tourism. The national department funds South African Tourism the national agency responsible for marketing South Africa. It aims to make tourism 'the leading economic sector in South Africa, and to promote sustainable economic and social empowerment of all South Africans'.[76] It shares the same national objectives as DEAT but it operates under an independent board. Other departments also contribute to the tourism sector. The national strategy for Broad-based Black Economic Empowerment (BBBEE) is designed to contribute to economic transformation, increase the number of black people that manage, own and control the country's economy and decrease income inequalities. BBBEE in the tourism sector is the responsibility of the

73   DEAT (1996): 23

74   DEAT (2001): 7

75   Department of Tourism (2010): 5

76   www.southafrica.net/sat/content/en/za/media-who-we-are accessed 7 July 2010

Tourism Empowerment Council of South Africa,[77] while overall national government responsibility rests with the Department of Trade and Industry. The national commitment to BBBEE has ensured that in South Africa there has been considerably more emphasis on the progressive economic and social agendas, and this has strengthened these two pillars in South Africa's approach to sustainable development through tourism. The particular history and diverse cultures of South Africa have shaped its structure of government and perspectives on sustainable development. In 2002 the provincial tourism organisation for the Western Cape hosted the first International Conference on Responsible Tourism in Destinations, which agreed the Cape Town Declaration. It was at Cape Town that South Africa embraced the Responsible Tourism ideal.

Local governance

Tourism takes place in destinations which are managed by local government on behalf of the communities which live there. Local authorities are composed of councillors elected by local communities to represent them and by administrative officials held accountable by those elected representatives. These officials have an opportunity to pursue objectives over a prolonged period of time, as long as they can carry the community and successive councillors with them. Policies which make a city more attractive to live in for residents will also benefit tourists. Streetscaping and the creation of green corridors in Delhi improve the city for residents, but also make it more attractive for tourists. In the UK park-and-ride schemes are generally introduced to ease city-centre congestion and to improve places for locals and commuters, but they also create a more enjoyable visitor experience for tourists, particularly where signposted walking trails are also created to manage visitor flow.

It is in a destination that the tourists, day-visitors and local people and businesses interact and that tourism is managed. With a shared focus on a place, with councillors and officers living locally and sharing the experience of the community, and with elected representatives and administrators working together for a prolonged period of time, there is a much greater chance that joined-up government[78] can deliver effective management of. In other circumstances, this does not naturally occur. As Kavanagh and Richards have

---

77   www.tourismbeecharter.co.za
78   As in §2.2 'Introducing a joined up approach' DCMS (1999): 13

argued, issues which are not the responsibility of one department alone are difficult to address. In national and local government around the world, when departments compete for resources and preferment, co-operation is not their natural reflex.

Councillors and officers operate within a legal, administrative and political framework contained in the constitution, national legislation and central government decisions about funding. The degree of local autonomy varies considerably from one destination to another and councillors can be held accountable at local elections. The Transition Towns movement in the UK, composed of groups preparing for a future with less oil and a changing climate, has been reluctant to address tourism[79] and has tended rather to see itself as an alternative to local government. From a Responsible Tourism perspective it is important to engage with those institutions and individuals who manage the places, exercise planning control, shape the place and pick up the litter. They have the opportunity to exercise responsibility.

One of the ways of exercising responsibility is to ensure that the growth of dwellings and tourism businesses are matched to the growth in the public infrastructure to service them. In Florida and Washington, new development is 'supposed to take place at the same time as the public facilities necessary to serve it are built'. This planned correlation ensures that tourism development does not proceed at a pace that results in degradation, and is called concurrency.[80] Land-use planning and development controls are important instruments available to local authorities for the management of tourism. For example, in Hawai'i there are opportunities to increase occupancy in the shoulder seasons, a challenge which has been addressed by destination marketing strategies. Bed occupancy rates have been increasing along with room rates and, in 2006, there were no plans for any accommodation of significant size to be developed for the following decade, thanks to zoning and planning constraints.[81] The restrictions on bed numbers resulting from these planning controls help avoid the problems of oversupply and maintain average bed occupancies. In Hawai'i the state government's vision for tourism commits first to 'honor the people and heritage of Hawai'i Island and second to 'support and enhance the quality of life for residents'.[82] It is arguable that these

---

79   Waddilove and Goodwin (2010) See also www.transitionnetwork.org
80   Bosselman, Peterson and McCarthy (1999): 44
81   Hawai'i Island Tourism Strategic Plan for 2006–15, Hawai'I (nd): 17
82   Hawai'I Island Tourism Strategic Plan for 2006–15, Hawai'i (nd): 4, www.hawaii-county.com/rd/HawaiiIslandTSP.pdf

controls do just that. In the Hawai'i Island Tourism Strategic Plan for 2006–15 'finding a sustainable balance' is identified as the critical issue facing tourism'. Paramount is the state's need to ensure Hawai'i remains 'a good place to live'. The plan asks 'how many residents and visitors can the state and each island support with infrastructure levels, natural resource constraints and resident tolerance'?[83]

Effective local management requires detailed, trustworthy evidence to inform decision-making. Whistler, the mountain resort north of Vancouver, has been attracting tourists for around a hundred years. In 1976 it adopted the first Official Community Plan and in 1994 there was a significant expansion in community participation. New developments would only be permitted if three conditions were met: if the development provided substantial benefits to the community and the resort; was supported by the community; would not have unacceptable impacts on the community, resort or environment. Whistler has a comprehensive monitoring plan which enables it to measure the way the community and its natural and social environment is changing, and includes an extensive resident survey, enabling the community to monitor its changing attitudes.[84] The Official Community Law Plan byelaw was passed in 1993 and consolidated in 2009 because of concern about the implications of the resort's growing from 30,000 bed units to 52,600.[85] The tracking information and progress against the targets is made public and is available on the Whistler website.[86]

Local development is clearly a political process. The Official Community Plan and its provisions for monitoring ensure there is appropriate information to inform decision-making, but the determination of what constitutes substantial community benefits and unacceptable impacts remain political decisions made by the community and its elected representatives: they determine the limits of acceptable change. On Kangaroo Island in South Australia, home to 4000 people and some of Australia's most accessible and photogenic wildlife, the local authority has consistently collected data on visitors, and resident perceptions of tourism, since 1996 to enable informed local decision-making. The authority's Tourism Optimisation Management Model (TOMM)[87] enables

---

83 Ibid. p. 7

84 Bosselman, Peterson and McCarthy (1999): 13

85 Official Community Law Plan Bylaw No.1021, 1993: 7

86 http://www.whistler2020.ca/whistler/site/explorer.acds

87 The TOMM management committee is composed of representatives from the Department for Environment and Heritage, South Australian Tourism Commission, Tourism Kangaroo Island, Kangaroo Island Development Board, Kangaroo Island Council, Kangaroo Island Natural

them to monitor the long-term health of the tourism industry and of Kangaroo Island: management is in the responsibility of national and local government and of the industry.

Anthony Climpson is employment and tourism manager at the UK's New Forest District Council (NFDC); in 1994, he was the tourism and publicity officer. The change in Climpson's role at NDFC is evidence of the importance of the work that he has done in developing an integrated approach to tourism development in local government. The tourism policy document, *Living with the Enemy*,[88] published in 1994, was provocatively titled, but it reflected the public mood of hostility to tourists and day-trippers. The NFDC argued that, far from being the enemy, tourists needed to become allies: 'if we are going to make tourism work for everyone's advantage, we need their help'.[89] The New Forest is largely common land, and controlling access has always has been an issue. In the 1960s, primitive roadside ditches and ramparts were not preventing motor vehicles degrading the forest habitat and, by the 1990s, there was an identified need for a more integrated approach. The district recognised its responsibility to balance the interests of visitors, the tourism industry, the community and the environment in what later became known as the VICE Model.[90] The VICE Model recognises the importance of visitor satisfaction and of a sufficiently profitable to enable reinvestment; yet it also values community acceptance and the protection of the environment. The VICE Model has been widely reused. It has the merit of adding to the triple bottom line a clear recognition of the importance of the visitor and their willingness to recommend the place. It understood that tourism needed to be managed in a way that respected the interests of the host and holidaymaker and that they should be on equal terms.[91] The challenge was – and remains – to find ways of managing the complexity of tourism, to manage the threats and to recognise 'that what is good for tourism can also be good for the quality of local life and vice-versa'.[92] In the New Forest, a partnership approach was adopted, managed by the local authority, which ensured that the interests and concerns of all the stakeholders were addressed. This engaged the public and private sector agencies and businesses in sustainable tourism management.[93] Tourism

Resource Management Board, the community and the tourism industry. www.tomm.info

88 New Forest District Council (1994)

89 New Forest District Council (1994): 2

90 Climpson (2005) see also www.thegreenforest.org

91 New Forest District Council (1994): 4

92 New Forest District Council (1994): 11 www.thegreenforest.org

93 Countryside Agency (2001)

is now seen as core business for the district, which now speaks of 'Our Future Together'.[94]

Local authorities in Cape Town have done as much as the national government to engage stakeholders and promote the Responsible Tourism strategy in their corner of South Africa. A 2009 survey of the attitudes of tourism businesses towards Responsible Tourism found that, despite generally positive attitudes, perceived costs, the highly competitive environment and a perceived lack of government support were preventing many from acting.[95] After consultation, led by the Tourism Department, the city of Cape Town decided to focus their efforts on the things which mattered to the local people and their environment. They did not leave it to the industry to choose the local priorities, although, as in the New Forest, the industry played a full role in the discussions. The agreement between the public and private sector stakeholders in Cape Town recognised that to achieve change at destination level there had to be focus, and that they needed to address the local social, economic and environmental priorities. Environmentally, water and energy efficiency were important, because of climate change, as well as a reduction in waste, and particularly in the numbers of plastic bottles. The economic priorities were local procurement and enterprise development in order to improve local livelihoods, while the social priorities were skills development, contributions to local job creation, training, health, conservation and community initiatives. Businesses and government departments in Cape Town have committed to these shared priorities, and to measuring their performance against a common set of indicators. Cape Town has based its local strategy on the national policy and the DEAT Guidelines[96] and is taking a multi-departmental approach involving planning, environmental managers, transport among others.

However important local government is to a place, tourism destinations do not always fit neatly into the political boundaries. Local authority boundaries rarely make sense either to tourists or to the management of destination and are often inappropriate for marketing. When diverse places are likely to be attractive to very different markets and are combined in one authority, each place's individual character can be undermined.

---

94 New Forest District Council published its tourism policy, *Our Future Together* in 1997 subsequently revised as *Our Future Together II* in 2009

95 See Frey and George (2010).

96 DEAT (2001).

Responsible destination marketing

Destination marketing organisations need to think hard about their triple-bottom-line impacts: the environmental impacts of paper and ink; about the social consequences of the images they present in words and pictures of the destinations they promote; the possibility of focusing on increasing earnings (yield) from tourism in the local economy and on the dispersal of visitors to benefit poorer and less visited areas. Marketing organisations should not be trusted to establish priorities – rather, these should reflect the priorities of the publicly accountable local authority. Their political masters need to hold them responsible for the expenditure of public money, and to ask whether the national and local interest is being well served by such marketing activity. There is a case for using marketing to spread the benefits to areas which need tourism to create employment and local economic development, rather than to increase tourism pressure in already-successful destinations. Match-funding for marketing campaigns too often benefits those businesses and places which are already successful. At the local level, the emphasis on growth can be problematic. Marketers are prone to dismiss 'lifestyle businesses' – those which are run by people who are motivated by the desire to live a satisfying life in particular place, rather than to maximise their earnings – for their lack of interest in marketing and growth: they may have neither motivation nor opportunity[97] to grow their enterprise, or to extend their season; they have achieved sustainability and see no need to grow. They are booked from year to year, with high repeat-visit and referral rates; a more enlightened marketer, less driven by numbers, might admire the control they have achieved over the sustainability of their business. Indeed, isn't a distinctive 'lifestyle' one of the major factors that draws us to destinations?

VisitEngland's *Enjoy Every Minute* campaign, launched in 2008, is unusual in that it recognises that locals can be 'tourists' in their own place. By this definition, tourism is being defined as the experience, the form of consumption, and not by the stay away from home. In UK employment law, workers have a minimum 20 days of vacation, 104 weekend days, 233 evenings and many spare hours, including lunch hours. Enjoy England's website and brochures encourage us to make the most of our lunch hour, marketing 60 minute experiences that will 'leave a warm feeling in the memory'. They recommend Nick Drake's grave, the Theatre of Small Convenience, the SnowDome, a lecture at the Royal Society, a swim in Pell's Pool and a visit to a Monkey

---

97 Constrained by planning regulations and capital.

Forest.[98] The campaign is noteworthy because it breaks down the distinction between tourists and locals – it offers memorable experiences in England for local residents, commuters, day-visitors, domestic and international tourists – all of whom are likely to use the same facilities and attractions.

The *Enjoy Every Minute* campaign runs counter to the prevailing marketing thinking that success is about attracting more and more tourists: tourism marketing campaigns are generally judged by the number of arrivals, so that is what marketers do (only rarely do they calculate yield or length of stay). It demonstrates that tourism marketing can help spread the benefits of tourism, and encourage locals to enjoy the tourism experience in their own place. Marketing and promotion are generally used to attract more tourists from existing markets to popular destinations, but they could (and perhaps should) be used to attract tourists to more marginal areas, spreading the benefits. Marketing can also be used to make tourism more responsible and to attract more appropriate tourists to the destination in order to meet Responsible Tourism objectives. This may extend to 'demarketing'[99] particular attractions that are in danger of being overwhelmed by visitors. For example, Clements argued that demarketing could be used to attract less rowdy and more appropriate tourists to Cyprus.[100] Marketers talk about 'attract and disperse' strategies – for example using London to encourage people to visit the provinces and spread the benefits. However, as regional tourist boards know, international holidaymakers have decided their travel plans long before they arrive, and have often pre-booked flights, accommodation and hire cars. They recognise that they need to do their own international marketing: more travellers need to have decided to include their region in their plans, because it is mostly too late after they arrive.

The first section of the Gambia's Responsible Tourism Policy[101] addresses the marketing of the Gambia. It recognises the need to differentiate the Gambia from other 'sun, sand and sea' destinations while 'attracting market segments

---

98 www.enjoyengland.com/ideas/enjoy-every-minute/sixty-minutes-ideas-one.aspx accessed 15 June 2010

99 Discouraging demand by ceasing to advertise or promote, spreading the message through PR that the attraction of place is over-visited and redesigning the product by bringing in timed-tickets or making access more difficult. This approach tends to be unpopular with tourism service providers who may prefer to increase prices.

100 Clements (1989). On demarketing see also Beeton (2003), (2006), Beeton and Benfield (2002); 11 methods for demarketing attraction identified by Benfield are listed.

101 Responsible Tourism Partnership, 2005. Available at www.artyforum.info/documents/gambia.pdf

which value the natural and cultural heritage assets' of the country. Yet the Gambia struggles with limited budgets to overcome the organic image.[102] Tourism marketing can adjust this with an induced image, but it is expensive and requires coordinated marketing activity over a number of years. Marketing plays a key role in determining who is attracted and what they know about the destination before they arrive. It could enable the Gambia to reduce its reliance on price competition in a crowded market place. It is through the national marketing effort and influencing what the brochure and travel writers say about a destination that a country can attract the kinds of tourists they wish to receive and host.

New Zealand has arguably done more than any other country to use its national marketing strategy to attract those tourists most likely to enjoy and benefit from its unique features. In 1998 the country's government started looking at what set it apart from other destinations, and began to identify the competitive advantage which could induce tourists to travel such long distances. The main draws for people to visit New Zealand were the geologically new landscapes, the unique culture and warm friendly people. The campaign focussed on the people in the landscape, visitors and locals alike, and had as core values in the strategy *kaitiakitanga*, meaning guardianship, care and protection of the environment, and *manaakitanga*, which expresses the responsibilities of hosts to welcome visitors and make them feel at home.

The 100% Pure New Zealand strapline was not an environmental claim: it was an experiential one. Tourism New Zealand (TNZ) backed the brand with a Quality Mark, and only subsequently added an environmental component.[103] It worked with the industry to ensure that high levels of visitor satisfaction are achieved; TNZ has grown the brand, recognising the importance of a sustained approach. In 2007 they launched *The Youngest Country*, a promotional film about the youngest country on earth,[104] that drew the viewer into the experience: 'close-ups of travellers' faces that illuminated the pleasures of kayaking, dining, walking, or drawing in the sand.' There was also a 'What's On' campaign to attract Australians across the ditch.[105] In the year to June

---

102 Gunn (1988) distinguished between the organic image, the product of non-commercial sources (newspapers, books, education, the media and the opinions of families and friends) and the induced image, that created by tourism marketing by tourism businesses and public bodies. Altering the organic image is expensive but creates durable change.

103 In 2010 Tourism New Zealand is planning to delink the two programmes following pressure from the trade.

104 See www.newzealand.com/travel/about-nz/history/history-immigration.cfm

105 Tourism New Zealand (2009): 50

2009, 9/10 visitors said that they were highly satisfied with their experience of New Zealand, and 97% said that they would recommend New Zealand to others.[106] The vision of the 2015 New Zealand Tourism Strategy, the result of collaboration between the national government and the trade association, is that tourism should be valued as the leading contributor to a sustainable New Zealand economy. It defines sustainable tourism as tourism 'that delivers maximum value economic, social, cultural and environmental, with as few unwanted effects as possible'.[107]

New Zealand's approach is simple and elegant: work out what the destination has to offer and the kinds of visitors who will enjoy the experience, and then market to them. High satisfaction and referral rates will follow. The evidence used for decision-making in New Zealand is strong, and the yield research undertaken for the new tourism strategy detailed. It identified private-sector and government yield, and quantified social and environmental impacts, as well as yield by tourist type – with coach tourists and independent travellers contributing the most added value, and campers imposing the highest national public-sector cost (though they contributed most to regional dispersal). In New Zealand the complexity is not hidden. The yield research showed that most residents still wanted to see more tourists in their home towns. However, the cost of carbon externalities, which was estimated, excluded international air transport.[108] The demand for Maori experiences continues to grow but there are still issues to be addressed around social inclusion in the industry, and there is the challenge of air travel and climate change.

Government, then, sets the administrative and legal framework within which destinations strike a balance between the interests of the current generation and the next. It also balances the competing interests of local communities, tourists and day visitors; and the originating market operators and the national and local tourism businesses. It manages the cultural and natural heritage assets, and defines where sustainability responsibilities. This is a political process, and, though tourism is an economic activity, they are in

---

106 http://www.tourismnewzealand.com/markets-and-stats/other-research/visitor-experience-monitor/overall-experience accessed 7 July 2010

107 Ministry of Tourism, Tourism Industry Association of New Zealand and Tourism New Zealand (2007): 5, 14

108 Ministry of Tourism, Tourism Industry Association of New Zealand , Tourism New Zealand, and Lincoln University (2007): 22 available on line at www.tourismresearch.govt.nz/Data--Analysis/Research-projects-reports-and-studies/Research-Reports/Yield-research/

close contact: all markets must be regulated. Governments enforces contracts, regulate behaviour, provide a legal framework for the market and provides the infrastructure necessary for the activity to occur – roads, airports, waste disposal. Governments impose (or should impose) the 'polluter pays' principle, and correct for market failure.

The corollary of this regulation is support. Tourism businesses look to government to support them and to provide the necessary infrastructure and security. Tourism businesses compete with other businesses and other stakeholders for the support of government, even managing to get government to fund the sector's marketing, at the same time as the trade associations lobby for a reduction in the tax and regulatory burden.

Sustainable tourism is an 'overtly political subject': it is about the distribution of resources.[109] Government intervention is required to facilitate tourism for the businesses which profit from it and to ensure the sustainability of destinations. Government regulations favour some and disadvantage others: there are winners and losers. Businesses and locals press for regulations to benefit themselves, or their interpretation of the public interest. In balancing the interests of competing stakeholders government makes political decisions: 'sustainable tourism is about who has the power – host communities, governments, the industry, and tourists – and how they use the power'.[110] And different constituencies of stakeholders have different access to skills and resources: some community voices are able, through relationships and connections, to make their voice is heard in private as well as in 'public conversations'.[111] Politics is about who gets what, when and how. Politics applies as much to tourism as it does to any other human activity, and inequalities of power often favour tourism.[112] The responsibility for strategy and future-proofing resides with communities, and the governments which they elect to look after the interests of their community

As we shall see in Part II, Responsible Tourism issues vary from destination to destination. Tourism needs to be managed in the destination to provide economic, social and environmental benefits and to minimise negative impacts, to ensure that the benefits are shared and the costs are borne in ways which are regarded locally as equitable, and to ensure that tourism contributes to

---

109 Swarbooke (1999): 41

110 Swarbooke (1999): 41

111 Bosselman, Peterson and McCarthy (1999): 30

112 Lasswell (1951)

making the destination a better place to live in. In a world of finite resources and increasing pressure from tourism growth, destinations need to consider how resilient[113] they are across the triple bottom line of sustainability. It is to these challenges that we now turn.

---

113 Bosselman, Peterson and McCarthy (1999) have addressed resiliency in their case studies (p. 19)

References

ABTA (2010) *Travel Matters: The ABTA Manifesto, London: ABTA.*

Bestard, A.B. and Nadal, J.R. (2007) 'Modelling environmental attitudes toward tourism', *Tourism Management,* **28** (3), 688–695.

Bosselman, F.M., Peterson, C.A. and McCarthy, C. (1999) *Managing Tourism Growth,* Washington, DC: Island Press.

Bramwell, B. (2004) *Coastal Mass Tourism: Diversification and Sustainable Development in Southern Europe,* Clevedon, Somerset: Channel View Publications.

British Museum (2009) *Annual Report 2008–9,* London: British Museum.

Butler, R.W. (ed.) (2006a) *The Tourism Area Life Cycle, Vol. I: Applications and Modifications,* Clevedon, Somerset: Channel View Publications.

Butler, R.W. (2006b) 'The origins of the tourism area life cycle', in R.W. Butler (ed.), *The Tourism Area Life Cucle, Vol. I: Applications and Modifications,* Clevedon, Somerset: Channel View Publications, pp. 13–26.

Clements, M.A. (1989) 'Selecting tourist traffic by demarketing', *Tourism Management,* **10** (2), 89–94.

Climpson, A. (2005) *Sustainable Tourism and the New Forest: A Simple Plan,* New Forest District Council and Local Government Association.

DCMS (Department of Culture, Media and Sport) (1999) *Tomorrow's Tourism,* London: DCMS.

DEAT (Department of Environmental Affairs and Tourism) (1996) *The Development and Promotion of Tourism in South Africa,* Pretoria: DEAT.

DEAT (Department of Environmental Affairs and Tourism) (2001) *Guidelines for Responsible Tourism,* Pretoria: DEAT.

Eade, J. (2002) 'Adventure tourists and locals in a global city, resisting tourism performances in London's "East End"', in S. Coleman and M. Crang (eds), *Tourism between Place and* Performance, Oxford: Berghan, pp. 129–139.

ECOMOST (European Community Models of Sustainable Tourism) (1994) *Planning for Sustainable Tourism,* Lewes: ECOMOST Project IFTO.

Ellitot, J. (1997) *Tourism Politics and Public Sector Management,* London and New York: Routledge.

Frey, N. and George, R. (2010) 'Responsible tourism management: the missing link between business owners' attitudes and behaviour in the Cape Town tourism industry', *Tourism Management*, **31** (5), 621–628.

Gunn, C. (1988) *Vacationscapes: Designing Tourism Regions*, New York: Van Nostrand Reinhold.

Hewison, T. (1987) *The Heritage Industry: Britain in a Climate of Decline*, London: Methuen.

Krippendorf, J. (1982) 'Towards new tourism policies', *Tourism Management*, **3** (3), 135-148

Krippendorf, J. (1987) *The Holiday Makers*, Oxford: Butterworth Heinemann.

Lasswell, H.D. (1951) *Psychopathology and Politics: Who Gets What, When, How*, New York: Free Press.

Lowenthal, D.(1998) *The Heritage Crusade and the Spoils of History*, Cambridge: Cambridge University Press.

Lyons, M. (2007) *Lyons Inquiry into Local Government: Final Report*, London: Stationery Office.

New Forest District Council (1994) *Living with the Enemy?*, New Forest District Council.

New Forest District Council (1997) *Our Future Together*, New Forest District Council.

New Zealand (2007) *New Zealand Tourism Strategy 2015*, Wellington: Ministry of Tourism.

Ringer, G. (ed.) (1998) *Destinations: Cultural Landscapes of Tourism*, London and New York: Routledge.

Schneekloth, L.H. and Shibley, R.G. (1995) *Placemaking: The Art and Practice of Building Communities*, Chichester: Wiley.

Squire, S.J. (1998) 'Rewriting languages of geography and tourism', in G. Ringer (ed.), *Destinations: Cultural Landscapes of Tourism*, London and New York: Routledge, pp. 80–100.

Tourism New Zealand (2009) *100% New Zealand 10 Years Young*, Wellington: Tourism New Zealand.

Urry, J. (1995) *Consuming Places*, London: Wiley.

Visit England (2010a) *England: A Strategic Framework for Tourism 2010–2020*, London: Visit England.

Visit England (2010b) *Keep it Real, Visit England*, London: Visit England.

Waddilove, A. and Goodwin, H. (2010) 'Tourism in transition? Incorporating tourism into the transition model', ICRT Occasional Paper 18, ICRT, Leeds.

WEF (World Environment Forum) (2009) *The Travel & Tourism Competitiveness Report 2009*, Geneva: WEF.

Wright, P. (1985) *On Living in an Old Country: The National Past in Contemporary Britain*, London: Verso.

Part II
Responsible Tourism in Practice

Tourism has positive and negative impacts. With scant attention 'on the ground' often accorded to the negative impacts, and a great deal of emphasis on the positive benefit, too little thought is given to the net benefit, and who captures it. Tourism cannot be isolated from other economic sectors and the tourism sector is only part of the economic and social activity occurring in a particular local environment. It is a central tenet of Responsible Tourism that sustainability is a local challenge: it is a challenge nearly everywhere but the solutions are local. Responsible Tourism is about engaging with the particular issues that arise in particular places as a consequence of tourism. If sustainability is about balancing the needs of environment, communities, visitors and the tourism sector, the optimal balance will be determined in destinations by the people who live there. That said, it is important to learn from experience elsewhere.

The second part of this book follows a traditional triple-bottom-line approach. Although in the last two years greater emphasis has been placed on the green aspect the sustainable tourism agenda, the Responsible Tourism agenda remains relentlessly three-pronged, recognising that the 1992 Rio settlement with its focus on environment and development is critical to achieving sustainability. The objective is sustainable development: developed countries and their populations cannot expect others to continue to live in poverty so that we can enjoy our existing and rising standard of living. Evangelical environmentalists, of all faiths and of none, rely on converting people to an eco-centric value system, one which is nature-centred rather than human-centred (or anthropocentric). This radical approach requires a shift in values and ethics on a broad scale, one which would accept, *as a basis for action*, that humans possess no greater intrinsic value than non-human nature. Our species is a very long way from accepting that ontological principle. It is just conceivable that the ethical basis upon which we live our lives may change and that developed country populations will accept a dramatic change in their material standard of living – but it does not appear likely. So we must do our utmost to preserve our standard of living while helping others achieve a similar one – hence the attraction of the Rio solution: sustainable development.

The social, economic and environmental impacts of tourism are experienced in destinations. The major exception to this generalisation is the impact of the journey between home and destination and, in particular, the greenhouse gases emitted through the burning of fossil fuels. Having looked at the case for Responsible Tourism, the development of Responsible Tourism in an originating market, the business case for taking responsibility, and Responsible Tourism management in destinations, we turn now to look at some of the particular sustainability issues and at how responsibility has been exercised in particular places.

Responsible Tourism is about social, economic and environmental sustainability. Sustainability cannot be reduced to the green agenda.

In the three chapters which follow, we follow the triple-bottom-line approach. The focus in Chapter 5 is on social issues which arise in destinations as a consequence of tourism, although there are other issues which affect our decisions about where to travel, in particular issues of human rights in Burma and a host of other countries.[1] Chapter 6 looks at economic issues, and Chapter 7 at environmental sustainability. Each chapter looks first at the range of issues which arise in destinations, and then gives examples of how responsibility has been taken for particular issues in particular places.

---

1 Some travel to raise these issues, others to support those promoting change in the destination.

5 Social Responsibility

Your everyday life is their adventure[1]

We take our holidays, and our business trips, in other peoples' places, in their homes. Experiencing another culture or society, however shallowly, is a significant part of the travel experience internationally and domestically. We seek that experience of other people's societies, their music, food, arts and crafts, their dress, customs, habits, attitudes and ways of life. While in theory we know that the societies we visit are probably as diverse and divided as our own, we easily forget that complexity. If for example we travel to Kerala, we glimpse something of daily life in Kerala – agriculture, religion, the public markets - but we also encounter Indians on holiday there, and other foreigners, visitors and workers, all discovering Kerala differently. People from many different societies and cultures are sharing a place: some born and brought up there, some who have migrated to live there, others who have chosen to visit as tourists or day-visitors. Their views on the place, and on the impact of tourism are formed by their experiences, some there, some carried pre-packaged from home or another place. It is in destinations that the diversity of local and outsider perspectives come into conflict about the impacts of tourism and what might be done to manage it.[2] Between the impact and the potential intervention to manage that impact are three fundamentally political questions. Is there agreement that the impact is an issue? Is there agreement about the cause? And, can agreement be reached, and responsibility accepted, to make a difference, reducing negative impacts and harnessing positive ones? Two further questions arise from the third: whose responsibility is it to make the change? Will they shoulder their responsibility?

Responsible Tourism addresses the established anthropocentric values and attitudes which are rather more widely held. It is difficult enough to secure changes in behaviour which benefit ourselves and other human beings; it is much more difficult to convert people to sacrificing their own wellbeing for the

---

1   Swedish NGO flyposting around the Slovenian National Assembly in 1998
2   For a discussion of the cultural basis of perspectives on sustainability see Robinson (1999)

greater good of biodiversity and nature – which requires more than support for charismatic, fashionable species, and the prevention of cruelty to animals. Responsible Tourism is reformist, its focus is on what can be done to reduce, mitigate and adapt within an anthropocentric mind set. It is pragmatic, it is about people taking personal and collective responsibility, and taking action to reduce their negative and increase their positive impacts, and those of others. Responsible Tourism poses the questions: What could you do? What is your responsibility? What can you do to encourage others to be more responsible? The latter question is inherently political, it is about accepting the responsibility to encourage others to reduce their negative and increase their positive impacts, but it is also about taking personal responsibility.

It may be true that we are unwilling to make large sacrifices, but there is much evidence to point to changing attitudes towards the sustainability of current patterns of travel. In July 2005 Richard Chartres, Bishop of London, pointed out that there is now an overriding imperative to walk more lightly upon the earth and that we need to make our lifestyle decisions in favour of doing so. He went on to say: 'Making selfish choices such as flying on holiday or buying a large car are a symptom of sin. Sin is not just a restricted list of moral mistakes. It is living a life turned in on itself where people ignore the consequences of their actions.'[3] Research commissioned by the British Air Transport Association conducted by YouGov in August 2006 found that 56% of respondents were concerned, and 12% very concerned, about the consequences of flying. 3% of respondents said they no longer travel by air because of their concerns and 10% said they had reduced the number of flights they took.[4] By February 2007 The Independent on Sunday was reporting that 1240 people had signed a pledge to give up flying altogether or to restrict themselves to one long-haul or two short-haul flights a year.[5]

Tourism takes place within particular consuming cultures. We have already looked at the example of the UK (in Chapter 2), but the consuming cultures which characterise originating markets are as diverse as the destinations consumed and consumed in.[6] Consumers are active subjects in the market place,

---

3   Quoted in the Sunday Times, 23 July 2006 'It's a sin to fly, says church'

4   YouGov Survey results based on a sample of 1955 adults representative of the British population available on line at www.bata.uk.com/Web/Documents/media/pubs/ BATAYouGovresultsAug06.pdf. The www.lowflyzone.org website is still functioning in February 2011; the other site www.flightpledge.org.uk has closed.

5   'Jet-setters pledge to ditch air travel to save the environment', The Independent, on Sunday 10 February 2007

6   See for example, Sharpley (2009): 97

and moral and political subjects in politics and civil society. When a consumer travels from a particular consuming culture, they carry these elements of their consuming behaviour with them from their home culture. Sassatelli makes these points, and underlines the significance of critical consumerism: 'the transnational and local/national dimensions of the phenomenon.'[7] We should be suspicious and critical of those who ignore the differences in originating markets as well as those who ignore the differences in destinations. There are global brands but they often mask significant local differences. For example, McDonalds in India does not sell hamburgers; in Germany it sells beer; in Canada it sells lobster; and in Costa Rica it sells rice and beans.[8] Consumer identities are not entirely globalised or homogeneous: 'globalisation and standardisation have in turn stimulated localisation and heterogeneity, contestation and resistance...'.[9] Social, economic and environmental responsibility is informed by a variety of national and peer-group discourses: different elements of the sustainability agenda matter to varying degrees to different consumers. This diversity cannot be ignored.

Tourism is conspicuous, it is easy to blame tourism for generating social change but the social impacts of tourism are difficult to disentangle from the broader processes of development and globalisation of which they are a part. There is quite widespread knowledge amongst local people even in areas which experience very little tourism of the problems caused by tourism: research conducted in Zimbabwe in 1995, for example, found that 73% of respondents in villages with limited contact with tourists felt that tourism had negative effects or caused problems. When asked to give examples, the most common reasons related to erosion of culture, the spreading of disease, prostitution, land degradation, resettlement and spying. This must be caveated by saying there are difficulties in translating 'tourist' into Shona and some respondents understood it as 'stranger' or 'migrant'. People were responding based on what they had heard about the potential negative impacts of tourism. When we asked more specifically about their concerns about tourism in their communities only 12% reported problems mentioning the erosion of culture and price rises for local goods. However, 85% wanted to see more tourists in their village.[10]

---

7   Sassatelli (2006): 220

8   http://trifter.com/practical-travel/budget-travel/mcdonald%E2%80%99s-strange-menu-around-the-world/ accessed 31 July 2010

9   Sassatelli (2006) : 226

10   Goodwin et al. (1997b) IV:§5.1.1:50–59

Similarly in the gateway towns to Komodo National Park in Indonesia, 93% of respondents said that they would be happy to see more tourists, and 89% said that they would be happy to see their children work in tourism. A third felt that tourism was damaging their culture; half did not like the way tourists dressed; only half felt that the whole community benefited from tourism and a quarter felt that only outsiders benefited. 27% felt that their family benefited and only 23% felt that tourism increased their income.[11] It is clear that local people have complex views about tourism; we should beware of those who argue that the community has a single view. Tourism elicits complex opinions and responses in individuals and more so in groups. Communities in destinations are made up of individuals who think for themselves and are, like us, capable of holding and expressing views which may be, or merely appear to be, contradictory.

One lesson to be learnt, then, is that it is important to identify causes precisely if intervention is to be effective. It is not possible to respond and exercise responsibility without being sure of the issue. Without an adequate definition of the problem effective intervention is not possible. I arrived in a village in northern Thailand with the owner of the lodge to be met by the Chief of the village complaining about a tourist having had sex with a 'girl' from the village. It transpired that the driver-guide of the vehicle which had brought a couple to the lodge had had sex with the village girl in the tourism car. The issue was not what it first appeared.

Isolating the negative social and cultural impacts of tourism from those of modernisation and the spread of popular culture from other areas is often difficult. It is important to disentangle tourism impacts from broader social and cultural change driven by inward migration, competition for land and the spread of new popular cultures from the impacts of tourism On Palawan in the Philippines, the qualified lawyer who ran the local NGO claiming to represent the interests of the Batak, the indigenous mountain people, suggested that it would be inappropriate for me to meet with them as contact may pollute them. When I asked how he talked with them he told me that he has a radio programme which enabled him to speak to them every Saturday morning; a one-sided conversation with a group less isolated from contemporary popular culture than one might expect: they listen to pop music too. Tourism is a problem to the Batak, they wear loin cloths which make them targets for tourists wanting an exotic photo, but settlement by lowland farmers and logging are much more significant pressures affecting the survival and culture

---

11   Walpole and Goodwin (2001): 163

of the Batak. Intervention in the way tourism is managed could prevent or reduce the numbers of tourists seeking to photograph the Batak in their loin cloths, but the social change being driven by their displacement by lowland settlers and by the spread of popular culture from Manila.

Awareness of the potential negative impacts of tourism does not necessarily correspond with there being negative impacts locally. The finger is often pointed at mass tourism, but 'alternative' forms of tourism are often no better than mass tourism – all forms of tourism can be more responsible than they are. Managed well, mass tourism may be more efficient and beneficial for local communities than fashionable eco-luxury, the negative impacts of which may include exclusion from natural resources now reserved for tourists. Communities are often economically poor because they have little to trade with richer people. For some, therefore, tourism may be the best opportunity they have to benefit from trade with those wealthier than them. It is responsible to consider tourism as one opportunity amongst others with benefits and negative consequences. If tourism is the best option for local development, or perhaps only the least bad, we must be careful to avoid denying others what we, the relatively wealthy, have in order to preserve what we want at their expense.

This chapter and the two that follow have a similar structure. The remaining part of this chapter will look at the socio-cultural issues that cause concern; Chapter 6 will examine the economic; Chapter 7, the environmental. Each will then discuss three or four of the issues in more detail. The particular examples reveal the complexity of the issues and the importance of paying attention to the particularities – to the evidence. Good intentions are salutary, but as the saying goes, the road to hell…. The concluding chapter provides an opportunity to reflect on the politics of the processes discussed in general in Part I and in particular in Part II and to offer some pointers to the efficacy of different approaches to achieving sustainability.

Defining social responsibility

When approaching a problematic tourism situation, the key questions are: what are the local priorities? What is the issue? Who can best do something about it? Whose responsibility is it, and how can people be encouraged to take responsibility for sustainability? Often the challenge is to achieve agreement amongst the stakeholders about the issues, and what can be done about them, and then to convince them that they can make a difference. It is not enough to endorse the principle of sustainability: stakeholders must accept responsibility – they need to accept that, if they are not doing something positive to alleviate it, they are at least in part the problem. Social sustainability is arguably the most difficult agenda. Here it is difficult to establish agreement about the issues to be addressed, let alone what could or should be done about them. It is the social agenda which reminds us most starkly that destinations belong to the communities who live there and they are unlikely to be of one view about the problems and how they may be best resolved.

Tourism has social impacts, both positive and negative, on the societies and cultures which experience tourism, whether as hosts or guests. In the academic literature, most attention is paid to the impact of the tourists on the places they visit, but we should not ignore the socio-cultural impact of foreign holidaymaking on the originating market. Consider for example the improvement in the quality and diversity of food in the UK which has paralleled the growth in foreign holidays since the 1960s. This is not to argue that the improvements in food culture in the UK over the last 40 years are entirely attributable to the British taking more holidays abroad, or for that matter more Italians coming on holiday to the UK. We should beware of such mono-causal explanations – even if they may seem obvious to us in our own place, about which we have more knowledge, than they are to us in other peoples' places. In this chapter we look at heritage and authenticity; at the issues of responsibility which arise in the host/guest encounter and what can be done to 'improve' the interaction; at the management of hedonistic tourism; and finally at putting something back: travel philanthropy and volunteering. This chapter no more than suggests an approach to a broad range of potential issues.

Tourism now pervades the everyday world. it is no longer adequate to think of tourism as an economic sector separate from other industries. Many places are on the tourist trail or not far from it, as Franklin puts it, 'the everyday world is increasingly *indistinguishable* from the touristic world … most of the things we like to do in our usual leisure time double up as touristic activities and are shared spaces. … much of our everyday lives are spent doing what tourists do, alongside tourists, and in what we might call a touristic manner.'[12]

VisitEngland's *Enjoy Every Minute* marketing campaign is founded on this shared experience between locals and tourists.[13] Tourists are generally spending more each day than they would at home, enjoying days and nights

---

12   Franklin (2003): 5, emphasis in the original, see also Sharpley (2009): 78
13   See above p. 175ff

of leisure. Tourism, being on holiday away from home, is different from having leisure at home, but there are important similarities which should not be ignored, as Franklin has argued, 'tourism has become a metaphor for the consumerist society'[14] in which the relatively wealthy live. However, as voluntourism shows, not all forms of travel and tourism are consumed in the same way.

Tourism is then a particular form of consumerism, taken in someone else's place. When we buy an experience our choice is shaped by availability, price and our expectations. Price determines our capacity to purchase and, along with availability, it determines our opportunity to purchase and to have the experience - an experience of 'the other'. Our expectations are shaped by our previous experience and by what we 'know' of the destination or activity. Encountering the other is not limited to tourism – it is possible to experience another culture, to experience the other, in an ethnic restaurant, in a cherry orchard during harvest time or by immersion in a novel or music. We can have a break without travelling very far, or at all. As Caitlin Moran said:

> leisure time has to be conducted within the following boundaries:
> a) 40ft from my children, b) between the hours of 6 pm and 1 am,
> Fridays only, and c) at a cost of no more than £30. Therefore, I like to
> get a very, very cheap bottle of supermarket whiskey – the kind that
> when you drink it, turns you into a pirate, closing one eye and shout-
> ing 'ARGH!' – sit down with a couple of chatty people and get a bit
> toasted.

Moran goes on 'If you are of a joyous mind, that kind of drinking is like a mini-break – as exhilarating an experience as spending three days sightseeing in Rome or walking Scafell Pike.'[15] Similarly, 'slumming it' – crossing to the dark side of the city to engage with prostitutes, drugs[16] and an under-culture, to experience squalid locales for amusement or to satisfy curiosity, does not require a long journey. We take our leisure in at home and away, away it is tourism. There are campaigns for safe sex, responsible gambling and drinking, and anti-drugs campaigns which address these experiences and encourage us to be responsible consumers.

Travel is not limited to physical relocation: we may transport ourselves through intoxication, like Caitlin Moran, through music, reading or a virtual-reality experience. However, when we are tourists, we reside temporarily in

---

14 Franklin (2003): 8

15 Caitlin Moran, The Times Magazine, 17 July 2010

16 Rojek and Urry (1997): 7

someone else's place. And when we do, we always take ourselves with us: '… I had inadvertently brought myself to the island.'[17] We travel to escape and to experience the other, but we rarely escape ourselves. Because we take ourselves with us when we travel, we may, cumulatively, have significant impacts in 'the others' place and there is potential for conflict as a consequence of differences of attitude and opinion about appropriate dress and behaviour, about the role of women, and about religion, ethics and other matters. As the opportunity to travel becomes available to the newly affluent in the emerging and emerged economies, tourists encounter not only their hosts but also other groups of guests who carry different cultures with them.[18] The slogan, 'Your everyday life is their adventure' was flyposted by a Swedish NGO around the Slovenian National Assembly in 1998. It reminds us that the everyday lives of people in destinations are a part, often a significant part, of the attraction. However, the tourism industry and tourists also contribute to 'the less tangible aspects of a place that give it whatever special appeal it has':[19] tourists contribute to the sense of place.

How we do this 'responsibly' is complex – it varies and may be contested between and within different consuming cultures. In the Cape Town Declaration, Responsible Tourism was placed in the context of the UNWTO's Global Code of Ethics. The attitudes of tolerance and respect for the diversity of religious and moral beliefs are 'both the foundation and consequence'[20] of Responsible Tourism. A responsible approach to tourism accepts that there may be debate about whether particular impacts are positive or negative. Ideas about responsibility reflect the diversity of our world, and the word carries subtle and sometimes significant differences of meaning between cultures. When we travel we experience societies and communities which may have very different values, tastes and attitudes to our own. That is what makes them other.

The challenges of social responsibility occur in both the originating society and the destination. Social exclusion results from inequality, infirmity,

---

17   de Botton (2002): 20

18   As recently as 2007 there was a towel burning incident in Italy. Put Germany + towels into Google for examples of resort conflicts between British and German tourists. There are cultural conflicts between Russian and British tourists too – see for example 'I hated the fact the hotel was full of Russians hardly any British people there so you just don't fit in.' http://www.tripadvisor.co.uk/ShowUserReviews-g297555-d1549428-r68148177-Tiran_Island_Hotel-Sharm_El_Sheikh_South_Sinai_Red_Sea_and_Sinai.html accessed 25 July 2010

19   Bosselman, Peterson and McCarthy (1999):15 They have a useful discussion of the challenges of managing common pool resources in Chapter 2, 'Planning for tourism growth'.

20   Cape Town Declaration (2002): 2 and 4

disability and the burdens of caring. Not everyone in society will have the opportunity to consume a holiday, and social tourism is about helping people to travel who would otherwise not have been able to. The European Union's Calypso Initiative is intended to assist underprivileged young adults, families facing financial or other pressures, people with disabilities and old people who cannot afford to travel or 'who are daunted by the challenges of organising a journey.'[21] This initiative reflects the European tradition of social solidarity and will contribute to extending seasonal employment.[22]

Responsible Tourism also endeavours to make tourism an inclusive social experience. It is not unusual for access to natural or cultural heritage sites to be charged at prices which exclude those who live in the vicinity and yet do not cover the full economic costs of the tourist's visit.[23] In these circumstances, tourists are being subsidised by local taxpayers or by conservation charities. Responsible Tourism, then, requires that tourism contribute to the costs of conserving the cultural heritage which tourists visit and use; and requires that access should be facilitated for people with disabilities and those who might otherwise be excluded for economic reasons.

It also works to favour other disadvantaged groups. Responsible Tourism combats sexual exploitation and the exploitation of children and endeavours to contribute to destination communities' wellbeing, health and education. Responsible Tourism 'provides more enjoyable experiences for tourists through more meaningful connections with local people, and a greater understanding of local cultural, social and environmental issues'; 'it is culturally sensitive' and 'engenders respect between tourists and hosts, and builds local pride and confidence.' The language is highly aspirational, as befits a movement that strives for 'better places for people to live in and for people to visit.'[24]

Sometimes, however, even with the best of intentions, the places we visit do not engage us – but is this their 'fault', or ours? The desire to experience the other is what motivates us to travel – although of course when we encounter the other we may be disappointed. If we are visiting a real place, a place where people live their everyday lives, the place will reflect the culture and behaviour of the residents and of the visitors. The Old Town of Lijiang is a

---

21 European Commission, DG Enterprise and Industry 2010 Calypso widens Europe's travel horizons, European Union, Luxembourg: 2

22 In the UK it is left to charities like the Family Holiday Association and Tourism for All or specialist charities such as those that send terminally ill children and their families on holiday.

23 Goodwin et al. (1997a): Vol.1 Chapter 4

24 Cape Town Declaration (2002): 3

UNESCO World Heritage site in Kunming Province which dates to the Song Dynasty. The Old Town is conserved and valued by domestic tourists who visit in large numbers. It contains many pavement restaurants and a replica Dutch Brown Café, and I was treated to competitive group singing by domestic Chinese tourists, including European football anthems and songs. Initially disappointed, I realised on reflection that the singing of European songs and the Brown Café's popularity with domestic Chinese tourists were as revealing of modern China as Blackpool's Golden Mile is of contemporary Britain. I preferred Lijiang, perhaps in part because it is not a part of my own culture.

It is not always easy to travel with an open mind. That early traveller Dr Johnson had it right: 'The use of travelling is to regulate imagination by reality, and instead of thinking how things may be, to see them as they are.'[25] Contemporary Lijiang is a product of its history, its residents and the predominantly Han Chinese who visit; it is their heritage. From a destination perspective, the challenge is to attract tourists who will 'fit in', who will enjoy what the place and its people have to offer, who will share the public spaces whilst creating the least conflict. Attracting those who identify with the place they are visiting has obvious advantages – they may become loyal repeat visitors or encourage their like-minded friends and relatives to visit and stay.

In the academic literature, discussions of social and cultural impacts generally focus on the tourists, the hosts or locals and the interaction between the two.[26] Tourism is an intrusive social process: outsiders temporarily reside in the destination and there are inevitable 'people impacts',[27] both positive and negative, depending both on the facts, and peoples' perception of them. In 1992, Mathieson and Wall made the point that studies of tourism 'cast little light on the nature of [social] impacts or the means for their investigation.'[28] In 2006 they repeated the point.[29] Little progress has been made in the intervening years, although many papers have been published. The problems of analysing the process of change and isolating the causal factors – let alone developing methodologies for attributing appropriate weight to different factors in particular situations – are intractable. Most of the literature is based on case studies which lead to generalisations from the particular, often contradicted elsewhere. The construction 'tourism causes' should always be read

25   Samuel Johnson, letter to Mrs Thrale quoted in Lamb (2009): 22
26   Affeld, cited in Mathieson and Wall (1992): 133
27   Wolf cited in Mathieson and Wall (1992): 133
28   Mathieson and Wall (1992): 134
29   Wall and Mathieson (2006): 222

with caution – which tourists? What kind of tourism? Where? The extent of impacts will be affected by volumes, the behaviours of tourists, the extent of the cultural divide, the resilience of the local culture(s) and many other factors.

The range of tourism impacts is as broad as the impacts which people have on each other, exacerbated of course by the fact that it is strangers and outsiders who are having the impacts in other peoples' places and that in many places they arrive en masse. To watch a cruise liner approach a small city and disembark into the heart of it, or to see the plane-loads of passengers being bussed to their hotels, leads to metaphors of invasion. Scale and volume do make a difference. Where tourists arrive in communities in large numbers, they alter the local market and, depending on how it is managed, the high street may become dominated by souvenirs and ice-creams. But it also depends on your point of view. Volume, concentration and proximity play a major role in shaping social and cultural impacts: in some environments people seek to be alone, in others such as street markets and festivals, we enjoy the crowds.

However, tourism's impacts are not evenly spread: there are 'honeypots' and there are places which receive very few tourists. The tourism textbooks identify a range of social issues which arise in destinations because of this: begging; inward migration to tourism honeypots; displacement for tourism development or the gazetting of a national park; airport art; overcrowding and congestion; prostitution; child abuse; crime; drugs; loss of privacy; the demonstration effect of tourist behaviour, which may introduce new ideas and lead to acculturation[30] or cause offence; alcohol consumption; bad language; pop music; hand-holding and public expressions of affection. It is difficult to disentangle the social impacts of tourism from the effects of the spread of Western popular culture, which has been an issue since the development of the movies and is now amplified by satellite television and the internet. The infrastructure of tourism is also used by drug traffickers to transport, launder and invest drug money.[31] Tourism brings development which is likely to increase dependence on non-local markets, international or domestic,[32] as does any export industry, and it can create new elites and alter the balance of power between genders.

The development of the Mahenye and Chilo Lodges in Mahenye, a Shangaan community in southern Zimbabwe, brought salaried employment, telephones,

---

30   Collins (1978):2 78, describes the cultural distance between host and guest generating cultural drift.

31   Gmelch (2004): 15

32   See below page 192ff

electricity and piped water and a contribution to household incomes levied on turnover. Six young women were employed as chambermaids.[33] They no longer carried water from the river twice a day, nor toiled in the fields, and they had incomes independent of their families, some earning more than their fathers.[34] The development of the two lodges brought significant change to the Mahenye community, not least because the improvement of the road brought a daily bus, providing transport and enabling them to take goods to market. Opinions differed about the changes: some female development-industry workers disapproved of women becoming chambermaids, holding the view that agricultural labour is nobler; older women disapproved of the changes in the dress of the young women; it is difficult to know what the fathers felt about the earnings and independence of their daughters. Development brings social change with advantages to some and disadvantages to others – some of the changes are approved of, and others are not. Stories abound of Maasai changing from their jeans[35] into their traditional costume behind a rock. Similar stories are not told about the Beefeaters in the Tower of London changing into their performance costumes, but only because tourists' expectations differ. There are pastiche villages created for tourism, in Kenya, as elsewhere, alternatively, it is possible to walk with a Maasai guide in the Rift Valley – the traveller can choose between very different experiences of the Maasai.

Tourism may bring salaried employment, independence from the family and a higher standard of living. It may also encourage destinations to differentiate themselves, resulting in increased local investment in tangible or intangible heritage. It may create economic opportunities which either discourage young people from leaving in pursuit of better jobs and employment prospects, or attract them back from the cities. Conversely, the growth of second home ownership and holiday lets can make housing unaffordable for local families and contribute to the creation of out-of-season ghost towns, resulting in the closure of the village school and local shops. The key question is whether, and to what extent, a community can use tourism to its advantage, and of how it defines its advantage. The issue is one of power and, as we have seen, the consumer is generally more powerful than the communities they visit. Tourism is inherently unequal. There are also issues within the community where the revenues may be captured by local elites, to the disadvantage

---

33   Goodwin et al. (1997b): IV §B3

34   Unpublished field notes.

35   Ralph Lauren has a Maasai Wash Jean – a 'rugged jean is designed for a trim, modern fit in a versatile wash and finished with subtle fraying for a well-worn casual look' www. ralphlauren.com/product/index.jsp?productId=3954698 accessed 30 July 2010

of others – whether by exclusion from tourism earnings or being prevented grazing or watering their livestock.

Tourists carry with them their values and the issues they feel strongly about. England has a National Society for the Prevention of Cruelty to Children and a Royal Society for the Prevention of Cruelty to Animals: animal welfare is important to the English and the British. One of the early initiatives taken by the UK's Federation of Tour Operators was on animal welfare. It matters to British consumers; they write letters to tour operators about it and make an issue of it. There have, for some years, been complaints from local people and international tourists, not only the British, about the traditional animal market on Las Ramblas, in Barcelona. The *ocellaires,* who sell birds as pets, developed their trade from La Boquería who sold fowl for the table. A Catalan law on the Protection of Animals was passed in 2003, making these activities and others illegal. The 150-year tradition of the *ocellaires* is ending, although it had evolved to include the selling of a wide range of pets, and few fowl. It has taken seven years for the law to be enforced. The stalls are re-opening selling tourists goods – sweets, ice creams, souvenirs – and local goods, such as *denominación* stalls and a Barça football club stall. Existing stall holders object to the increased competition. The change has occurred because the issue was raised by locals and foreigners[36] on the grounds of both animal welfare and human health: dead animals were alleged to have been thrown into the rubbish. Born Free is a UK NGO that works internationally to stop wild animal suffering and protect threatened species in the wild. Born Free has corporate partnerships with tour operators and with airlines, and has been active in Barcelona in pressing for the implementation of the law.[37] There are parts of the community who are not happy about the change. One of the stalls carried an open letter to visitors: '*Dear visitors, This is a city where people work and live, not a theme park. Stores in 'La Rambla' have a 150-year history, before you arrive, we were very happy, Please show some respect for the city and its inhabitants.*'[38]

Yet the fight over cultural sensitivity and tradition runs both ways – even in the same territory. Writing on a tourism website, Xinoxano (from the username,

36   I am indebted to Robin Barden for this example. The UK's Born Free Foundation campaigned on the issue with local NGOs, www.bornfree.org.uk/news/news-article/?no_cache=1&tx_ttnews[tt_news]=414. For a Catalan campaign site, www.ramblesetiques.com

37   www.adn.es/local/lleida/20091201/NWS-1814-Ecologistas-Ramblas-britanicos-protestan-animales.html accessed 27 July 2010

38   http://barcelonasights.blogspot.com/2010/01/all-change-for-las-ramblas-animal.html accessed 16 July 2010

presumably a Catalan), looks forward to the day when bullfighting is banned in Catalonia[39] and suggests that it is the tourists who provide the revenues to keep the *corrida* alive, reporting that the 'ring is nearly always half empty and 70% of the attendance are ignorant tourists, many of which leave the ring before the fight is finished absolutely disgusted, some crying or dizzy of the bloody butchery they have witnessed'.[40] Is bullfighting a distinguished local tradition or a tourist trap?

In Canada, the Vancouver Humane Society campaigns against rodeo arguing that fear, stress and pain are caused to the animals and that the 'risks and the suffering they endure are especially unacceptable, given the unnecessary and frivolous nature of rodeo as entertainment'.[41] They too have sought to elicit the support of visitors for their campaign,[42] which has focused on the Calgary Stampede, a not-for-profit community organization that seeks to preserve and promote western heritage and values and which organises an annual ten day festival. The Vancouver Humane Society enlisted originating-market tour operators in communicating their concerns to international visitors. These animal welfare rows draw on debates about authenticity and heritage, and raise questions about the difference between large commercial events like the Calgary Stampede and small-town and ranch rodeos, which are claimed to be more authentic and representative of current ranching activity. These local events are economically important to relatively marginal communities and, it is argued, represent current rural Albertan culture as well as historic western Canadian culture. There have been changes at the Calgary Stampede, as a result of monitoring of the event by the Calgary Humane Society and the Alberta Society for the Prevention of Cruelty to Animals.[43] Similarly, the debates about zoos, shark diving, swimming with dolphins, dancing bears and snake charming will continue: they are issues, there are conflicting views about it and tourists are deployed by one or both sides. Where tourists provide a market, they contribute to the continuation of the practice, but of course the acceptability of different forms of animal abuse varies between different

39 Legislation was passed in late July 2010 which has banned bull fighting in Catalonia from January 2012.

40 www.virtualtourist.com/travel/Europe/Spain/Catalunya/Barcelona-274654/Tourist_Traps-Barcelona-Bullfights-BR-1.html accessed 27 July 2010

41 www.vancouverhumanesociety.bc.ca/rodeos.html accessed 16 July 2010

42 The UK online travel agency ResponsibleTravel.com has backed the Vancouver Humane Society's campaign.

43 Laura McGowan of ICRT Canada drew this conflict to my attention and provided the background

originating markets – we take our ethics with us when we travel. These questions will not easily be resolved.

Tourists are often bemused when they encounter hostility from locals, and are puzzled or offended to be treated as an intrusive pest, a status accorded to them on account of their own behaviour or that of other tourists – they do not realise that they are seen as part of a mass. In 2009, there were reports of residents blocking the runway at Easter Island's airport to demand limits on the numbers of tourists[44] In June 2010 there were reports of graffiti being used to designate tourism lanes in the tightly packed Gothic district in Barcelona to create space for 'normal' Barcelona residents.[45] But it is not only the locals who may be offended; visitors have long taken and expressed offence at the behaviour of tourists. Arriving at Lanthony Priory in 1870, the Reverend Francis Kilvert, perhaps because his taking of lunch at the local hostelry, had been delayed by other visitors, wrote rather grumpily in his diary:

> What was my horror, on entering the Abbey, to see two tourists with staves and shoulder belts all complete posturing amongst the ruins in an attitude of admiration, one of them of course discoursing learnedly to his gaping companion and pointing out objects of interest with his stick. If there is one thing more hateful than another, it is being told what to admire and having objects pointed out to one with a stick. Of all the noxious animals too, the most noxious is the tourist. And of all tourists, the most vulgar, ill bred, offensive and loathsome is the British tourist.[46]

The issues arise from conflict about seemly behaviour. If parties of French school children are noisy and disrespectful in Canterbury Cathedral, it may cause annoyance to other tourists or to locals, but it becomes an issue only if the behaviour is challenged, or if people feel that something should be done. Inappropriately dressed tourists who disembark from a cruise boat into the cultural and commercial heart of an Islamic city will cause offence, the more so if they then visit a mosque. But it becomes an issue only when offence results in demands for something to be done. The issue may then be raised by local people, or members of the same society who may not be local, or by domestic

44 http://inform.com/world/easter-island-locals-block-flights-tourism-protest-634819a accessed 26 July 2010

45 www.guardian.co.uk/world/2010/jun/13/barcelona-rebels-against-tourist-invasion accessed 26 July 2010

46 Fitton (1995): 159

or foreign visitors. Sometimes groups of tourists and locals stand together seeking change opposed by others. Rarely will there be unanimity about any issue – it is an issue because there is conflict occasioned by real differences in values and ethics. There is also a temporal dimension: the attitudes of visitors and locals change over time, as do our perceptions of destinations.

Our perceptions of a destination are formed by many forms of media, by what we are told by friends and family and by our own experience of the destination. When I first visited the city of York, more than 30 years ago, there were very few tourists there outside of a short summer season. Now I perceive the city centre as dominated by the visitor economy: it has changed and so have I. The judgment that a place has been spoilt depends on the comparison being made. Each generation discovers Paris, Carnaby Street or the Taj Mahal, unencumbered by memory and perhaps with a different concept of authenticity: there is a ratchet effect as each generation discovers a more crowded and touristified La Rambla in Barcelona, Trafalgar Square in London or Montmartre in Paris. The locals also come to terms with the change in their own way, often deserting a site or location as it becomes a tourism zone. Efforts are made to preserve sense of place, such as in Barcelona where there is a movement to defend the unique character of La Rambla[47] and the authorities have been given powers to close down illegal tourist apartments. There has been a moratorium on the building of new tourism accommodation and ordinances have been introduced to restrict the souvenir shops in residential areas close to tourism honeypots.

It is difficult to generalise about social impacts, difficult to distinguish change which results from tourism, and there are differing perceptions between groups. Determining who or what is responsible for causing change, who can take responsibility for intervening or even what a responsible intervention might be, is for debate in particular local circumstances.

Heritage and authenticity

Reflecting on contemporary perceptions of Britishness, Korte and Muller, state: 'Cultural identity involves myth-making; it is fictional and always constituted through storytelling, in particular through "the role of the stories we tell ourselves about the past in constructing our identities in the present".'[48]

---

47   There is an association *Amics de la Rambla* seeking to defend the unique character of La Rambla

48   Korte and Muller (1998): 15

History is rewritten and reinterpreted, generation by generation and heritage, like history, is contested. As Lowenthal has argued 'heritage today peddles a wider range of goods to more buyers than ever before ... the medieval relic trade out-did any modern scam. What *is* novel is the mistaken notion that such abuses are new and hence intolerable.'[49] Domestic and international visitors are a significant part of the market for heritage, which now conveys a broader, plural view of the past than that narrowly purveyed by old in school text books. There is bad interpretation of the past, as heritage and history, but there are numerous good examples.[50] The development of heritage sites for paying visitors in Coalbrookdale in England has developed our understanding of the Industrial Revolution, just as the District Six museum, Robben Island in Cape Town and the Constitutional Court on Constitution Hill in Johannesburg have spread awareness of what apartheid meant, as well as the post-apartheid aspirations of a newly democratic South Africa. Tourism brings an audience and a source of funding – understanding and education is the purpose. Commodification is essential to the maintenance of heritage: unless a great deal more public funding becomes available, heritage sites rely on visitor fees and trading profits from the associated shops and cafés.

It has been argued that mass tourism caters to the 'imagination of others', and that mass tourism 'routinely recycles dying industries, dead sites, past colonial relations, and abandoned ethnographic tropes to provide industrial parks, living historical villages, and enactments'.[51] In a country such as Britain, the redevelopment of coal mines, iron foundries, potteries and dockyards as mixed-use educational and leisure sites, as heritage, has been significant both for the conservation of our built environment and for the visitor economy in our post-industrial society.

Authenticity has, perhaps, always been negotiated – a middle-ground between actual history or heritage experiences and the tourist's perceptions or aspirations. Cohen, for example, argued that the 'communicative staging' of experiences which are inherently authentic for tourists.[52] New cultural developments achieve a patina of authenticity over time, a phenomena he described as 'emergent authenticity'.[53] Societies often stage, manufacture and charge international and domestic visitors for culture, such as at Stratford-on-Avon

---

49   Lowenthal (1998): 101 emphasis in the original.
50   For some bad examples see Lowenthal (1998): 103, and Chapter 5.
51   Bruner and Kirshenblatt-Gimblett (1994): 435
52   Cohen (1989)
53   Cohen (1988)

or the Globe Theatre in London, and charge for it. This is co-modified culture, culture packaged for sale, as is the theatre in the West End or Broadway. Without a paying audience theatre is rarely sustained. Dependent though London's Theatreland is on coach parties of visitors, it is not criticised in the same way as other tourism attractions – perhaps because the audience is mixed and locals are also present. The Flora Macdonald Scottish Highland Games are held in North Carolina, a long way from Scotland, but tourists have regarded it as authentic.[54] The Great Dorset Steam Fair[55] has been held every year in the fields near Blandford and attracts 200,000 domestic and international visitors to a heritage festival of steam and nostalgia. Staged authenticity for sure, but one where many of the audience are also performers.

Bruner has argued that all tourists are not the same but that 'scholars in the field tended to reduce the variety by seeking the essence of the tourist experience' as a quest for authenticity, a transition from home to elsewhere, a form of neo-colonialism or a 'gaze'. As Bruner sees it: 'Exceptions to the generalizations were common, rendering questionable their usefulness; one was never sure when or where the general propositions were applicable.' He goes on to argue that more recent scholars have relied less on 'typologies and monolithic generalizations' although there is still a tendency to 'homogenize local tourist displays' and 'a single form of tourism becomes associated with one ethnic group in a given locality...' His conclusion is provocative: 'Tourism scholarship thus aligns itself with tourism marketing, in that scholars tend to work within the frame of the commercial versions of the sites. Grand statements about the nature of tourism in Bali or Africa or even more broadly in the "Third World" are sometimes the result......'[56]

Yet the interplay of these forces, while potentially destructive, is more complex than this statement suggests, and to be specific to each local manifestation. Wall and Mathieson argue that carving did not play a significant part in the life of the Canadian Inuit until demand from tourists resulted in an 'upsurge in Inuit carving' and the development of art prints.[57] Yet, looking at a similar phenomenon from a different point of view, Ryan and Crotts report that tourist demand for Maori art has resulted in a regeneration of their traditions: its commodification has provided resources to maintain the culture, and the

---

54 Chhabra, Healy and Sills (2003), although there were important differences in perceived authenticity among different visitor groups

55 www.gdsf.co.uk

56 Bruner (2001): 881

57 Wall and Mathieson (2006): 275

Maori have maintained a relatively high degree of control. Aboriginal art from Australia has prospered in part because of tourism, which has contributed to its international success.[58] This contrasts with Bali where work by Francillon revealed an increasing tendency for religious symbols and rituals to be used for tourism and trivialised. Here outbound and inbound tour operators, guides, hotels and tourism offices can take responsibility by encouraging tourists to buy from local artists and crafts people and encouraging visitors to engage with local cultural life while avoiding the tourist traps. Tourism can be used to re-instil pride in their cultures amongst the youth of First peoples by demonstrating that their culture is valued by others and that it can provide livelihoods.

Cultural Studies has increased academe's understanding of the complexity of 'travelling cultures'[59] and there is an increasing awareness of cultural diffusion and hybridity.[60] People, cultures and objects migrate. Tourism is only a part of many much broader cultural encounters. The notions of home and abroad, of ours and theirs, have become, or have become to be recognised as over-simplistic: '[T]ourist cultures are a complex of relationships that occur with, through, and in space – both real and imagined.'[61] Baudelaire's concept of the *flâneur*,[62] someone who wanders to experience other places as an immersed outsider, becomes increasingly relevant. As experiential travel becomes more common the 'framework is … expanded from one concerned with disassociated 'gaze' to emphasise a more engaged set of experiences and imaginings …'[63]

Visitor satisfaction, a product of the gap between expectation and experience, is an issue for destinations and for outbound tour operators. It is a particular challenge in an industry which competes by creating expectations about the experience. Some tourists are very concerned about authenticity, particularly some anthropologists, but 'authentic' is a powerful and very slippery word. Reisinger and Steiner state that scholars should abandon the concept and the term because there is no agreed common grounds for

58   See for example http://aboriginalart.com.au and Myers.

59   Said (1983) and Clifford (1992)

60   See for example Rojek and Urry (1997): 4

61   Wearing, Stevenson and Young (2010): 2

62   ''The crowd is his element, as the air is that of birds and water of fishes. His passion and profession are to become one flesh with the crowd. For the perfect flâneur, for the passionate spectator, it is an immense job to set up house in the middle of the multitude, amid the ebb and flow of movement, in the midst of the fugitive and the infinite', Baudelaire (1986): 9

63   Wearing, Stevenson and Young (2010): 2

its existence, meaning or importance.[64] For tour operators and destination managers this is not an option, since the commercial imperative is to meet expectations – a difficult task if one doesn't know what those expectations, or the particular definition of the contested notion of authenticity, are. Tourists may arrive with expectations and a desire for authenticity which requires that local people do not change the way live, and yet development is surely their right. Tour operators and local tourism businesses can responsibly contribute to that aspiration, but the responsibility to determine the character of the place rests with the communities and their government.[65]

The *Alarde* is a local parade held each year in Fuenterrabia, Spain. Greenwood suggests that 'by making it into a tourist package, it is turned into an explicit and paid performance and can no longer be believed in the way that it was before.'[66] Others have pointed out that cultural traditions evolve and occur within societies which are themselves changing.[67] In Faversham we have a Hop Festival which is a modern creation. It is neither new nor traditional; although after 20 years, perhaps it should now be considered a tradition.[68] The Edinburgh Festival is both a cultural and commercial success, and tourism is a major part of many arts festivals, supplementing the local market and providing a justification for funding support from public agencies.

Host/guest encounters

The host/guest encounter is inherently unequal. In many cultures, from the Bedouin to Benedictine monasteries, tradition required that travellers who asked for shelter should be treated as honoured guests: the stranger would be housed, fed and taken care of. It was also expected that hospitality was a reciprocal relationship and that guests would treat their hosts with courtesy and respect. Hospitality has become a global industry, one in which travellers and tourists are accommodated in hotels, lodges and guest houses. Staff now routinely provide hospitality services to guests who, having rented a room, act as though they own the property. The relationship is unequal because of the social status of the hospitality worker and the guest, the routine provision of hospitality services and the superior attitude of the guest who has pur-

---

64   Reisinger and Steiner (2006)

65   www.travelifecollection.com accessed 1 August 2010

66   Greenwood (1977): 179

67   See for example Wilson (1993)

68   http://thehopfestival.com

chased service. Hotel guests with the least experience of hotels can be most demanding to accommodate, often arriving with unrealistic expectations.

The host/guest relationship is inherently complex, affect by, among other factors, the scale, forms of tourism, extent of interaction, novelty, economic importance and the extent of the cultural and behavioural divide. de Kadt identified three functional types of interaction between hosts and guests: economic encounters where goods are being purchased or a service provided; encounters where there is leisure proximity, on a beach or in an audience; purposeful encounters where there is an intention to exchange ideas.[69] 'Bumsters'[70] in the Gambia and beach boys in Kenya engage with tourists in all three ways – a conversation developing into a trading opportunity and playing football with tourists.

Is this kind of response typical? Doxey argued that the response of residents to tourists resulted in varying degrees of resident irritation which change over time through euphoria, apathy and irritation, ending with antagonism. This model suggests that the community moves as one through the cycle, although others have argued that all four attitudes may exist at the same time.[71] Dogan, for instance, identified five types of response that could coexist in a destination: resistance, retreatism, boundary maintenance, revitalization and adoption. Later work recognised that there will be a range of views and behavioural responses and coping strategies in any destination.[72] These typologies have provided labels for intervention and management, but have not provided intervention strategies.

There is often a considerable difference of wealth between tourists and the people they meet in destinations. Whether in the developed or developing world, the relative deprivation[73] can be significant: market opportunities are created which may cause envy and resentment. The USA has significant numbers of poor people but they are not encountered as tourists, nor are they often portrayed in the popular media. Tourists are not necessarily representative of the populations from which they arrive. Krippendorf asked:

Don't we occasionally get the impression that local people are fed up

---

69 De Kadt (1979): 50

70 A word they use to describe themselves as well as by others to describe them.

71 Mathieson and Wall (1992): 139

72 For example, by Ap and Crompton (1993) and Brown and Giles (1994)

73 The concept of relative deprivation was coined by the American sociologist S.A. Stouffer and colleagues in the 1940s, see also Runciman (1966)

with tourism? They want to shake off the dictatorship of the trade, take their destiny into their own hands, make their own decisions and participate in their development. What they want above all else is to shape their own environment as a place for themselves and not as a playground for other people. The locals are getting near to rebellion.[74]

Some may be, but for many tourism creates opportunities for economic development and for some the transformation of their lives. In the Gambia, the development of a relationship with a *tubab*, a tourist, creates commercial opportunities, but it may also result in gifts for the bumster and his family, schooling for a younger child in the family, a scholarship to college or university or marriage. The relationships between female tourists and young Gambian men range from holiday romance and marriage to prostitution, but there are plenty of couples returning to visit family to demonstrate that the stereotypes, although persistent, are just that – stereotypes. Bumsters are often relatively well educated, and to be successful they need to be linguistically capable. Many speak more than one European language well and act as guides. As Smith has pointed out, the guides who come from the community act as cultural brokers: as 'marginal men'[75] they are likely to become acculturated and may experience conflict with their own communities as a result. Cultural brokers can play a major role in managing tourists and their impacts, but their effectiveness in this management role is diminished if they identify too closely with their clients.

In communities, teachers and parents can discourage children from begging and address tourism in schools. Communities can do a great deal to manage tourism impacts responsibly. Their effectiveness in so doing so is dependent on the strength of their own social structures and ability to stand up to the industry, which is often politically well connected. Communities often struggle to identify and defend a collective community interest against the demands of the industry. In Morocco, most of the country's mosques are not open to tourists and the tourist police work to reduce hassle and unofficial guiding.

Like local guides, tour operator representatives, guides, couriers and tour leaders play an important role in demonstrating and encouraging responsible behaviour which can be achieved without preaching. Many tour operators engaged in Responsible Tourism provide advice and guidelines that encourage their tourists to take responsibility for their social impacts – for example, by purchasing traditional local crafts, asking permission to take photographs

---

74 Krippendorf (1987): xvii–xviii
75 Smith (1977): 48

of people, learning a little of the local language, respecting the local dress code, not giving sweets to children and avoiding extravagant displays of wealth. As tourists are responsible for some of the greatest impacts in the destination, it is essential to modify their behaviour, and operators do this by raising awareness and engaging their clients in a better experience, offering more meaningful connections with local people,[76] and building repeat business. Some operators have monitored and reported on the impacts of their trips;[77] others, recognising that they organise high-impact holidays, have taken responsibility and adapted their management strategies.

Hedonistic tourism

Eighteenth century Brighton offered an escape for the Prince of Wales from his father's disapproving court. Jane Austen captured the allure of the seaside resort:

> In Lydia's imagination a visit to Brighton comprised every possibility of earthly happiness. She saw with the creative eye of fancy, the streets of that gay bathing-place covered with officers. She saw herself the object of attention to tens and scores of them at present unknown … she saw herself seated beneath a tent, tenderly flirting with at least six officers at once.[78]

The coming of the railway made Brighton more accessible to day visitors and weekenders and, like Blackpool, it became synonymous with anonymous hedonistic escape. Tourism developed in Las Vegas in the 1900s because of the coming of the railroad, and was augmented by the nearby Hoover Dam in 1935, a major publicly funded tourist attraction. However, the biggest draw was surely the legalisation of gambling in 1931, which led to the development of the casino-hotels and 'Sin City' – a city in which gambling, clubbing,

---

76   See for example Exodus 'you have as important a role as we do' www.exodus.co.uk/responsible-travel/your-role? There is also Explore's approach: 'No lectures…we want you to relax and enjoy yourself whilst you're on holiday. No-one would want their enjoyment at the expense of others or to damage the beautiful places they are travelling to'. www.explore.co.uk/responsible-travel/what-you-can-do.htm. Neilson offer tips 'We all have a vested interest in protecting these locations, but how can we all play our part? Well, the old proverb every little helps is certainly true. Imagine, for example, if all our guests refused one plastic carrier bag from a shopkeeper during their holiday. That would mean around 100,000 plastic bags would fail to make it to landfill sites each year.' www.neilson.co.uk/Responsible-Travel-Our-Tips.aspx accessed 3 August 2010

77   See for example Intrepid www.intrepidtravel.com/ourtrips/rt/research.php

78   Austen (1813) Chapter 41

prostitution and alcohol are available 24 hours a day. It even has its own code of conduct: *'What happens in Vegas, stays in Vegas'*. Managing tourism in hedonistic resorts poses particular challenges.

In a reflective piece in the Daily Telegraph in 1985, Skidmore, himself formerly a Club 18–30 rep at Middleton-on-Sea, wrote of binge drinking, lewd behaviour, drunken brawls and league tables of sexual conquest.[79] As Skidmore argues, there is money to be made in this market, and the resorts and tour companies 'have to take some responsibility for the behaviour of young people on holiday.' Local authorities have criticised drunken youths but historically 'have taken little action for fear of damaging a lucrative trade'. Travel companies and the party destinations 'may not be responsible for creating the monster, but they have certainly fed it a plentiful diet'.[80] They have facilitated and encouraged its growth. Choices have been made by tourists, tourism businesses in originating markets and destinations, and local authorities – they are all responsible for their choices.

Getting drunk and having sex are traditional holiday objectives of some tourists and with the advent of cheap flights, the trade moved abroad. Destinations can also be portrayed as victims. In the summer of 2003, Faliraki was subject to considerable adverse publicity in the UK press following the killing of one British holidaymaker by another. Tribe argues that tourism in Faliraki and Newquay has morphed from sun, sand and sea to Sin, C and Sound. Sin includes 'rowdy and noisy behaviour, litter, vandalism, swearing, urinating and defecating in public, vomiting and fighting. Some of these have been immortalised in the names of cocktails such as "Sex on the Beach", "Slow Comfortable Screw Up Against The Wall", "Red Headed Slut" and "Skip And Go Naked".' 'C' refers to drugs and alcohol and 'Sound' to music and clubs.[81] In August 2003, two Blackpool policemen flew to Rhodes, armed with their experience of British youth at the seaside. Superintendent Andy Rhodes was

---

79   Middleton-on-Sea, a small village in Sussex close to Bognor Regis, was one of the first attempts to create a self-contained holiday camp for tourists. The 'New City' opened in 1922 in a former seaplane factory. It changed hands several times, and by the 1970s it had a private beach and swimming pool and dancing every night, by the 1980s it was popular with visitors from the north of England. In the 2004 Parish Action Plan, tourism is not mentioned, the village is changing from a holiday area to a residential area, and the holiday centre has become residential, converted to houses and apartments. Middleton-on-Sea Parish Action Plan 2004 Countryside Agency and Action for Rural Sussex

80   Skidmore (2003), 'As reps, we encouraged drinking among the clients', Travel Telegraph, 23 August 2003, www.telegraph.co.uk/travel/728171/As-reps-we-encouraged-drinking-among-the-clients.html

81   Tribe (2005): 6

reported in *The Guardian* as having said that the TV documentary, *Club Reps*, had suggested to young people that 'they could come to Faliraki and do what they want… It has increased trade but brought a problem in terms of behaviour.' He added that 'aggressive' promotions of alcohol, bar crawls by up to 500 people and inadequate policing had encouraged the bad behaviour.[82]

Young British people abroad have in some parts of the world earned a very poor reputation.[83] The TV series *Club Reps*, which ran on mainstream television in the UK from 2001 to 2004 established 'Faliraki, Kavos, Malia and Agia Napa as freelance zones of promiscuity'.[84] In July 2003 there was a report of a group sex competition on the beach in full view of family holidaymakers in the late afternoon: the reps involved lost their jobs.[85] Kavos in Corfu is heavily dependent on tourism revenues and its image is closely associated with alcohol and sex. Interviewing those engaged in tourism in Kavos, Balomenou found broad agreement that it would be better for Corfu to have more independent tourists and to be offering more cultural and activity holidays. People accepted that the publicity was negative for the island, yet, off the record the interviewees argued that young people have to go somewhere – 'Why not Kavos?' – and although locals point out that they make money from tourism, there was 'common ground that more tourists would come to Kavos next year due to these incidents.'[86] Balomenou heard reports that even the police were afraid to go to Kavos, that there were many unlicensed businesses operating there and that the bar and club owners are largely responsible for the situation, as they profit from it. Measures such as increased policing and stricter environmental health, licensing and planning controls were seen as repressive and unwelcome.[87]

Closer to home in the UK, Newquay in Cornwall has been criticised for encouraging the youth market by allowing plentiful cheap accommodation, fast-food outlets, pubs and clubs, and neglecting facilities for family holidays. It has led to the town's inclusion on the 'humorous' website Chavtowns,[88] which makes fun of down-at-heel places in the UK. Tribe quotes the site:

82 'TV show blamed for yob antics in Faliraki', The Guardian, 1 September 2003

83 'Binge drinking rapes squalid deaths Club 18–30 insider reveals horrific truth about Britons abroad', Daily Mail 13 August 2008

84 Balomenou (2003): 20

85 www.thesun.co.uk/sol/homepage/news/article82014.ece The reps side of the story was also published www.mirror.co.uk/news/2003/08/03/we-re-so-ashamed-98487-13249600/

86 Balomenou (2003): 53

87 Balomenou (2003): 54

88 www.chavtowns.co.uk

Just imagine you have a picturesque fishing village on top of a dramatic Cornish cliff. How do you oversee its development? Well if you are in Newquay you build lots of drab hotels and guest houses, fill the High Street with a load of tacky arcades and cheap surf shops and generally make it mega appealing to chavs![89]

As Tribe notes, reactions like these 'suggest that people have a misguided view about the powers of planners and planning mechanisms.' However, abdicating responsibility, a lack of planning and leaving development or decline entirely to market forces, has consequences: cheap multiple-occupancy accommodation attracts particular kinds of holidaymakers and they are likely to drive away others. Eventually local authorities are pushed to restore the balance. In Faliraki, there were a number of high-profile arrests, including five tour reps; pub crawls and drinking in the streets were banned. In Newquay, more police were deployed and they were given additional powers to designate exclusion zones and fixed penalty notices.[90]

Once a destination gains a hedonistic reputation it is very difficult to move away from it: the established businesses rely on the kind of tourism for which they have a reputation and other opportunities are generally incompatible with party tourism. There is a strong case for enclaving and isolating it. The responsibility for the development of a place like Kavos or Faliraki belongs to the local authorities,[91] council, police and other agencies. Guide-book writers, airlines, travel agents and tour operators in the originating markets also have responsibilities – they can encourage or discourage particular tourists and behaviours. Partnership with local businesses and those who attract and bring tourists to the destinations helps, but the management of the destination is ultimately the responsibility of the local authorities. The problems in Corfu are not new: a couple of decades previously there were similar problems in Benitses, a small fishing village with a population of 1000. In 1985 a crowd of English tourists is reported to have dragged the body of a beheaded donkey through the nightclubs of the area. A decline in demand for low-quality accommodation had resulted in the arrival of low-value, alcohol-fuelled tourism, which filled the rooms and contributed to the destination's downward spiral. The local council and businesses in Benitses struggled to reposition the destination and move it up market, and Benitses now attracts

---

89   Tribe (2005): 10

90   Tribe (2005): 13. Police officers will be able to arrest misbehaving revelers if they refuse to leave 'designated zone'.

91   And in protected areas National Park Authorities

mainly families and couples. There is now only one nightclub; all the revellers now go to Kavos[92] The local authorities took responsibility in Benitses as they are beginning to in Kavos.

Originating market operators cannot and should not avoid their responsibility for the way they market destinations and the advice they give their travellers. British tour operators have become increasingly involved in managing the behaviour of their clients in destinations. Club 18–30 carries approximately 80,000 holidaymakers to 12 destinations in the Mediterranean every summer, and is well aware of the negative images that have been associated with its brand in the past. There have been significant changes in the last few years. In order to remain the number one youth travel operator the company must re-invent itself as often as its customers do, to remain in tune with new music, new attitudes and new fashions. Thousands of 18–30 year olds spend the most important weeks of their year on a Club 18–30 holiday. The company aims 'to give young people the fun that they need, at the price that they want and with the service that they deserve'.[93]

Club 18–30 has built a valuable and powerful relationship with its holidaymakers, creating a mutual respect that it is now using to promote more responsible behaviour amongst its customers whilst still providing the ultimate holiday experience. Pre-departure information is provided to customers through ticket books, the website and e-flyers covering everything from safe sex campaigns with the Department of Health, advice on drugs through the 'Be Frank' campaign, alcohol awareness through Drinkaware[94] and targeted messages via the Foreign Office's Know Before You Go campaign. In resorts, these campaigns are brought to life through information posters in hotel receptions. Free bottles of water are available from the Drinkaware partnership, with sensible drinking messages printed on them. In the welcome meetings, reps brief holidaymakers on local issues and the laws that they should be aware of. It is also working with the UK government and others to connect with young people and understand their behaviour better. Club 18–30 has facilitated research with young people on holiday in Kos and Turkey to help the Foreign Office understand which campaign messages work best within the age group. One key message is that holiday insurance becomes invalid when the holidaymaker is under the influence of alcohol. In 2006, the company was

92 Balomenou (2003): 20–23, see also www.benitses.org and www.realholidayguides.com/benitses.htm

93 Personal communication, Club 18–30

94 www.drinkaware.co.uk

a key partner in developing the Travel Foundation's 'Make a Difference While You Party' campaign – a campaign to raise awareness among young people about ways to minimise their negative impacts in resort. In 2010, 170 Club 18–30 reps and managers received training from the Department of Health, Drinkaware and the Foreign Office and learned about sustainability in destinations through the Thomas Cook sustainability team. In Kavos the Club 18–30 team are worked with local bar owners to 'Keep Kavos Clean' and reduce the amount of broken glass in the streets and their relationship with local business people and authorities considerably improved. Club 18–30 have worked hard to ensure that their holidaymakers have a better, safer, holiday and to develop mutual respect between the tourists and the local community.

The economics of tourism are powerful. For sun, sand, sea and sex tourism, resorts operate in a buyer's market dominated by tour operators exercising buying power on their tourists' behalf. Once a destination moves down market, it can be very difficult to reverse the trend. It is better to avoid the trap of becoming a party destination – if that is what the local authorities and communities agree. The growth of budget airlines and availability of cheap hotels and alcohol has fuelled the growth of stag and hen parties in cultural capitals from Dublin to Amsterdam, Krakow to Vilnius. More robust policing, tighter licensing and efforts to fill the hotel beds at weekends with a different market segment will all help to address the problem, but the destination first needs to agree that it is an issue that must be dealt with. Then the relevant authorities must take responsibility and insist that the originating market operators, the media and others take theirs, and contribute to change.[95]

Philanthropy and volunteering

Philanthropy and volunteering are social responses that are often triggered by travel; the travel experience can generate an impulse to put something back, to give back to the peoples and places visitors have encountered. The currencies of tourism are money and time; they are donated to the people and places which have been experienced through tourism, in part because travellers and holidaymakers recognise that they have more of both than most of the people they encounter in the destination. There is an impulse among returned tourists and travellers towards accepting some level of personal responsibility for 'their' destination. This responsibility sometimes takes the

---

95 For example Amsterdam in 2007–08 reduced the size of its red light district see www.digitaljournal.com/article/250264

form of donating to appeals for familiar destinations and sites, or establishing small charities when they return home; sometimes people realise that they have the skills and contacts to develop local tourism. Local initiatives in the hotel, meanwhile, may include fundraising for ambulances or the education of children – 48% of visitors arriving in the Gambia in 2001, a country with a high proportion of repeat visitors, were carrying gifts.[96] It is not unusual to see a middle-aged white couple sat at the side of the road talking with their taxi driver: they may have had the car shipped out to a bumster who has become a taxi driver and who will drive them round when they come on holiday each year. People-to-people aid is significant in the Gambia, as it is in other destinations where holidaymakers repeatedly return.

Travel philanthropy is best defined broadly as 'the donating of money, in-kind resources (office equipment, flights, accommodation) or time (mentoring or volunteering), occasioned by or facilitated by travel'.[97] Companies are increasingly encouraging and facilitating it, recognising that clients expect it, that staff take pride in companies that do this, and that it contributes to fulfilling the corporate social responsibility agenda. Research undertaken in 2009 identified £160 million raised for causes in destinations or in originating markets.[98] However, concerns are now being raised about increasingly popular charity challenges, which impose costs and other burdens on the experience destinations while raising funds for charities at home. In July 2010, the Lake District National Parks Authority was considering asking charities to cover some of the costs of the environmental damage done by charity events on Scafell Pike.[99]

Although Internet forums[100] report many examples of dissatisfied clients there is a tendency to be very forgiving of the travel companies and other organisations providing volunteering opportunities abroad, or so-called 'voluntourism'. They are generally given the benefit of the doubt because of the ostensibly philanthropic aims of the organisation, and dissatisfied volunteers rarely use the same criteria and methods that travellers and holiday-makers

---

96 Bah and Goodwin, unpublished research.

97 Goodwin, McCombes and Eckardt (2009): 4

98 Goodwin, McCombes and Eckardt (2009): 4; Hall and Brown (2006): 130

99 Goodwin, McCombes and Eckardt (2009): 66–70 and www.thirdsector.co.uk/News/FundraisingBulletin/1019618/Lake-District-National-Park-Authority-may-ask-part-challenge-profits/95C44D51AA8FA99C54783813F47E1CFE/?DCMP=EMC-FundraisingBulletin accessed 3 August 2010

100 There is a list at http://haroldgoodwin.blogware.com/blog/_archives/2011/2/11/4749386.html

use to claim recompense.[101] However, the situation with voluntourism is far from ideal. I have come across many instances of volunteers replacing local employees, of volunteers demanding transport and other resources, as well as reports of buildings being knocked down to be built again by the next group of volunteers or remaining unfinished, the promises to volunteers and communities left unfulfilled.

Volunteering is complex and it raises difficult questions about who benefits. The young gap-year volunteers, focused on their curriculum vitae, are likely to have different motivations and capabilities from a retired or career-break teacher or health worker with substantial experience and developed skills. However, altruism is rarely entirely disinterested: gap-year, retired or mid-career volunteers are all likely to feel good about their volunteering. Peopleandplaces[102] matches volunteers with work placements abroad and campaigns for responsible volunteering. The volunteers do not replace local labour, and every volunteer must meet all the costs of their volunteering so as to not impose on the community, with a minimum of 80% of the cost of the placement being spent in the host country. Each volunteer is part of an ongoing, sustainable project, where they talk with previous volunteers and are able to maintain contact afterwards, thus ensuring continuity. There is a long way to go to ensure responsible practice in the overseas volunteering sector. Not all volunteers who will work with children or vulnerable adults are screened, and host countries need to be more assertive about what they regard as acceptable and responsible practice.[103] Companies, NGOs and charities offering volunteering experiences abroad operate in very different ways, and the status of the organisation is no guarantee of responsible practice. Potential volunteers are well advised to remember the principle of *caveat emptor* and to enquire carefully about the practices of the organisation with which they intend to travel. One of the reasons why people volunteer is to contribute to the community, it is particularly important to ensure that the community, or at least the relevant part of it, has been consulted and their volunteering is welcome; ask whose idea was the project and who runs it.[104] I have come across

---

101 Goodwin, McCombes and Eckardt (2009): 6

102 I should declare an interest, I am non-exec Chair of People and Places founded to establish a new benchmark for responsible volunteering. It is how I would like to see all volunteering companies run. www.travel-peopleandplaces.co.uk

103 www.travel-peopleandplaces.co.uk/About.aspx?category=20 South Africa has guidelines. www.fairtourismsa.org.za/pdffiles/VoluntourismCodeofGoodPractice.pdf

104 There is a useful list of questions at http://www.travel-peopleandplaces.co.uk/About.aspx?category=20

examples of situations where volunteers have been unwelcome, subsequently discovering that the local teacher had been sacked to create a volunteering opportunity or where the local community asked for no more volunteers to be sent, since they were eating all their chickens.

Communities are rarely of one mind in their attitudes to tourism, but as Murphy pointed out a quarter of a century ago:

> Many destination area attractions are public property or public goods, and the hospitality needed for a memorable visit must come from members of the public as well as employees of the industry….. It is the citizen who must live with the cumulative outcomes of such developments and needs to have greater input into how his community is packaged and sold as a tourist product on the world market. [105]

There is a democratic deficit in the way most destinations are managed for tourism, with very limited opportunities for broad community engagement in decision making about tourism, too often the interests of local tourism businesses and their international partners prevail. In theory, the destination belongs to the people who live there, but theoretical ownership bestows very limited influence.[106] Tourism planning is usually in the hands of outsiders: the developers and investors, national governments and the development banks which fund the master plans. As Krippendorf said, 'the local population are regarded merely as landowners or as a reserve of labour, not as people entitled to participate in decision making'.[107]

Tourism may contribute to the growth in international understanding, it can also lead to 'mistrust, resignation and aggressive dissatisfaction'.[108] We can take some individual responsibility for this by the way that we choose to travel and the way that we behave, and we should expect operators in the originating market to take their responsibilities seriously too. In destinations responsibility has to be exercised through the local authorities: it is the elected councillors and officers and the other local authorities who have the power and must use it properly. Local residents can demand that they take responsibility; originating market operators can encourage them to take responsibility; political engagement is required. The destination belongs to the communities who live there.

---

105 Murphy (1985): 16
106 See for example Haywood (1988); Robinson (1999); Jamal and Fetz (1999)
107 Krippendorf (1982): 142
108 Krippendorf (1982): 142

References

Austen, J. (1813) *Pride and Prejudice*

Bah, A. and Goodwin, H. (2003) 'Improving access for the informal sector to tourism in The Gambia', Pro-Poor Working Paper 15, Pro-Poor Tourism, London.

Balomenou, N. (2003) 'The way Kavos, in Corfu, Greece is presented and marketed as a tourism destination and the impacts on the local community', unpublished MSc dissertation, University of Greenwich.

Baudelaire, Charles (1986): *The Painter of Modern Life and Other Essays*. New York and London: Da Capo Press.

Bosselman, F.M., Peterson, C.A. and McCarthy, C. (1999) *Managing Tourism Growth*, Washington, DC: Island Press.

Botton, de, A. (2002) *The Art of Travel*, London: Hamish Hamilton.

Bruner, E.M. (2001) 'The Maasai and the Lion King: authenticity, nationalism, and globalization in African tourism', *American Ethnologist*, **28**, (4), 881–908.

Bruner, E.M. and Kirshenblatt-Gimblett, B. (1994) 'Maasai on the lawn: tourist realism in East Africa', *Cultural Anthropology*, **9** (4), 435–470.

Chhabra, D., Healy, R. and Sills, E. (2003) 'Staged authenticity and heritage tourism', *Annals of Tourism Research*, **30** (3), 702–719.

Clifford, J. (1992) 'Travelling cultures', in L. Grossberg, C. Nelson and P.A. Treichler (eds), *Cultural Studies*, New York: Routledge, pp. 96–116.

Cohen, E. (1988) 'Authenticity and commoditization in tourism', *Annals of Tourism Research*, **15** (3), 371–386.

Cohen, E. (1989) 'Primitive and remote: hill tribe trekking in Thailand', *Annals of Tourism Research*, **16** (1), 30–61.

de Kadt, E. (1979) *Tourism – Passport to Development?*, New York: Oxford University Press

Doxey, G.V. (1976) 'When enough's enough: the natives are restless in Old Niagara', *Heritage Canada*, **2** (2), 26–27.

Fitton, M. (1995) 'Does our community want tourism? Examples from South Wales', in M.F. Price (ed.), *People and Tourism in Fragile Environments*, Chichester: Wiley, pp. 159–174.

Franklin, A. (2003) *Tourism: An Introduction*, London: Sage.

Gmelch, S.B. (2004) *Tourists and Tourism*, Long Grove, IL: Waveland Press.

Goodwin, H. (1998) 'Sustainable tourism and poverty elimination', discussion paper for the Department for the Environment, Transport and the Regions and the Department for International Development, London.

Goodwin, H.J., Kent, I.J., Parker, K.T. and Walpole, M.J. (1997a) *Tourism, Conservation and Sustainable Development: Vol. I, The Comparative Report*, London: Department for International Development.

Goodwin, H.J., Kent, I.J., Parker, K.T. and Walpole, M.J. (1997b) *Tourism, Conservation and Sustainable Development: Vol. IV, the South-East Lowveld, Zimbabwe*, London: Department for International Development.

Greenwood, D.J. (1989) 'Culture by the pound: An Anthropological perspective on tourism as a cultural commodity'. In VL Smith, *Hosts and Guests: The Anthropology of Tourism* (2nd edition.), (pp 171-185) Philadelphia: University of Pennsylvania Press

Haywood, K.M. (1988) 'Responsible and responsive tourism planning in the community', *Tourism Management*, **9** (2), 105–118.

Jamal, T. and Fetz, D. (1999) 'Community roundtables for tourism-related conflicts: the dialectics of consensus and process structures', *Journal of Sustainable Tourism*, **7** (3 & 4), 290–313.

Korte, B. and Muller, K.P. (1998) 'Unity in Diversity Revisited: Complex Paradoxes beyond Post-modernism' in *Unity in Diversity Revisited? British Literature and Culture in the 1990's*, Korte, B. and Muller, K.P. (eds), Tubingen: Gunter Narr Verlag.

Krippendorf, J. (1982) 'Towards new tourism policies', *Tourism Management*, **3** (3), 135-148

Krippendorf, J. (1987) *The Holiday Makers*, Oxford: Butterworth Heinemann.

Lowenthal, D.(1998) *The Heritage Crusade and the Spoils of History*, Cambridge: Cambridge University Press.

Mathieson, A. and Wall, G. (1992) *Tourism: Economic, Physical and Social Impacts*, Harlow: Longman.

Murphy, P.E. (1985) *Tourism: A Community Approach*, New York: Routledge.

Reisinger, Y. and Steiner, C.J. (2006) 'Reconceptualising object authenticity', *Annals of Tourism Research*, **33** (1), 65–86.

Rojek, C. and Urry, J. (eds) (1997) *Touring Cultures*, London: Routledge.

Said, E. (1983) *Orientalism*, London: Routledge.

Sassatelli, R. (2006) 'Responsibility and consumer choice: framing critical consumerism', in J. Brewer and F. Trentmann (eds), *Consuming Cultures, Global Perspectives, Historical Trajectories, Transnational Exchanges*, Oxford: Berg, pp. 219–250.

Sharpley, R. (2000) 'Tourism and sustainable development: exploring the theoretical divide', *Journal of Sustainable Tourism*, **8** (1), 1–19.

Sharpley, R. (2009) *Tourism Development and the Environment: Beyond Sustainability*, London: Earthscan

Smith, B. (ed.) (1977) *Hosts and Guests: An Anthropology of Tourism*, Philadelphia: University of Pennsylvania Press.

Tribe, J. (2005) *Runaway Tourism*, International Conference on Tourism Development and Planning (ATEI), Patras, Greece

Walpole, M.J. and Goodwin, H. (2001) 'Local attitudes towards conservation and tourism around Komodo National Park, Indonesia', *Environmental Conservation*, **28** (2), 160–166.

Wearing, S., Stevenson, D. and Young, T. (2010) *Tourist Cultures, Identity, Place and the Traveller*, London: Sage.

Wilson, D. (1993) 'Time and tides in the anthropology of tourism', in Hitchcock *et al.* (1993), pp. 32–47.

6 Economic Responsibility

Only connect the prose and the passion...[1]

E.M. Forster

There is a general assumption that there is positive economic impact from tourism, oft-claimed to be the world's largest industry. Economic benefits may include foreign exchange 'hard currency' earnings; taxation revenue; modernisation through infrastructure development and contact with the international economy; and increased local demand for goods and services, which creates business opportunities and employment. The adage 'it is not tourism until it is sold' is an important reminder that tourism is both an experience and a commercial activity. But there are also negative economic impacts to be considered.

The challenge is to ensure that tourism is used by the destination to contribute towards making it firstly, a better place to live in, and secondly, a better place to visit. Tourism is an export industry, which can exploit the destination or be used by people in the destination to improve their livelihoods. Responsible Tourism accepts that tourism is a consumer driven activity, purchased and provided in a very competitive market, a market in which the consumers (and the tour operators who purchase on their behalf) are generally more powerful than the producers (in the destinations). Tourism as an economic activity is likely to grow for the foreseeable future, despite the challenges of our finite world. Ironically those activities in destinations which are able to secure the highest prices are those which benefit from having secured access to a limited resource – for example, gorilla viewing in Rwanda, or where consumers purchase exclusivity in a resort or spa and the supply is controlled in order to maintain a premium price.

At Responsible Tourism's economic core is 'harnessing tourism for local economic development, for the benefit of communities and indigenous peoples'.[2] The central tenet of the Responsible Tourism movement is that all forms of tourism can tourism can be improved by taking responsibility

---

1   E.M. Forster, *Howards End*
2   Cape Town Conference (2002): 2

for the economic impacts of tourism – they can be made more economically sustainable by avoiding or reducing the negative impacts and maximising the positive ones. Travellers and holidaymakers, guides, excursion providers and attractions, accommodation and transport providers, tour operators can all can contribute to this. Employing local people on good terms and conditions, training them so as to ensure their progression and buying locally produced goods and services make a difference in the destination, with individual consumers and businesses able to make a significant difference. The chef at the Hotel des Milles Collines in Kigali, Rwanda, was unable to purchase jams made from local fruits for the hotel breakfast tables, so he worked with local women to create the product, and imported the jars on their behalf, exemplifying what an individual can contribute. Similarly, the holidaymaker who shuns the high-margin goods brought in from beyond the local area for sale in the hotel shop, and instead goes to meet with and buy from a local craft producer, makes a difference. He or she also has a more interesting experience. The hotel owner or manager who invites local craft producers to sell in the hotel on a rota provides another facility to the guests, contributes to the local economy and builds goodwill with the hotel's neighbours. None of this is particularly difficult and often it improves the destination experience. In each of these examples someone took responsibility to improve the local economic impact.

It is not always so simple, and it is not sufficient to look only at the positive impacts. If the purchase of crafts result in the loss of hardwood trees or endangers species, if tourism development on the beach denies access to fishermen, or a herdsman access to water, there will be negative environmental and economic impacts. Judging whether the wellbeing of a community has been enhanced though tourism is inherently more complex than considering the impacts at the individual or household level. In development processes, there are generally both winners and losers. Responsible Tourism must, therefore, require a net-benefit, triple-bottom-line, approach, and emphasise the importance of enabling access to the industry for those excluded from it.

Tourists create economic opportunities for tour operators and agents in originating markets. They operate in a competitive market where, for most products, supply comfortably exceeds demand – there are far more destinations in the world than there are people to travel to them. The consumers are the primary beneficiaries of that competition; it is a buyer's market. Tourism also presents advantages for destinations. There are no tariff barriers, other than visa charges imposed by the exporter, on the sale of tourism services.

There are opportunities for local producers to capture the full end-consumer value in the destination. When a tourist buys a locally made carpet in Nepal more of the value is captured in Nepal than if the carpet is purchased abroad. Tourism can bring infrastructure investment, and the means to pay for it, through foreign exchange earnings.

Aside from these very direct benefits, tourism is best understood as a market that creates demand for a wide range of goods and services which are not always obviously to do with tourism. It creates work for bakers and refuse collectors, demand for printing and plumbing, and a hundred other trades and services. By definition, tourists come from elsewhere to consume in a local economy. To the extent that tourism demand stimulates local production, it generates economic development.[3] Where tourists purchase locally produced craft, local production increases, linkages are greater, employment is increased and the multiplier will be higher. Where tourists are offered, and purchase, crafts imported into the area, because the quality is better or the margins for local traders are higher, the leakages are greater. The money is being spent in the local economy but it leaks straight out, particularly if the trader is sending money home or spending their earnings on imported goods.

The economic objectives of different stakeholders vary: entrepreneurs see business opportunities; communities gain employment; national governments and regional development agencies seek to maximise arrival numbers in order to grow the economy, and to maximise foreign exchange earnings and tax revenues. National governments place great emphasis on foreign exchange earnings, which can be used to repay foreign loans and purchase capital goods or arms,[4] and sometimes seek to rebalance the trade deficit on tourism by encouraging residents to holiday at home.[5] It is surprisingly rare for governments to calculate the net foreign exchange earnings from international arrivals by subtracting the import costs incurred by the sector from foreign currency revenues. There are, of course, other costs which arise from tourism.[6] Yield research in New Zealand found NZ$429 million (US$313 million) net financial benefit for central government. The same research found that for local government tourism was largely cost neutral and that in the

3   For the contrary view, see Judd (2006).

4   Tourism is widely regarded as the major source of the foreign currency that enabled the industrialisation of Spain through the import of capital goods, Harrison (1978): 156

5   For example in the UK, see above: 138

6   See for example Dwyer and Forsyth (2007); Jayawardena and Ramajeesingh (1989), and Jackson (2006).

'private sector many firms produce lower yields than other firms or sectors across the economy and compared with the opportunity cost of capital'.[7]

Tourism is an export industry. Tourists, domestic or international, are an export market for any local community. The consumption of the product occurs locally, but it is paid for with money from outside the locality, providing an additional market for goods and services which may be produced or supplied locally. Tourists bring money from abroad or from another geographical area of the domestic economy to the local market; their purchases are exports from the local economy. This can also be seen as a weakness, any export industry is dependent upon the maintenance of demand in a market which may be remote and capricious – the more so when the industry is dependent upon discretionary high value leisure spend, or where tourism is the mono-crop.[8]

Those Caribbean islands which were major producers of sugar and tobacco became dependent on tourism for foreign exchange revenues as changes in consumer preferences, and sugar beet subsidies, reduced demand for the Caribbean export staples. It can reasonably be argued that tourism is more fickle than the demand for sugar and that the product is not so fungible – not so mutually interchangeable – as sugar or tobacco, which can be exported to anywhere that there is demand, tourists have to be attracted to the Caribbean, which then is under a burden to prove its particular attractiveness to them over other destinations that offer palm trees, sun and sandy beaches.

Like any other monoculture, places which rely too heavily on tourism risk becoming dangerously dependent. Both modernisation and dependency, or under-development, theory have value for understanding the development processes which occur through tourism. Modernisation theory expresses the view that tourism brings development in its wake through integration into the international economy, and introduces modern and commercial values. Dependency or under-development theory argues that, to the contrary, the dependency of the industry on international arrivals traps the destination in under-development.[9]

Elements of both processes can coexist spatially and temporally. In the Gambia for example, tourism has brought dependency on export markets for the sale of a 'sun, sand and sea' product which is in oversupply, one where

---

7   Ministry of Tourism, Lincoln University, Tourism New Zealand and Tourism Industry Association (2007): 16, 28–29

8   Selwyn in Boissevain and Selwyn (2004): 57

9   For a discussion of these competing theoretical perspectives applied to tourism, see Harrison (1992): 8–11

producers are weak. However, the groundnut market, the Gambia's other export opportunity, is also one which trapped the Gambia in dependency: that industry has declined. Tourism has created the opportunity for the development of local accommodation, lodges, apartments and homestays, The flight-only options on the charter planes are important to Gambians for education, business and social purposes. They have contributed to the modernisation and diversification of the economy.

The flight-only option is one route through which the Gambia can differentiate itself from other sunny destinations. To the extent that a destination is able to differentiate the experience it offers to potential consumers, it can avoid commodifying its product and the resulting extreme competitiveness that results. This is extremely difficult, but not impossible, in the 'winter sun', and 'sun, sand and sea' markets within charter operating distance of the northern European originating markets. The Gambia, for example, is promoting the cultural experiences which it has to offer in order to stand out from the numerous other sunny destinations within five or six hours of northern Europe. Business in the sector is highly competitive. The fact that the traveller has to come to the destination is a risk – they may cease to come for reasons beyond the control of the destination – but it is also an opportunity for additional sales in the destination. Research in the Gambia in 2001 revealed that tourists were spending an average £25 per day in cash in the local economy and one third of that was going to the informal sector, but they were also leaving with an average of £23 unspent from the spending money that they had brought with them.[10]

As we are constantly reminded by the sector, travel and tourism occurs globally. This obscures the fact that neither the products nor the markets are global. The global marketplace is a myth: For example, McDonalds in India does not sell hamburgers; in Germany it sells beer; in Canada it sells lobster; and in Costa Rica it sells rice and beans.[11] Destinations are different one from another, and those which are undifferentiated face higher levels of competition. In addition, there is tremendous diversity between consuming cultures around the world. The jet engine, charters and the budget carriers have enabled more people to travel internationally but their choice about where to travel is shaped by cultural and historical preferences, the availability of transport (principally air routes) and the costs in time and money. The

10 Bah and Goodwin (2003): 19
11 http://trifter.com/practical-travel/budget-travel/mcdonald%E2%80%99s-strange-menu-around-the-world/ accessed 31 July 2010

effective demand, the number of people able and willing to purchase a holiday at the current price, is limited and potential travellers in different originating markets will have very different international destination priorities. Between 2000 and 2008, the global average annual growth in international arrivals was 3.8%. International arrivals grew by 1.9% in the Americas and 3.2% in Europe, 60% in Asia Pacific, 7.3% in Africa and 10.6% in the Middle East. International travel expenditure is still dominated by Europe, which has seven of the world's top 10 source markets. The United States is the second largest market, and China, fifth. International arrival figures reveal that in 1990, 80.5% of all international travel was intra-regional; in 2008 the figure was still 78.4%.[12] The growth in international arrivals and the focus on the headline figures distorts our view of the market; domestic travel is far more significant in most, although not all, destinations.[13] Responsible Tourism development requires a focus on domestic and regional tourism, and it is similarly imperative to remember that, for the vast majority of travellers, the length of their trip is constrained by flights booked in advance and their holiday entitlement. If a tourist is to spend additional time in one area of a destination or region they will probably spend less elsewhere. If tourists are passing by, even in large numbers, they are unlikely to stop, unless the visit can be accommodated within their time budget and their pre-planned travel arrangements.

Economists use a range of different methodologies[14] to determine the economic impacts of travel and tourism; most famously, Tourism Satellite Accounts (TSAs) are used to demonstrate the importance of the sector to government. [15] TSAs aggregate the value of expenditure by tourists and the value of economic activity by tourism and tourism-related business. The more of the tourist spend that recirculates locally, the greater the value of that initial tourist spend to the local economy. Economists measure this recirculation effect and calculate multipliers – the higher the propensity to consume locally produced goods and services, the higher the multiplier. Generally the multiplier is used in macro-economics to enable the calculation of aggregate demand impacts. This methodology has been widely used in tourism to demonstrate the scale of demand and the importance of the sector. Those B&Bs and hotels which serve a local breakfast in the New Forest are contributing to the incomes of farmers,

---

12   UNWTO (2009): 10

13   In small and economically poor countries those who can afford a holiday often prefer to travel internationally rather than domestically.

14   There is a useful summary in Mitchell and Ashley (2010): 109–116

15   Eurostat/ OECD/WTO/UN (2008); Libreros (2006)

butchers, bakers and millers.[16] Those who use local tradesman, plumbers, electricians, builders and decorators are also increasing the local multiplier. Expenditure by and on behalf of tourists in a local economy increases the aggregate level of demand. Multipliers tend to be higher, the larger and more diverse the economy for which they are calculated, because there is a greater likelihood that the direct and indirect tourism revenues will be respent in such an economy and that the induced expenditure, that of employees in the sector, will be spent on goods and services from within the local economy if it is large and diverse. A small island with a limited range of agricultural production and a limited craft sector is not able to sustain a multiplier as high as that of a destination such as Turkey where much of the accommodation is locally owned and built with locally sourced materials, where the tourists consume locally produced food and drinks, and where local crafts satisfy the demands of tourists.

The language of leakages and linkages is more useful than that of multipliers in thinking about responsibly managing the economic impacts of tourism: the multiplier is merely a measure of the extent to which tourism expenditure recirculates in the local economy. The multiplier increases when the leakage is reduced and linkages are increased. The larger the proportion of the goods and services consumed by tourists which are produced locally the greater the local economic benefit and the larger the multiplier. Leakages occur whenever goods and services are imported to fulfil the demands of tourists, or businesses that sell to tourists.

The trend from some source markets towards more experiential holidays – holidays in which there is a greater propensity for holidaymakers to consume local food and beverages, to prefer locally produced souvenirs, to purchase from local craftspeople and to stay in small locally owned accommodation increases linkages and therefore the multiplier. In general, an import substitution strategy, where goods and services imported into the local economy to satisfy tourism demand are replaced with local goods,[17] will reduce leakages so long as the goods or services are competitive in quality and price and meet demand. The Gambia is Good project has successfully substituted locally grown fruit and vegetables for previously imported produce, thus spreading the benefits of tourism beyond the tourism area to the benefit the rural poor with no access to tourism.[18] Tour operators and accommodation providers

---

16 www.thenewforest.co.uk/breakfast.html
17 See for example Saville (2001) on Humla.
18 Sharpley, (2009b) and Mitchell and Faal (2007)

can make a contribution by sourcing locally, encouraging their suppliers to do so too, and enabling their guests and passengers to buy local.[19]

The costs of an export industry include marketing, transport and retailing of the product to the consumer; of the value of a coffee sold in Starbucks in London or New York, only a tiny fraction reaches the producer. Even with fairly traded coffee, only a few pence of the retail price reach the producer, and most of the premium is captured in the distribution chain.[20] Tourism is an export industry: people from outside the local economy are attracted to spend money locally. Marketing, transport and retailing entails leakage, whatever the export – and tourism often creates opportunities of additional linkages when tourism businesses and tourists purchase in the local economy. The leakage critique of the tourism industry[21] is persistent, but overstated. It is unreasonable to identify airfares, distribution, sales and marketing costs as leakages; although it is possible to reduce leakages by using a national or local airline but this makes sense only if the airline is not subsidised by destination taxpayers. Similarly it is generally more economically efficient to use businesses in the originating markets for sales and marketing.

The repatriation of earnings by employees or profits by owners and shareholders remains an issue, but it is often more complex than it appears. The repatriation of profits may be considerably less significant than the loss of sales value which occurs when the payments are received offshore and the company in the destination invoices a lesser amount to the offshore company. If expatriate labour is employed and the earnings are repatriated there is leakage. When Nile valley workers are employed in Sharm el Sheik and send most of their earnings home that is leakage from the local, but not from the national economy.[22] Migrant labour is also widespread in the industry – in London bars, hotels in the British countryside and in the hospitality sector in Arabia, to name just a few examples. Many Arab countries now have policies designed to increase the proportion of non-expatriate labour employed in the tourism industry, and some businesses are committed to ensuring career progression for local employees. The private sector can make a significant contribution

19   Schwartz et al. (2008)

20   See Harford (2006): 33, 'Cafédirect paid farmers a premium of between 40p and 55p per pound of coffee. That relatively small premium can nearly double the income of a farmer But since the typical cappuccino is made with just a quarter-ounce of coffee beans, the premium paid to the farmers should translate into a cost increase for Costa of less than a penny a cup.'

21   See for example www.leaplocal.org/leakage-from-tourism.html accessed 6 August 2010

22   Goodwin (2007): 68–70

by training for career progression within the company and prioritising the employment of local labour. However, it would be irresponsible to create a situation where earnings for hotel staff or guides, wages and tips, are greater than those of doctors and head teachers. As in Cuba, where for many years the tourist peso has been worth 20–25 times the local peso – and therefore a well-tipped barman comparatively earns a fortune. Terms and conditions of employment in the tourism sector are an issue, but they need to be relevant and realistic in the local context. It is responsible to provide locally relevant advice about tipping by for example ensuring that travellers know what a local schoolteacher earns.

The tourism sector has significant numbers of lifestyle businesses, owned and managed to provide comfortable sustainable livelihoods rather than to maximise profit.[23] Often the businesses identify strongly with the destinations, the experiences they provide and the activities which they facilitate, and are consequently more likely to take a responsible approach. They may be less 'professionally' run and they may welcome the quiet off-season, and frustrate destination marketers seeking to drive up visitor numbers – since they have reached individual sustainability and do not wish their businesses to grow. Whether lifestyle businesses are good or bad for destination depends on circumstances, and local views about the purpose of tourism. If tourism is seen as an additional income that should not be permitted to change the area, lifestyle businesses may be seen as a good thing; if by failing to create enough jobs, they contribute to young people drifting away, they may be seen as undesirable.

If demand begins to outstrip supply, an increase in demand for tourism goods and services may cause local inflation. Residents in the gateway towns of Komodo, in the Lesser Sunda Islands of Indonesia, reported price increases as a negative consequence of tourism. Where supply is inelastic, for instance, with hotel rooms, increased demand will generally result in price increases, although they affect tourists rather than the local community. An increase in the size of the local market for souvenirs may suck in craft items from outside of the local economy. Imports which undercut local producers but provide additional margins for retailers, whether in the local shops or in a craft market, are also harmful. The growth in the tourism economy can also attract migrant labour, either because of shortages of labour locally, or because it is easier or

---

23 Although research in New Zealand found no evidence that lifestyle businesses had lower financial yields than businesses with a stronger commercial focus (Ministry of Tourism et al.2007: 1).

less expensive to bring in skilled labour from outside the area than to train locally; occasionally, local attitudes may deem tourism jobs inferior. Tourism honeypots may also attract informal sector traders from further afield, increasing local competition.

The increased demand which tourism represents can therefore have negative impacts in a local economy. Tourism may also reduce access to the natural resources where for example local fishermen are no longer able to access the beach and marine resources, or displace people when land increases in value because of tourism demand. Sometimes existing community members achieve a good price and relocate or develop a tourism business. But it is a sobering experience to meet a family, in a beautiful bay on Palawan, who sold their land for US$100 to a local entrepreneur, who now has title and will benefit from resort development there, leaving the original owners landless. Higher land or property values benefit those who sell, on Palawan or in a Cotswold village, but the community and future generations lose access to housing, land for farming or beaches and marine resources. An asset can be sold only once by a member of the local community – although with time the purchaser may become a part of the community.

Economic impacts depend very much on what type of tourists visit the destination. The choices made by National Tourist Boards (NTBs) about target markets will, unless they are very incompetent, exert considerable influence on who is attracted and who arrives in the destination. Different market segments will purchase different accommodation, patronise different attractions, retailers and food and beverage providers. For tourism businesses, the profile of visitors being attracted to the destination is of considerable concern. The influence of established businesses on NTBs, exacerbated by the increasingly popular match-funding of marketing campaigns, advantages larger and already successful businesses in established areas – areas which, local residents may think – are already receiving too many visitors, from the perspective of local residents.

It is still relatively rare for destinations to have reliable information about the value of particular tourist demographics. The spending patterns of different groups of tourists often vary significantly and the results are often counter-intuitive. New Zealand is looking to increase visitor spend by attracting tourists beyond the peak season and by more closely targeting those likely to be satisfied by the experiences the country has to offer.[24] New Zealand's yield

---

24   New Zealand Ministry of Tourism (2007) 2015:14

research revealed that backpackers generate higher residual income because they spend their money in sectors that have higher than average return-on-investment such as youth hostels and recreational activities; camping tourists spend a substantial amount on rental vehicles which are also high yield. Independent travellers and coach tourists generated lower residual income.[25] This does not mean that hotels in New Zealand are necessarily unprofitable, and they would obviously argue for further international marketing to attract independent travellers and coach tourists. Research conducted in Puerto Princesa in the Philippines in 1998 revealed that Filipino tourists arriving on the Airbus from Manila were spending more per day than the international tourists, although the international tourists and backpackers were spending more in the destination because they stayed longer.[26] A lack of reliable data on the spending patterns of different tourists hinders responsible policy making as stereotypical generalisations about the 'value' of different kinds of tourists are often locally inaccurate.

The capacity of a destination to manage the development of tourism, to maximise positive and minimise negative impacts, is a function of its competitive advantage and the strength of its local governance, Can the local authority, for example, manage the growth in the supply of accommodation to avoid both shortages and oversupply, or to develop sufficient appropriate skilled labour locally to discourage inward migration? It may be that slow and steady growth in demand for small scale accommodation will result in more of it being owned locally or by incoming owner operators who settle. Rapid externally financed investment tends to result in ownership and control being outside of the community. Where the business is locally owned it is more likely that profits will be reinvested or spent locally.

Master-planning is still relatively common in tourism funded by international development banks and development agencies. The emphasis is on infrastructure investment – airports, ports, cruise handling facilities, resorts, hotels and major attractions – intended to increase international arrivals, to grow the sector and create employment and tax revenues. The expectation is that infrastructure investment will be funded by loans to the public and private sector serviced and repaid from foreign exchange revenues. The master plan and strategy are generally developed by consultants working for national governments, funded by loans or grants, consultants who will identify bank-

---

25 Ministry of Tourism/Lincoln University/Tourism New Zealand/Tourism Industry Association (2007): 25–26

26 Unpublished consultancy research, Goodwin, 1998.

able projects with a market justification. However, many plans are not implemented because they 'are too complex, financially impractical, and somewhat disconnected from the institutional arrangements of particular destinations… The process of master-planning seems rarely to generate a sustainable consensus among the stakeholders about objectives and strategy sufficient to permit successful implementation.'[27] Achieving sufficient consensus amongst the stakeholders to secure change is a major challenge. In the 1990s, Malta attempted to reposition itself as a cultural heritage destination, amid growing awareness of the need to conserve the island's ecology and cultural heritage. However, it struggled, with factors constraining change including inertia, the cost of intervention and opposition from entrenched business interests.[28]

As with the issues of social sustainability, it is clear that a responsible intervention needs to be based on a sound understanding of the dynamics of the local situation.

Oversupply

The tourism sector is not isolated from developments in other industries nationally and internationally. Leisure and business travel is vulnerable to economic recession and cuts in government expenditure that reduce demand. In Ireland, the industry's vulnerability was increased by government intervention, which encouraged oversupply. Between 2004 and 2008 the number of available hotel rooms in Dublin increased 38%, from 12,800 to 17,700.[29] Between 1995 and 2008, the room stock increased by 211%, and, at the peak of the boom in 1998, 27 hotels opened – more than two per week. This hotel building boom was fuelled by EU grants and tax breaks for hotel construction in designated urban renewal areas.[30]

Average room rates were flat in Ireland between 2000 and 2008, but in real terms they fell 75% in the same period. Hotels had to cut rates to maintain occupancy and revenue per available room fell 33%. Since 2008, prices have declined severely, 26% year on year to 2009 alone.[31] A report by Bacon & Asso-

---

27 Yasarata et al. (2010): 346 and discussion 346–347
28 As identified in Foxell and de Trafford (2010)
29 Estimates are based on information from the CSO's Country of Residence Survey (CRS) and Fáilte Ireland's Survey of Overseas Travellers and the Visitor Attitudes Survey published by Research & Policy Development, Fáilte Ireland, October 2009
30 McManus (2001): 112
31 Bacon (2009): 25–27

ciates has concluded that the hotel sector is now insolvent, that the new-hotel sector has been insolvent since 2005, and that since 2002 new hotels have on average been insolvent from construction. Oversupply and weaker demand has produced a deep crisis. With an oversupply of hotels rooms and the impact of the recession the country has seen the emergence of 'zombie hotels'. These are hotels owned by banks which have foreclosed on the developers: although bankrupt, they must be kept open to maintain capital allowances, and avoid a tax liability due to a clawback of allowances already paid out by government. The problem of oversupply is not being addressed and, as prices are pushed down to non-viable levels, insolvency spreads through the industry.

Of a total of 59,000 hotel rooms in Ireland, approaching a quarter needs to be closed urgently, varying according to which forecast of future demand is used. This is a consequence of falling demand and oversupply. Yet 15,600 rooms have been introduced since 2005. As hotels cut prices to maintain occupancy and cash flow, competitors follow and prices spiral downwards. The impact of the recession and the decline in demand has been significantly exacerbated in Ireland by the growth in the bed stock as more and more investors sought to benefit from the destination in a 'tragedy of the commons' exacerbated by government taxes and subsidies. As Bacon & Associates say:

> ... the potential for excess capacity to undermine the sector is a classic market failure – the potential downside would be borne by the whole sector including the existing hotels while the upside would accrue to the investor in new stock. Excess investment is the inevitable result of such a situation, particularly when further promoted by planning considerations and the easy availability of debt.[32]

Bacon & Associates' report concludes that failure to foreclose damages the long-term interests of the hotel and tourism sectors: the excess supply needs to be taken out of the market.[33]

This is an example of a tourism sector crisis generated by a construction boom based on subsidised supply-side factors, a classic 'tragedy of the commons' scenario where individual businesses seek benefit at the expense of the group and act with irresponsible consequences – just like the mayor I spoke to in Greece.[34] It may be argued that this is simply market economics: inves-

---

32 Bacon (2009): 44

33 Bacon (2009): ii–v. The report suggests that on the debt to value ratios there has been no justification for new rooms since 2001 (p. 37)

34 See above page 18

tors see an opportunity and take it. It is irresponsible in this case because the government has distorted the market. It is a tragedy of the commons because when supply outstrips demand all may become unsustainable. The immediate losers in Ireland were institutional, although the victims of the economic crisis, occasioned in part by the unsustainable boom in property development, were those made redundant or who had their wages and benefits cut. They had not caused the boom, nor would they have been significant beneficiaries of it. They were the major victims of the bust exacerbated by irresponsible subsidised lending and investment.

Where loans are taken out by the economically poor, the impact of irresponsible lending is more immediately damaging. Kuelap, an impressive Chachapoyan archaeological site dating from AD 800, is a slowly emerging destination in northern Peru. Only 30 years ago it took two months to walk there; it is now accessible by road and will one day rival Machu Picchu, which is 600 years younger. In the early 1990s, a Peruvian bank provided a loan to a group of local farmers in Maria, adjacent to Kuelap, to build a small hotel. The loan was apparently secured against their farms and the farmers had been assured that the bank would bring tourists. Visiting shortly after the hotel had been opened, I was there when the proud new owners realised the gap between the loan repayments and their revenues from guests.[35] It was a sobering experience to watch as the realisation dawned of the scale of the problem and their intractable indebtedness. The same bank had funded a further 10 households to develop guest accommodation on the road to the mountain top archaeological site, creating an oversupply which undermined the financial sustainability of the properties and making the borrowers very vulnerable to foreclosure. The bank has created oversupply in a very limited market. Beware of banks offering to bring tourists.

All-inclusives

All-inclusives are attractive to holidaymakers concerned about the value of their currency and whether or not they will be able to afford to buy a beer in the destination. In the UK market in 2011, a cashless all-inclusive holiday is alluring. There is no need to worry about the cost of meals and activities and the booze is free at the point of consumption. For families an all-inclusive holiday removes the stress of children wanting spending money for ice creams,

---

35 Community engagement in tourism development around Kuelap has been written up by Wood (2005): 11

drinks and activities. All-inclusive products are also attractive to agents as their commission earnings reflect the higher initial spend. Back in the 1960s, all-inclusives were popular in the British market because of sterling's weakness, and booking an all-inclusive made the government-imposed £50 limit[36] on spending money more tolerable. Since the economic crisis of 2008, there has been rapid growth in all-inclusives outbound from the UK, and they are sold in most originating markets. The older traveller from Canada, for example, goes to all-inclusive resorts in Cuba to escape the winter. The range of all-inclusive holidays is very broad, including purpose-built resort complexes and theme parks.[37] All-inclusives are understandably popular with consumers, and consequently with tour operators and agents.

Yet all-inclusives are often criticised. It is frequently argued that the spending which might have benefited local communities in the destination is controlled by the tour operator and may never reach the local producers. Another criticism is of the tourists' isolation from the local community – although as we saw in the previous chapter there are some forms of hedonistic and licentious tourism from which local communities may prefer to be isolated. More traditional products, such as luxury hotels offering full-board and half-board packages, also discourage guests from venturing far from the hotel, but local communities express concern about not being able to access tourists, who have very little incentive to leave their all-inclusive oasis. Some commentators argue that whilst the enclave character of an all-inclusive may be a response to harassment, it can also create resentment and exacerbate the problem.[38] Swarbrooke provocatively asks whether all-inclusive and self-contained resorts are the new apartheid, since they may have been built on land from which the original local community was forcibly displaced. Enforcing the separation of tourists and local communities, he argues, gives 'greater rights to the immigrant tourists than to the indigenous community'.[39]

All-inclusives are not new. Early package holidays to Spain were often all-inclusive; facilitated by the easing of restrictions on charter flights in 1960 and loans from British operators for infrastructure development. Prices were keen and growth was rapid. There had been holiday camps in Britain in the 1930s[40] and full-board has always been an option in hotels. Club Med

36   Using the RPI this equates to £694 in 2009. See www.measuringworth.com
37   Swarbrooke (1999): 330–333
38   Chambers and Airey (2001): 112
39   Swarbrooke (1999): 332
40   The first Butlins opened in Skegness in 1936

developed the concept globally in the 1950s. The original Club Méditerranée proposition was that the guests paid one price in advance for their holiday that covered accommodation, food, drink, entertainment and activities, tips and airport transfers. The first luxury all-inclusive was established in Jamaica in the mid-1970s.[41] In Jamaica, in particular, this model has been profitable and all-inclusives have prospered.[42]

The stereotypical all-inclusives is sold on price: they offer a cheap holiday and consequently often have a down-market image. However, the concept has diversified. There are luxury cruise products offering very high staff-to-client ratios, five-star services and yachting style which are also all-inclusive. There are exclusive, all-inclusive honeymoons, and all-inclusive skiing and scuba diving. The traditional African game safari is one of the most exclusive of any all-inclusive holidays; even if the guests visit a craft market, the operator will have transported them there. Enclave tourism,[43] as typified in the all-inclusive holiday, isolates tourists from other tourism businesses, restaurants, bars and activity providers, restricting the opportunities for the tourists' spend to reach small enterprises and sole traders in the local economy; discretionary in-destination spend is reduced and even the sightseeing trips may be controlled.

The case against all-inclusives is persuasive, sufficiently so for the Gambia briefly to ban them.[44] However, circumstances alter cases. Sometimes, tourists' behaviour is perhaps best contained within the walls of a resort; enclaving may be the best way of containing tourism pollution. It may also make it possible to attract tourists to destinations that are not otherwise able to draw in significant volumes. For the economic development of local communities, through the creation of employment and enterprise, the key issue is the extent of the local economic linkages. An all-inclusive that employs local people to provide activities and entertainment, sells local beers, spirits and juices, makes local ice cream, encourages the development of local crafts and markets them within its walls, sources its table linen and uniforms from local women's co-operatives, helps farmers to develop their agriculture and guarantees a market, recruits and trains local staff to fill management positions... this is a very different proposition. It is important that we look at the impacts of the

---

41   Issa and Jayawardena (2003) and Chambers and Airey (2001)

42   Chambers and Airey (2001)

43   'Tourism enclaving' refers to a process of the spatial and social segregation of tourists from residents', Schmid (2008): 105

44   Scheyvens (2002): 169–170 – the ban lasted October 1999 to December 2000 because of concern about the loss of tourism to competitors.

all-inclusive enterprise as a whole and that we do not focus solely on the form and marketing strategy; particular all-inclusive products should be judged on their local net impacts. Stereotyping leads to poor decision-making.

Community-based tourism

Community-based tourism or CBT, is a form of tourism that enjoys widespread and pernicious support. It, too, should be judged on its outcomes. CBT has been promoted as a means of bringing economic development to rural communities for three decades and it enjoys continuing popularity with donors, despite the absence of evidence for its efficacy. CBT has been so popular that it has rarely been subjected to critical review, and its continuing popularity is a consequence of a failure to monitor and report outcomes. Donors have been content that the lodge is built; it matters not whether it provides sustainable livelihoods. Back in 1992, Butler argued 'for rational, objective evaluation of the merits and problems of all forms of tourism' and pointed out that alternative tourism initiatives often 'penetrate further into the personal space of residents' and 'expose often fragile resources to greater visitation'. Their proponents need to be able to demonstrate the positive impacts of the initiatives and to be candid about negative impacts.[45] Butler's words of caution ought to be heeded; not all forms of alternative or appropriate tourism are necessarily responsible.

CBT is a concept used flexibly, but in the literature it is generally used to refer to 'tourism owned and/or managed by communities and intended to deliver wider community benefit'; the term is applied to community tourism enterprises that are designed to benefit 'a wider group than those employed in the initiative'.[46] The large majority of CBT initiatives are lodges, with donor funds being secured for the purchase of materials and to fund the NGO or other agency that will develop the lodge with a community. The community provides free labour, in return for eventual employment in the lodge and a community benefit. Donor tend to favour this approach because the community is investing in the project: it is making an in-kind contribution by providing unpaid labour. There is perhaps an assumption that the labour of the economically poor is free, and a lack of recognition that investing their time in building a lodge means that they are unable to gather food or engage in subsistence agriculture. If the investment does not pay off in earnings, they have been robbed of livelihood. The community takes all the risk.

---

45 Butler (1994): 46 and 39
46 Goodwin and Santilli (2009): 4

This would not matter if CBT projects were successful. They are certainly successful for NGOs and donors in that they get funded and are built. Unfortunately there is little evidence that they deliver for communities who rarely, if ever, gain sustainable livelihoods, let alone secure any return on their investment in construction and training. In my experience, it is rare for those working with the economically poor or with small enterprises to recognise the opportunity cost of participating in meetings and training where the donors and NGOs are likely to be the only people in the room being paid to be there.[47] Reviews by Mitchell and Muckovsky, ResponsibleTravel.com and Conservation International suggest that average bed occupancies of CBT projects are close to 5% and that most fail once the funding ceases. This is most commonly because of poor market access and governance.[48] An extensive search by Goodwin and Santilli identified only six CBT projects that were economically sustainable and two of those were joint ventures – many were still donor dependent.[49] The research also identified significant collective community earnings generated by non-CBT initiatives.[50] Donors should expect reports on the outcomes of the projects they fund and those that implement them should be held to account. CBT is a good idea, but there is little evidence that it works.

Given this clear track record of failure, one wonders why people continue to build lodges. There are more viable alternatives. In La Yunga in Bolivia the CBT lodge attracted just 60 visitors in a year. After the implementing NGO had withdrawn, the community conceived of and developed a day walking trail primarily for the local market using the lodge only to provide lunches. They made a good return on their investment, without any donor or NGO assistance.[51] Where communities are able to find a market, for example through a commercial operator, they are more likely to be successful.[52] One can only hope that NGOs, donors and other proponents of CBT think to place this, and other critical success factors to such projects, higher up their lists of priorities when planning their activities. It is irresponsible not to be concerned with the

---

47   Although they may be paid travel and provided with lunch, the time is rarely recompensed. It is, after all, an in-kind contribution.

48   Quoted in Goodwin and Santilli (2009): 4

49   Goodwin and Santilli (2009): 7. The research sought to identify as many successes as possible.

50   Baltit Fort 60%, Manda Wilderness Lodge 30% and Yachana Lodge 60% – Goodwin and Santilli (2009): 6

51   Goodwin and Santilli (2009): 12

52   See for example www.villageways.com

outcomes, particularly since the investment in the projects that is demanded by the donors of the communities; at the moment, it is only the communities that risk becoming the real losers.

Poverty reduction through tourism

In 1998 the British Department for International Development (DFID) commissioned a discussion paper on Tourism and Poverty Elimination in the context of the Millennium Development Goals.[53] The potential of tourism for poverty reduction[54] had not previously been championed by a government development agency, but following further work commissioned from Deloitte,[55] during which the term Pro-poor tourism (PPT) was coined, DFID briefly championed the approach. Pro-poor tourism won support at the UN in 1999, at the Seventh Session of the Commission on Sustainable Development. The idea was subsequently taken up by UNWTO and the Dutch development agency SNV.[56]

Pro-poor tourism, echoing the concept of pro-poor growth, was defined as tourism which brings net benefits to the economically poor. The Pro-Poor Tourism Partnership[57] asserted from the beginning that any form of tourism could be pro-poor: all that was required was that the economically poor must be the beneficiaries, not the objects, of tourism.[58] Again, measuring the outcomes for the target groups – reporting the net benefits for the economically poor (however that is locally defined) is essential.

Many involved from the start have been aware of the fate of CBT and ecotourism, popular ideas that have both failed to deliver what they promised (we shall turn to ecotourism in the next chapter). The PPT research was published online in order to share findings and to encourage reporting. As Scheyvens recognised in 2007, the various approaches to PPT adopted by development agencies, 'do not share the same vision of poverty reduction through tourism'

---

53 Goodwin (1998)

54 It has long been discussed by tourism academics, see for example de Kadt (1979) and Harrison (1992)

55 Bennett, Roe and Ashley (1999)

56 UNCSD (1999), WTO (2002, 2004), by 2004 the approach had been narrowed to focus on seven mechanisms, the market and livelihoods orientation all but disappeared.

57 The PPT partnership comprised Ashley, Goodwin and Roe, see Ashley, Roe and Goodwin (2001)

58 PPT is not the same as poorism, see Goodwin (2009)

as that of the PPT Partnership.[59] Many of those who adopted the language, both amongst the funders and the implementers, continued with business as usual. PPT was co-opted to the cause of CBT and ecotourism, and, with little engagement with the private sector, these approaches have continued to fail.[60] The failures of bad PPT approaches are clear: 'Neither the practitioners nor the funders have been willing to account neither for the expenditure of development funds nor the use of the valuable time of the economically poor in receiving training or participating in implementing projects.'[61] Too often, those involved in PPT schemes fail to calculate the net benefits of the work – whereas this is exactly what must be done to determine who the actual beneficiaries are and to ensure that the negative impacts are taken into account.[62] The PPT Partnership saw tourism as an additional livelihood opportunity for communities rather than as alternative; it was important that tourism fitted with existing livelihoods and that PPT was developed in thriving destinations, where tourists already existed as an additional local market for the goods and services of the economically poor. It was never intended that tourism take on the whole economic burden of lifting communities out of poverty.

As Harrison has argued '...PPT projects have simply not delivered benefits, or adequate benefits, to the poor, and ... the term 'pro-poor' tourism is a misnomer'.[63] Despite there being some obvious truth in this – demonstrated by the failure of many schemes – there are still very few published examples of the outcomes of initiatives, without which the efficacy of the approach cannot be judged.[64] In the PPT Partnership's 2005 and 2006 Annual Register, we called for examples which could demonstrate net benefits for the economically poor. Yet very few came. In 2007, we wrote in the editorial: '...we still do not have enough examples of initiatives with clear demonstrable impacts ... we lack case studies which demonstrate the mainstreaming of tourism and poverty reduction strategies'.[65] We still lack those examples, because

---

59   Scheyven (2007): 243.

60   See for example the critique by Harrison (2008) and Goodwin's response in Third World Quarterly (2008) and Goodwin (2009).

61   Goodwin (2008a): 58

62   This approach drew on earlier work on tourism and livelihoods. See for example Ashley (2000). Tao and Wall (2009) have argued that when tourism is introduced into a community, it is important that it complements rather than displaces existing activities.

63   Harrison (2008): 860–861

64   Saville (2001); Bah and Goodwin (2003); Goodwin (2007) and Harrison and Schipani (2007).

65   PPT Partnership (2007): 1 and Mitchell and Ashley (2010): 27. The PPT Partnership no longer publishes an Annual Register for want of documented examples to include.

practitioners have not been required by the funders to prove the efficiency or efficacy of their interventions.[66] There has been a lack of accountability and of responsibility. Pro-poor tourism, as an idea, is a good and necessary one. Yet we are still living in hope for its widespread implementation in a responsible manner.

Only connect

If there is one thing that these examples should teach us, it is that tourism will not necessarily bring development to a country or region. Hotels and resorts can be developed, profits can be made and tourist arrivals can grow without economic development occurring. It is possible to develop tourism products without local economic development[67] – indeed some forms of tourism in wild and remote areas are perhaps best organised in that way. For tourism to bring local economic development there needs to be extensive local economic linkages, employment, increasingly skilled employment, and dependency needs to be avoided.

The tourism sector needs to be judged not by demand but by its effectiveness in providing livelihoods, contributing to the local economy and the net benefits to destinations. Size is not the real issue. It is the impacts of the industry that matter. Sharpley has recently suggested looking at more broadly at the flow of benefits to the destination.[68] This approach has the great merit of putting local communities and their environment at the heart of the calculation and placing the emphasis on net local benefit, where the negative socio-cultural and environmental costs are included in the assessment. Tourism should be judged against other opportunities for economic development, destination by destination and business by business, and the judgement needs to be based on net impacts including the socio-cultural and environmental impacts. Tourism is often the development option of last resort, selected when there is nothing else. We should not be surprised when in those circumstances it fails.

In *Howards End*, E.M. Forster writes about the Wilcoxes, an Edwardian business family and Margaret's efforts to help build 'the rainbow bridge that

---

66   Goodwin (2008a): 57

67   See for example Sharpley (2009a): 178

68   He suggests focusing on the different capitals used in livelihoods analysis at the destination level. Sharpley (2009a) 180–183.

should connect the prose in us with the passion. Without it we are meaningless fragments, half monks, half beasts, unconnected arches that have never joined into a man.'[69] With a degree of responsibility, business can address the issues of poverty and development, and increase its contribution to making better places for people to live in. Every year in the Responsible Tourism Awards[70] we see inspiring examples of tourism businesses which are maximising their contribution to the local economy by employing local people, training them for more senior roles, sourcing goods and services locally, encouraging their visitors to spend in the local economy, mentoring and growing local businesses and through their own and their clients' philanthropy. Tourism must connect the power of business with some passion, and a broad responsibility agenda.

---

69 Forster (1910) Howards End, Chapter 22

70 www.responsibletourismawards.com. Take a look at Nihiwatu in Indonesia, Guludo in Mozambique and Rivertime Resort and Ecolodge, Laos, three successful businesses which are making a big difference to the livelihoods of their employees and communities. There are many more.

References

Ashley, C. (2000) 'The Impacts of Tourism on Rural Livelihoods: Namibia's Experience', Working Paper 128, ODI, London.

Ashley, C., Roe, D. and Goodwin, H. (2001) *Pro-Poor Tourism Strategies: Making Tourism Work for the Poor*, London: PPTI, Pro-Poor Tourism.

Ashley, C., Goodwin, H., McNab, D., Scott, M. and Chaves, L. (2006) *Making Tourism Count for the Local Economy in the Caribbean*, London: Pro-Poor Tourism and the Caribbean Tourism Organisation.

Bacon, P. (2009) *Over-Capacity in the Irish Hotel Industry and Required Elements of a Recovery Programme*, Wexford: Peter Bacon Associates. Available at www.ihf.ie/documents/ HotelStudyFinalReport101109.pdf

Bah, A. and Goodwin, H. (2003) 'Improving access for the informal sector to tourism in The Gambia', Pro-Poor Working Paper 15, Pro-Poor Tourism, London.

Boissevain, J. (ed.) (1996) *Coping with Tourists: European Reactions to Mass Tourism*, Oxford: Berghahn.

Boissevain, J. and Selwyn, T. (2004) *Contesting the Foreshore: Tourism, Society and Politics on the Coast*, Amsterdam: Amsterdam University Press.

Butler, R.W. (1994) 'Alternative tourism: the thin edge of the wedge', in V.L. Smith and W.R. Eadington (eds), *Tourism Alternatives*, Chichester: Wiley, pp. 31–46.

Chambers, D. and Airey, D. (2001) 'Tourism policy in Jamaica: a tale of two governments', *Current Issues in Tourism*, **4** (2–4), 94–120.

de Kadt, E. (1979) *Tourism – Passport to Development?*, New York: Oxford University Press.

Dwyer, L. and Forsyth, P. (2007) 'Measuring the benefits and yield from foreign tourism', *International Journal of Social Economics*, **4** (1–3), 223–236.

Eurostat/OECD/WTO/UN (2008) *Tourism Satellite Accounts: Recommended Methodological Framework*, New York: UN (Sales no. E.01.XVII.9).

Foxell, E. and de Trafford, A. (2010) 'Repositioning Malta as a cultural heritage destination', *International Journal of Culture, Tourism and Hospitality Research*, **4** (2), 156–168.

Goodwin, H. (2007) 'Measuring and reporting the impact of tourism on poverty', in Tribe and Airey (eds), *Developments in Tourism Research*, Oxford: Elsevier, pp. 63–74.

Goodwin, H. (2008a) 'Tourism, local economic development and poverty reduction', *Applied Research in Economic Development*, **5** (3), 55–64.

Goodwin, H. (2008b) 'Pro-poor tourism: a response', *Third World Quarterly*, **29** (5), 869–871.

Goodwin, H. (2009) 'Reflections on 10 years of pro-poor tourism', *Journal of Policy Research in Tourism, Leisure and Events*, **1** (1), 90–94.

Goodwin, H. and Santilli, R. (2009) 'Community-based tourism: a success?', ICRT Occasional Paper 11, International Centre for Responsible Tourism, Leeds.

Harford, T. (2006) *The Undercover Economist*, London: Little, Brown.

Harrison, D. (1992) *Tourism and Less Developed Countries*, Chichester: Wiley.

Harrison, D. (2008) 'Pro-poor tourism: a critique', *Third World Quarterly*, **29** (5), 851–868.

Harrison, D. and Schipani, S. (2007) 'Lao tourism and poverty alleviation: community-based tourism and the private sector', *Current Issues in Tourism*, **10** (2 & 3), 194–230.

Harrison, J. (1978) *An Economic History of Modern Spain*, Manchester: Manchester University Press.

Issa, J.J. and Jayawardena, C. (2003) 'The "all-inclusive" concept in the Caribbean', *International Journal of Contemporary Hospitality Management* **15** (3), 167–171.

Jackson, L.A. (2006) 'Ameliorating the negative impacts of tourism: a Caribbean perspective', *International Journal of Contemporary Hospitality Management*, **18** (7), 574–582.

Jayawardena, C. and Ramajeesingh, D. (1989) 'Performance of tourism analysis: a Caribbean perspective', *International Journal of Contemporary Hospitality Management*, **15** (3), 176–179.

Judd, D.R. (2006) 'Commentary: tracing the commodity chain of global tourism', *Tourism Geographies*, **8** (4), 323–326.

Libreros, M. (2006) *Designing the Tourism Satellite Account (TSA) Methodological Framework*, Madrid: WTO.

McManus, R. (2001) 'Dublin's changing tourism geography', *Irish Geography*, **34** (2), 103–123.

Mitchell, J. and Faal, J. (2007) 'Holiday package tourism and the poor in the Gambia', *Development Southern Africa*, **24** (3), 445–464.

Mitchell, J. and Ashley, C. (2010), *Tourism and Poverty Reduction*, London: Earthscan.

New Zealand (2007) *New Zealand Tourism Strategy 2015*, Wellington: Ministry of Tourism.

New Zealand Ministry of Tourism, Lincoln University, Tourism New Zealand & Tourism Industry Association (2007) *Enhancing Financial and Economic Yield in Tourism*, Wellington, New Zealand: Ministry of Tourism

Pro-Poor Tourism Partnership (2007) *Annual Register*, London: Pro-Poor Tourism Partnership.

Robinson, M. (1999) 'Collaboration and cultural consent: refocusing sustainable tourism', *Journal of Sustainable Tourism*, **7** (3 & 4), 379–397.

Saville, N. (2001) 'Practical strategies for pro-poor tourism: case study of pro-poor tourism and SNV in Humla District, West Nepal', PPT Working Paper 3, Pro-Poor Tourism, London.

Scheyvens, R. (2002) *Tourism for Development: Empowering Communities*, Harlow: Prentice Hall.

Schwartz, K., Tapper, R. and Font, X. (2008) 'A sustainable supply chain management framework for tour operators', *Journal of Sustainable Tourism*, **16** (3), 298–314.

Sharpley, R. (2009a) *Tourism Development and the Environment: Beyond Sustainability*, London: Earthscan.

Sharpley, R. (2009b) 'Tourism and development challenges in the least developed countries: the case of The Gambia', *Current Issues in Tourism*, **12** (4), 337–358.

Swarbrooke, J. (1999) *Sustainable Tourism Management*, Wallingford: CABI.

Tao, C.H. and Wall, G. (2009) 'Tourism as a sustainable livelihood strategy', *Tourism Management*, **30** (1), 90–98.

UNCSD, (1999), UN Commission on Sustainable Development, Seventh Session, 19030 April 1999. Agenda Item 5, 2f, Economic sector/major group: tourism, E/CN.17/1999/L.6 29n, United Nations, New York

WTO (2002) Tourism and Poverty Alleviation, Madrid: UNWTO

WTO (2004) Tourism and Poverty Alleviation: Recommendations for Action, Madrid: UNWTO

Yassarata, M., Altinay, L., Burns, P. and Okumus, F. (2010) 'Politics and sustainable tourism development – can they co-exist: voices from North Cyprus', *Tourism Management*, **31** (3), 345–356.

7 Environmental Responsibility

infinite growth of material consumption in a finite world is an impossibility.

Schumacher[1]

Although Responsible Tourism and the sustainability agenda cannot be reduced to the green agenda, the environmental challenges that confront us are pressing and serious. Rio was about environment and development; the Cape Town Declaration called for negative environmental impacts to be minimised, for tourism to make a positive contribution to the conservation of natural heritage and to the maintenance of the world's diversity. According to the Cape Town declaration, environmental concerns should be managed 'throughout the life cycle of tourist establishments and operations – including the planning and design phase'. It also called for the sustainable use of resources, and for waste and over-consumption to be reduced; for tourism and tourist activities to be managed within the environment's capacity to absorb them without damage; and for tourism to be used to promote environmental education and awareness amongst tourists.[2]

Krippendorf's first book, *Die Landschaft Fresser* (*The Landscape Devourers*) about the problems of tourism in the Alps in 1975. It is only necessary to visit parts of the Alps and the Mediterranean coast to understand the transformation wrought on the landscape by tourism, particularly in areas which attract large numbers of holidaymakers and second-home owners. Tourism takes place in all of the world's different environments: in deserts and rainforests, on and around lakes, rivers and seas, in the mountains and deep canyons, on snow and sun-soaked beaches. Most of the potential environmental impacts are local: the issues vary from place to place and different forms of tourism and tourist activities have different impacts. Fundamental to Responsible Tourism is the principle that the destination belongs to the people who live there, and their descendants. It follows from this – and it was enshrined in the Cape Town Declaration – that: '… different destinations and stakeholders will have

---

1   In *Small is Beautiful*, first published in 1973
2   Cape Town Conference (2002): 4

different priorities...' Each is unique,[3] and environmental impacts need to be prioritised and managed locally, including solid and liquid waste and the consequences of irresponsible disposal, such as seepage, downstream and sea pollution. Only greenhouse gas emissions have non-local impacts, although cumulative loss of habitats and species may result in global extinctions.

Inevitably, this chapter addresses climate change and tourism, but the environmental agenda is not exclusively about the use of fossil fuels and emissions of greenhouse gases. There are other issues which must also be considered. Tourism like other industries causes pollution – light and noise, solid and liquid waste, and through the consumption of water and fossil fuels – and it destroys natural habitats through infrastructure development and use of construction materials. Species are consumed as souvenirs and food, and tourism may introduce exotics – invasive flora and fauna which may negatively affect the local ecology. The leisure and recreational activities of tourists – skiing, climbing, diving, wildlife viewing, snorkelling, yachting and a host of others – all have environmental impacts which need to be managed. In theory, tourism can contribute to conservation and the maintenance of biodiversity, but ecotourism remains little more than a good idea. There are major gains to be had by greening businesses but the case for certification, or green labelling, is less robust. The chapter concludes by asking what responsible aviation might look like.

The tourism sector of the world economy is large – it consumes resources and has negative impacts, both in transporting tourists from the originating markets, and in the destinations. The World Travel and Tourism Council claims that the travel and tourism economy represents 9.2% of global GDP, and forecasts that it will grow at an average annual rate of 4.4% over the next decade.[4] The UNWTO's Davos Declaration, agreed in 2007, accepted that tourism accounted for about 5% of global CO_2 emissions, and also accepted the responsibility to address a quadruple bottom line – adding climate responsiveness to the canonical three.[5] If you are tempted to argue that 9.2% of global GDP creates only 5% of emissions and that the industry is therefore carbon efficient, don't. The figures are not comparable easily in this way.

The World Travel and Tourism Council, with the UNWTO, has through satellite accounting established that the travel and tourism sector is large.

3   Cape Town Conference (2002): 2 and Sharpley (2009a): 179
4   WTTC (2010): 5, the estimates include suppliers to the sector.
5   UNWTO Davos Declaration, 3 October 2007: 1

Their success has drawn it to the attention of environmentalists. Travellers and tourists are almost by default engaged in conspicuous consumption. Even if they are consuming less than they would at home, they are probably still consuming more per day than their hosts; add the environmental impacts and carbon costs of long- or short-haul travel, and the sector's share of the world's construction spend (primarily on building hotels), and travel tourism can be presented as the world's largest industry *and* a big cause of greenhouse gas emissions and global warming.[6] The sector sometimes appears to feel that it is being unfairly criticised, but it has worked hard to create awareness of its scale and it is characterised by conspicuous consumption, it made itself a target for environmentalists. The key issue is not how big the sector's contribution is to greenhouse gas emissions, it is big. We do not need to have a precise figure for how big it is to begin to measure how much its carbon efficiency is improving and whether its emissions are growing or falling, they need to fall.

Travel makes global inequality more apparent, as do other elements of globalisation. As Jared Diamond has pointed out, people in the Third World aspire to First World living standards, developing these aspirations through broad media access and observing First World visitors to their countries. ... [N]o one at the UN or in First World governments is willing to acknowledge the dream's impossibility: the unsustainability of a world in which the Third World's large population were to reach and maintain current First World living standards.[7]

Diamond's seminal work on *Collapse* is subtitled *How Societies Choose to Fail or Succeed*. We make choices every day in a finite world, which imposes what Diamond terms 'the cruellest trade-off that we have to resolve: encouraging all people to achieve a higher standard of living, without thereby undermining that standard through overstressing global resources.'[8] In his comparative study of the collapse of previous civilisations, Diamond identifies eight causal factors: deforestation, habitat destruction; soil degradation; water management; overhunting and overfishing; overpopulation; the impacts of introduced species; and increased per capita impact of people. To this list he adds four new ones: anthropogenic climate change, energy shortages, the build-up of toxins in the environment and full human utilisation of the Earth's photosynthetic capacity.

---

6   If it is a major constructor, then it must take responsibility for its share of the global production of cement. Cement contributes about 5% of global greenhouse gas emissions. World Business Council for Sustainable Development (2002): 13

7   Diamond (2005): 495–496 and WWF (2008)

8   Diamond (2005): 496

In a finite world, growth is constrained by increasingly expensive resource costs. Without very major increases in how efficiently we use our resources, the costs of production will rise, threatening commercial viability and squeezing margins. In addition, increasing production of biofuels may displace food production. Beddington, the UK Government's Chief Scientific Adviser, has warned of a 'perfect storm' of food shortages, scarce water and insufficient energy resources that threaten to provoke mass migration, cross-border conflicts and public unrest.[9] Like Diamond, Beddington is pointing out that the problems we face as we push up against the limits of a finite world are complex and interconnected. Since the 1920s we have known from quantum physics that the lack of certainty is a fundamental. Werner Heisenberg's 'Uncertainty Principle' was memorably articulated in Schrödinger's fable of the cat, which may be alive or dead depending on the random decay of a single atom. Chaos theory addresses the non-linear dynamics of complex systems and asserts that relatively simple or small changes can cause complex and large-scale changes – the concept popularly captured as the butterfly effect.[10]

We live in a complex world, one beset by feedback loops, where changes may amplify of reduce the impacts of some changes. Inherent in the science of complex systems is an element of uncertainty, life is uncertain, business leaders and politicians know about the problems of managing uncertainty, even though they may not be very good at it. In the face of Beddington's identification of a potential perfect storm we would be wise to adopt a precautionary approach. Or, as the Rio Declaration put it: 'Where there are threats of serious or irreversible damage, lack of full scientific certainty [should] not be used as a reason for postponing cost-effective measures to prevent environmental degradation.'[11]

Concern about climate change is not new. Fourier first described the way in which the atmosphere traps radiated heat in 1827, and Arrhenius postulated the 'enhanced greenhouse effect' in 1896, arguing that increasing concentration of greenhouse gases would result in global warming. In August 1965 the first landmark conference on the 'Causes of Climate Change' took place in Boulder, Colorado, and in 1971 the US National Academy of Sciences estimated that a doubling of greenhouse gas concentrations in the atmosphere

9   Beddington (2009)

10   This phenomenon was discovered by Lorenz when running climate model simulations and by Poincare studying astronomical systems in the 1880s.

11   Rio Declaration on Environment and Development, June 1992 Principle 15 General Assembly A/CONF.151/26 (Vol. I) available at www.un.org/documents/ga/conf151/aconf15126-1annex1.htm

would raise average temperatures by between 1.5°C and 4.5°C. The United Nations established the Intergovernmental Panel on Climate Change (IPCC) in 1998, and in 2007 the IPCC concluded that 'warming of the climate system is unequivocal', the evidence being based on increases in global average air and ocean temperatures, rising global average sea levels and the widespread melting of snow and ice.[12] Global anthropogenic greenhouse gas emissions have increased 70% between 1979 and 2004 and the rate of emissions is still growing.[13]

Science proceeds by a process of contest and debate and there are generally dissenting voices. Where those dissenting voices have utility for particular interests and are able to secure funding and media attention, they are voluble. The earth's climate is a complex system and change is not linear. Even so, eleven of the twelve years 1995-2006 rank amongst the twelve warmest years in the instrumental record since 1850.[14] The US Department of Commerce acknowledges that the 1980s was then the warmest decade on record, followed by the 1990s, and that the 2000s were warmer still. Our planet's climate is becoming warmer and its weather more extreme.[15] Arguments will persist about the extent to which the causes of climate change and global warming are caused by humans, despite the ever-growing body of empirical research that points towards human activity as its main driver; this should not detract from the fact that our own pollution of the atmosphere is the only cause that we can realistically do anything about.

As a species, we are slowly coming to terms with the finite nature of our world; the realisation that our land, freshwater lakes and rivers, our atmosphere and oceans do not have an unlimited capacity to absorb and lose our waste. Landfill taxes in the developed world are driving recycling and encouraging the export of waste to less developed countries, countries eager for the raw materials contained in the waste, and with less stringent health and safety regulations. The growth of manufacturing in India and China in particular has brought us cheaper consumer goods, but already commodity prices are increasing and the BP oil spill in the Gulf of Mexico in 2010 has demonstrated the environmental and economic costs of extracting oil from a more hostile and pristine environment. The era of cheap oil and fossil fuels

---

12   IPCC (2007): 30

13   IPCC (2007): 36

14   IPCC (2007): 30

15   US Department of Commerce (2010): 5

driving economic development is fast approaching its peak,[16] if it hasn't already passed. Unsurprisingly, this will have serious effects for everyone involved in the tourist industry. For instance, Becken has looked at the implications of peak oil for tourism in New Zealand, which will need to refocus its marketing efforts on regional originating markets and away from the UK, Germany and the USA.

International regulation is not currently doing enough to help us develop sustainably and with respect for the environment. The Copenhagen Climate Conference in December 2009 was widely regarded as disappointing; the Copenhagen Accord was scrambled together in the closing hours of the conference and is vague, with no legal standing. The Rio Earth Summit in 1992 was founded on the principle of environment and development; sustainable development sought to offer the prospect of economic development to the world's economically poor and to conserve our planet's environment at the same time. In Copenhagen that strategy was severely challenged, if not undermined, by the unwillingness to address climate justice. The high levels of greenhouse gases in the atmosphere are in large part a product of industrialisation; those countries which industrialised first benefited from cheaper raw materials and fossil fuels and from the unrestricted discharge of greenhouse gases and other pollutants. It is argued therefore that the burden of reduction should therefore rest on industrialised countries, and particularly when the current emissions for developed countries are calculated on production not consumption: it is convenient, for example, that the greenhouse gas emissions caused by continued consumption of steel in developed countries is charged to the carbon accounts of the developing countries where the steel is produced. We are outsourcing the pollution caused by our consumption. Copenhagen failed to address the 'common but differentiated responsibilities' principle[17] and there was little or no progress on allocating responsibility for greenhouse gas emissions. The developing world demands the right to develop and the developed world demands equitable cuts; Copenhagen failed because of the impasse.[18] Countries, industries and businesses are reluctant to

---

16   See the Oil Depletion Analysis Centre http://odac-info.org

17   Based on Principle 7 of the Rio Declaration which clearly provides a normative framework in this respect: 'The developed countries acknowledge the responsibility that they bear in the international pursuit of sustainable development in view of the pressures their societies place on the global environment and of the technologies and financial resources they command'. See also Article 3 of the UN Framework Convention on Climate Change

18   The debate continues; see for example Greenhouse Development Rights http://gdrights.org/ UNWT0s. Sustainable Tourism and Elimination of Poverty initiatives are one example of attempts to square the circle.

pay the costs of polluting our atmosphere: they all fear that their own restraint would only hand the advantage their competitors and that they would watch others remove any good that their own sacrifice would do. It is a classic – the ultimate – tragedy of the commons and one that could be terminal for many of us. What then are the implications for the tourism sector?

Climate change will have a range of direct and indirect impacts in destinations. Climate is a major driver of tourism demand, but tourism is dependant on many other physical, ecological and economic systems, so seasonality and the changes in water supply, biodiversity, the frequency of extreme weather events, erosion, desertification and water shortages will all have their implications. Cost increases are likely as a result of climate change in many destinations and originating markets; heating, air conditioning, snow-making, food and insurance, and the mitigation responses, whether through consumer choice or regulatory action, will be expensive, and reduce the amount of carbon-intensive travel we do. It also appears very probable that there will be a significant reduction in global income, and therefore on tourism spend. Changes in the global climate will lead to major changes for the whole sector, and those changes will have different local consequences. In many destinations, the people are already beginning to adapt.[19] In very few, if any, originating markets or destinations is it sensible to plan for the future on the basis of business as usual and assume growth based on rising living standards around the world. Travel and tourism as we currently know it were the product of cheap transport, fuelled by fossil fuels, and that era is coming to an end.

The impact of any trip varies, according to the amount of fossil fuel burnt; decisions by consumers and tourism businesses about how they construct and facilitate their holidays, particularly travel and accommodation, make a significant difference.[20] Detailed research on the environmental impact of tourism to the Seychelles found that 97% of the energy consumed was as a result of air travel to the destination. Gossling *et al.* concluded that any 'strategy towards sustainable tourism must … seek to reduce transport distances … [and that] any tourism based on air traffic needs … [is] to be seen as unsustainable'.[21] As the cost of international air travel increases, it is likely that the growth in long-haul travel will slow and stall and that intra-regional travel will continue to predominate. The best estimates suggest that the tourism sector, including

---

19   UNWTO/UNEP/WMO (2008): §6.2, see for example advice on climate proofing businesses in southern England www.climateprepared.com

20   UNWTO/UNEP/WMO (2008): §6.4

21   Gössling et al. (2002): 208

day excursionists, contributes around 5% of global greenhouse gas emissions. Of that total 5% of greenhouse gases, accommodation is responsible for around 20% and transport contributes 75%. Air transport is estimated at 40% of the total and car transport 32%. Mitigation is essential, but there are other policy imperatives too, including economic development and the rights of people to holidays. It should not be forgotten that some holidays cause very limited greenhouse gas emissions. Short-haul city travel now looks more environmentally friendly than it did,[22] and ecological footprinting in rural Tuscany suggests that, if the transportation to the destination is excluded, the tourist footprint is very similar to that of residents. Arrival transport accounts for 86% of the total tourism impact.[23]

The consumption of air travel is very unequally distributed within and between countries; Gossling and Nilsson suggest that frequent flyers may, through air travel alone, cause emissions amounting to twelve times the global annual per capita average. But reducing our flying will have negative effects too. Relative price increases and a decline in international arrivals would have significant impacts on small island states, such as Jamaica, that are heavily dependent on tourism; in these circumstances, low carbon, high-yield destinations will have market advantage.[24]

There are four approaches to mitigation: reducing the consumption of fossil fuels, improved efficiency, greater use of renewables and carbon sequestration.[25] The challenge to reduce greenhouse gas emissions is important across the whole economy. We must put processes in place to deal with tourism's emissions as a part of national and international strategies to reduce emissions from all sources. Energy efficiency regulations apply equally to office blocks as to hotels – the challenges of heating and cooling are similar. I sat with a group of hoteliers for lunch in Cape Town and was surprised that they were not concerned about the pollution caused by air-conditioning in their hotels: electricity looks clean at the point of consumption – the carbon pollution caused by generating electricity is not visible from the hotels. Given the prices which hotels are able to charge in many destinations, and the relative marginality of energy costs to operating costs, the impact of rising resource

22 Dolnicar et al. (2010)

23 Patterson et al. (2007)

24 Gossling and Nilsson (2009)

25 Sequestration takes carbon out of the atmosphere and locks it away for a long period of time in a reservoir or carbon sink, for example saline aquifers, or an aging oil field. The oceans and photosynthesis also absorb carbon dioxide but do not necessarily lock it away. It is important to remember that sequestration through photosynthesis is not instant.

costs will hit local people first: the hoteliers will only notice any impact on their profits when it has already become prohibitively expensive to those outside their doors. The conspicuous consumption, characteristic of the sector, raises a stark inequality between the developed and the developing world, between rich and poor, within and between societies. It is irresponsible and unsustainable.

Communities around the world rely on government, particularly local government and parks authorities, to manage the environmental impacts of tourism in the destinations, from the physical effects of construction to the management of recreational nuisances such as trampling and litter. Many of the environmental impacts which need to be managed in a destination are the same as those which need to be managed for the local population: waste, sewage, building controls and greenhouse gas emissions from fossil fuel consumption. Tourism does not take place in a separate autonomous system, nor should it. Tourists engage in the same kinds of behaviour as they do at home, except that they may do more while at leisure and they may do it in places which are not as well equipped to manage the impacts. The challenge is to manage these impacts without necessarily having the tax base or the technical capacity to do so. For example, there is no capacity to deal with waste batteries in many parts of the world and traditional forms of sewage management can easily be overwhelmed.

Environmental Impact Assessments, one part of many current systems for managing tourisms impacts, often are not up to the job. Tourism developments, as with other large scale building and infrastructure projects, are increasingly subject to EIAs. These vary significantly from one place to another and the competence of those monitoring them also varies. There is anecdotal evidence of EIAs being completed post-construction, when the certificate is required for a licence. EIAs are required for individual developments rather than for larger areas involving a number of developments, so the cumulative effect is not controlled. EIAs do not effectively hold anyone to account for the impacts of development nor do they build the foundations for ongoing environmental monitoring.[26]

Water scarcity, too, is a major and growing issue in some parts of the world. The tourism sector consumes water in the offices, bedrooms, kitchens, gardens, pools, spas and bathrooms used by staff and guests. Climate change, population growth, deforestation, the use of irrigation in agriculture and the use of water in industry are leading to our increasing dependence on fossil

---

26   Wall and Mathieson (2006): 155 and 301–305. See also Zubair et al. (2010) on the Maldives

water. Fossil water is consumed when water is extracted from ground sources faster than it is replenished. Water has been fundamental to the growth of civilisations, and one of the greatest luxuries is to be able to turn on a tap and drink water at will.[27] The common solutions are all short term and may exacerbate the problem for others: dams create major problems with water flow downstream and often result in others being short of water; desalination is very energy intensive, expensive[28] and bad for greenhouse gas emissions; piping water is also energy intensive, unless it is downhill all the way; and pumping water out of the ground risks fossil water being consumed. One lodge owner in the Gambia reported that the water table was dropping by a metre per year and that he had deepened his well three times.[29] If it is necessary to go deeper for water, then fossil water is being consumed; that is unsustainable and, year after year, it is irresponsible.

In most places, tourism is not the major cause of water shortages, although it is seasonally significant in some places.[30] Irrigation for agriculture may appear a virtuous use, but where irrigation is involved and the produce is exported, then large amounts of 'virtual water' are being exported too. In Cyprus, Malta, Egypt, Morocco, Tunisia and parts of Spain, water shortages are acute. In Mallorca by the late 1980s it was reported that 'aquifers were exhausted, water demand was increasing, the coastal areas were immersed in an intensive urbanisation process, and at some beaches the coastline was retreating'.[31] Most tourists in arid and hot areas will not notice if it is drier one year than another but when water tankers arrive on the ferries, as was the case in Barcelona in 2008, the holidaymakers notice and it reaches the foreign media.[32]

People and tourist businesses around the world are beginning to be forced to adapt to what is becoming their new reality. The Kasbah du Toubkal in the High Atlas in Morocco has provided potable water to its neighbours in the village and assisted with the redevelopment of the village hammam that provides public washing and toilet facilities. Increasingly, accommodation

---

27 For the broader debate see Bell, and Solomon. Starr (1991) has written about water wars.

28 Kalogirou (2001)

29 Goodwin and Walters (2007): 15

30 'due to the simultaneous occurrence of low precipitation, high evaporation and increased demands for irrigation and tourism.' Angelakis et al. (2003): 61 and Iglesias et al. (2007)

31 Garcia and Servera (2003): 288. They concluded 'that the dwelling capacity of the island has been exceeded and the present levels of water demand and beach degradation are not sustainable.' (p. 298)

32 Nash 'Arid Barcelona forced to import water', The Independent, 11 April 2008

providers are providing potable water to their neighbouring communities. &Beyond has distributed thousands of hippo water rollers to communities in Africa, enabling them to carry water on wheels to their village. Water scarcity is increasingly recognised as an issue[33] by global business, one which involves reputational risk as well as raising ethical concerns, but businesses in the tourism sector have done relatively little to address the water issue. The Travelife programme encourages hotels to reduce water consumption and reuse grey water for irrigation; hotels can make very significant savings.[34] It's one way that hoteliers and operators can encourage their clients to be responsible about how they use water and increase savings:[35] to encourage guests to do their bit, hotels and operators need to be seen to be doing theirs. There is little point in a guest being exhorted to re-use their towel if there is only a bath in the suite, or an unaerated shower, or if they have to waste gallons of water before it runs hot. In these situations, the effort guests are asked to make pales in comparison to the waste, and they will feel discouraged from taking responsibility. The business will damage its reputation if it is seen to be hypocritical about saving the environment, failing to take responsibility themselves, passing it to the guests. How difficult is it to put a hippo,[36] or a brick, in the cistern? Those operators who are building relationships with their clients to generate repeat business and encourage referrals are best placed to be influential. Goldstein *et al.* demonstrated, through experiment, that when the room card informed guests that 75% of previous guests who had stayed in the same room had reused their towels, 49% reused their towels; up from 35% with the standard environmental message.[37] The normative dimension matters: peer group pressure works, it affects behaviour. In some areas, restaurants are now charging for tap water with the proceeds going to water charities. This raises not only raise money, but awareness of the issue, with debate around the dining tables about whether or not this is acceptable. Such debate contributes to creating change.

Waste water is also an issue, although people prefer not to talk about it. Reviewing tourism development on Pacific islands, I would request to meet

---

33   See the Lloyds Bank risk site: www.lloyds.com/360 and www.lloyds.com/News-and-Insight/360-Risk-Insight/Research-and-Reports/Climate-Change/Global-Water-Scarcity

34   Green Hotelier, Issue 50 Water Management and Conservation, International Tourism Partnership, London

35   For example Neilson Holidays who advise their customers 'Save water – and in doing so save the power needed to heat it. Take a shower instead of a bath and reuse your towels.' www.neilson.co.uk/Responsible-Travel-Our-Tips.aspx accessed 20 August 2010

36   It does not take more than 6 litres to flush a toilet.

37   Goldstein et al. (2008): 477 and 475

with local sewage treatment managers and be met with blank incomprehension – nobody had previously wanted to talk with them about tourism. I spent three weeks on Pacific islands and never once entered the sea, the pollution was often visible floating in an out on the tide. In the UK, Surfers Against Sewage campaign against the discharge of raw sewage into the sea where it poses a health hazard.[38] There have been problems with sewage contamination of the seawater around Boracay in the Philippines; in 2009 a new joint venture company was formed to tackle the freshwater and sewage issues and to improve the quality of the sea bathing around the island. In Mumbai, a city with major water shortages, hotels are reported to pay 16 times more than standpipe users for their water, as much as local racecourses.[39] In 2009, piped water supplies in some areas were reduced to 45 minutes a day and the supply of water to swimming pools in five-star hotels and clubs was reduced. In a city like Mumbai hotels will always be able to buy water, but the more responsible, like the luxurious Orchid Hotel, fit aerators to all taps, which reduce water flow but not the experience, and also recycle wastewater.[40]

Managing solid waste has become a major issue in the developed world, a major challenge, both in tackling the aesthetic issue of litter and the more serious and long-term problems of environmental pollution and disposal. Plastic waste persists in the environment and presents a particular hazard to terrestrial and marine life: deaths caused by litter are an unintended consequence of irresponsible behaviour, but one for which the perpetrators should be held to account. Pre-industrial waste was mainly organic and rotted away; when dumped in water courses, the sea or rivers, it biodegraded. Contemporary waste is less likely to rot – and there is far more of it. In many places the tourism sector organises beach clean ups, and some operators run tours like *Clean up the Nile*: they discourage travellers from taking packaging with them and encourage them to take home their plastics and batteries to be recycled. Hotels can offer battery and plastics recycling as well as reducing the waste produced by their operations. Owners and managers are beginning to take responsibility, but as research in Wales has found, local authority support is essential both to facilitate and incentivise action to responsibly reduce and manage waste.[41]

The main emphasis in environmental work has been on the supply-side

---

38   www.sas.org.uk

39   Sule (2004): 5

40   EUHOFA/IH&RA/UNEP (2001): 131 and 132. If you are in Mumbai ask to see the sewage treatment plant on the roof.

41   Radwan et al. (2010)

as businesses and destination managers seek to manage the impacts of ever increasing numbers of tourists and their activities. There is an alternative set of approaches which seek to achieve sustainability by permitting development within the carrying capacity of the ecosystem. It is generally possible to increase the carrying capacity of any particular environment with visitor management and site hardening, and limits set in management plans are often ratcheted upwards. Governments share an interest in maximising revenues from tourism, but paradoxically, it is only when the resource is privatised that owners can restrict supply, create exclusivity and increase revenues. This may help to keep visitor numbers within the carrying capacity of the ecosystem, but even in these limited cases, return may be maximised at well above optimum visitor levels, and long-term damage is not avoided.

As Liu has argued in his critique of sustainable tourism development, the sector is both supply-led and demand driven: 'successful development in the long term necessitates a balance of supply and demand in terms of range, quality, quantity and price'.[42] Demand needs to be constrained. Marketing, the management of demand, plays an important role in sustaining tourism by channelling tourists to more resilient places, and visitor management can be used to 'select or deselect tourists, control their flows and influence their behaviour through promotion and education'.[43] In its current strategy, New Zealand's national tourism strategy has set priorities to protect and enhance the environment, which range from facilitating consumer choice on environmental performance to reducing waste and carbon emissions, and has identified other national strategies with which businesses in the sector will comply.[44]

It should be a surprise to no one that the importance ascribed to the environment by different national groups varies: we have peer groups, live in families and communities and we are part of societies which all contain a range of views about environment and environmental relationships. Anyone concerned to encourage environmental responsibility forgets this at their peril. Research for the Canadian Tourism Commission compares the attitudes of nine international markets with the Canadian domestic market. There are clearly methodological issues, which are addressed in the report, but there are also clearly significant differences amongst potential long-haul travellers from

---

42 Liu (2003): 462

43 Liu (2003): 463 and above pp.147]

44 New Zealand Ministry of Tourism, Tourism Industry Association of New Zealand and Tourism New Zealand (2007): 48–49 and 70–71

these markets. Respondents were asked to agree, or not, with the statement: 'For an equivalent experience I am more likely to choose an environmentally friendly travel option over one that is not'. Results showed that the Chinese (80%) and Koreans (72%) say they are the most environmentally friendly; next came the Mexicans (65%) and the French (62%), the Japanese (45%), Canadians (43%) the Germans came in at 39%, the USA at 38%, the Australians at 32% and the British at 29%.[45] When asked if they would be willing to pay more for an environmentally friendly experience, the percentages all dropped, but the same countries remained at the top and the British and Australians were still the least likely to pay more for an environmentally friendly option. Culture matters, values vary by originating market, consumer preferences vary by market: there is no global market. In the destination, the socio-cultural background and environmental attitudes of owners and managers, as well as cumulative peer group pressure, all affect the willingness of enterprises to take responsibility for their environmental impacts. Bauer, Wong and Lai concluded from their work in Cebu in the Philippines that 'there seems to be a strong influence of the owner's background on environmental performance…'.[46]

Greening businesses

Businesses adopt environmentally responsible practices for the sake of their reputation, to be seen to be doing the right thing, generate consumer loyalty, to be good neighbours, secure a license to operate, manage risk and to reduce costs, and to generate additional profits. Owners and managers also adopt good environmental practises because it is the right thing to do and it engages their staff. Going green makes good sense to an increasing number of businesses and most of the advice on how to do so is available free on the web. The UK regional body South West Tourism points out to businesses that increased efficiency and reduced waste save them money, that using local products adds consumer value to their offering, and increases their appeal and resilience in the market: 'Taking action now will make you better prepared for the higher costs and tougher legislation predicted as well as the impacts of a changing climate.'[47] Visit England launched *Better Tourism* in the summer of 2010 to provide free online advice to tourism businesses about how to secure their sustainable future.[48] It makes sense, and is in the public interest,

---

45   Canadian Tourism Commission (2010): 23

46   Bauer et al. (2002): 7

47   www.swtourism.org.uk/business-support/save-money-go-green/ accessed 21 August 2010

48   www.better-tourism.org

to make freely available the information about how to green a business: it contributes to halting the tragedy of the commons. This approach dates back to the first post-Rio initiatives, including the UK's Green Audit Kit, developed by the South Devon Green Tourism Initiative in 1993.[49] It was businesses that engaged in these early greening initiatives that sought recognition for their efforts through certification and badging. Peer-group pressure and support is often important in encouraging and assisting the adoption of responsible practises throughout the supply chain – there are examples from CoaST in Cornwall to Kangaroo Valley in Australia.[50]

Some progress has been made, but the tourism sector is largely character-ised by small businesses, which are often not able to invest in environmentally friendly changes where the pay-off could be over a year or more in the future. The larger hotels, meanwhile, are beginning to make significant progress, but for the smaller hotels and guesthouses finance is a bigger challenge. Hotels and resorts are built for resale: the original owner and developer have no interest in building to make long-term environmental savings. Building regu-lation is essential to remove this market failure and ensure that energy, waste and water concerns are addressed right from the planning stage. It is unwise to leave the sustainability of a destination to individual businesses. Where local authorities are unable to protect the environmental integrity, resort and lodge operators buy larger tracts than they need and exclude others – how else can they protect the environmental resource on which they depend from the next less scrupulous investor?

Conservation and ecotourism

The creation of national parks began with Yellowstone as recently as 1872. It was heralded as a wilderness to 'be held for public use, resort, and recreation'.[51] In most of the world, the presumption is that national parks are wildernesses without human population: however very few areas of the world have not been inhabited.[52] Protected areas are also social spaces: as Jeff McNeely Chief Scientist at IUCN states, what 'many conservationists still refer to as 'pris-tine' landscapes, 'mature' tropical forest or 'untouched wilderness' are, in

---

49 Dingle (1993)

50 Cornwall Sustainable Tourism Project, www.cstn.org.uk, and the Kangaroo Valley Kangaroo Valley Tourism Association which also has a code of ethics, www.kangaroovalleytourist.asn.au

51 Muir (1912): 115

52 McNeely (1994)

fact, mostly human cultural artefacts.'[53] For the communities who inhabited those wildness areas, when the 'protection' arrives, the continued use of their pantry[54] becomes a crime and respected hunters become poachers overnight. Wildlife and habitat, protected for hunting and for non-consumptive recreation, in turn brings roads and tourism infrastructure.[55] In the 1980s attitudes began to change and in 2003 a 'new paradigm' was established for protected areas, with the Durban Action Plan calling 'for a halt to forced resettlement and involuntary sedentarization of indigenous peoples without their free, prior and informed consent.'[56]

Tourism can, it is argued, provide potential livelihood opportunities for indigenous communities in and around protected areas, as well as an economic reason to create and manage parks. As early as 1972, Myers had argued that tourism could provide an incentive for conservation and the establishment of National Parks; Budowski argued in 1976 that there was a symbiosis between conservation and tourism. In 1982 the International Union for the Conservation of Nature affirmed that 'tourist potential' was an important factor in the selection of protected areas.[57] Research by Zebu and Bush (1990) found that tourism formed part of the management strategy of 75% of the park managers they surveyed. Wells and Brandon reported in 1992 that many Integrated Conservation and Development Projects (ICDPs) had promoted tourism in order to generate funds for conservation and to generate enhanced income for local communities. They concluded that only a very limited number of protected areas attracted significant numbers of tourists and that they failed to generate sufficient revenues for local communities to attract much popular local support for parks.

Ecotourism has been a persistent idea and it remains attractive. The idea is simple: it is low-impact nature tourism that contributes to the costs of conserving habitats and species and provides revenue to local communities, which encourages them to 'value and protect their wildlife heritage areas as a source of income'.[58] However, the injunction to 'take only photographs and leave only footprints', is inadequate. Ecotourism has to benefit conservation by making a net contribution to the costs of conserving habitats and species

53 Ghimire and Pimbert (1997): 6
54 Colchester (1997): 101 and Dowie (2009): 21
55 Bonner (1993): 193
56 World Conservation Congress, at its 4th Session in Barcelona, Spain, 5–14 October 2008, 4.048, Indigenous peoples, protected areas and implementation of the Durban Accord.
57 Goodwin (2000): 97
58 Goodwin (1996): 288

within, to avoid damaging the habitat or species, and to financially benefit local communities. There is a substantial literature on recreational damage to terrestrial and marine habitats and species, damage which ranges from species collection to the trampling of vegetation and physical damage to coral, as well as garbage and human-waste pollution and species disturbance. The direct impacts of tourism on wildlife include displacement, accidental killing and the disruption of feeding and breeding that results in a failure to reproduce. The extent of the problem for particular species will depend upon the nature and intensity of the tourism they experience, their resilience and capacity to adapt.[59] For instance, Malaysia is concerned about coral bleaching as a result of increased water temperatures. As bleaching increases the vulnerability of coral to divers, the Malaysians have in 2010 closed twelve reefs, including the very popular Kedah, Terengganu and Pahang dive sites, to prevent damage and allow time for recovery. The closure will cause short-term financial pain but contribute to the conservation of the reefs and the long-term prosperity of the dive industry in Malaysia.

The Bengal tiger is in serious decline in India: in April 2010 Dr Rajesh Gopal, head of India's National Tiger Conservation Authority, expressed concern that the reserves were small and prone to tourist disturbance. There were reports of tigers becoming extinct in 16 reserves and, consequently, the Environment Ministry was reported to have ordered India's states to wind down tourism at some reserves. M.K. Ranjitsinh, chairman of the Wildlife Trust of India was reported as saying that tourists in vehicles and on elephants were destroying the high grassland in which tigers hunt and the Environment Minister, Jairam Ramesh, was reported to have said that unregulated tourism was as much a threat to the tiger as hunting. He singled out Corbett National Park as having degenerated because of tourism: surrounded by luxury resorts and growing local populations with which the tigers compete for space and increasingly trapped in reserves, there is less contact between isolated tiger populations for breeding.[60] Tour Operators for Tigers (TOFT) responded by arguing that the best tiger habitat exists in the tourism zones, and that tigers and prey sense the security of these habitats. Moreover, TOFT estimates that Machali, a famous Ranthambhore tigress, generated US$130 million in 11 years.[61] But there is no estimate on what the tourism sector has contributed

---

59 Mathieson and Wall (1992): 105–112 and Roe et al. (1997)

60 Rhys Blakely, 'India to stop tiger tourism in attempt to prevent species extinction', The Times, 28 April 2010

61 TOFT Press Release India's Nature Tourism Bites Back, 30 April 2010

to conservation. Following discussions with the Ministry of Tourism, which feared the impact on visitor numbers, Ramesh announced the development of guidelines for tourism in tiger reserves and said that the Ministry was 'not at all interested in stopping tiger tourism'.[62] Tourism triumphed.

Nature-based tourism, particularly where charismatic mega fauna are involved, is very valuable, and not just to the wildlife tourism operators but to the tourism sector as a whole. In the protected area it is not possible to distinguish the impacts of ecotourists from the others. They use the same vehicles and lodges and encircle the same animals, and the impacts are the same or worse if, by getting closer and deeper into the park, they cause more disturbances in areas with lower visitation. It is clear that a few companies do make significant contributions to conservation but most do not: they retain the value for themselves.

There has been little rigorous research on ecotourism, Weaver and Lawton recently assessed the field as still being in a 'state of adolescence'.[63] The adolescent is suffering from neglect, and as Buckley has pointed out Weaver and Lawton 'specifically excluded any attempt to evaluate its practical achievements or outcomes.'[64] One piece of research conducted ten years ago for the International Year of Ecotourism found that the concept was hardly used in the UK marketplace.[65] Tourism to national parks appears, from the limited research available, to be subsidised by other budgets;[66] there is little or no evidence of increased support from local communities protected areas thanks to the revenues they bring in or the livelihood opportunities they create. To achieve support the volume of tourism in the park would probably endanger what it was intended to protect. Perhaps it is best not to look too closely. The idea of ecotourism remains seductive; donors still support ecotourism projects and conservationists hang on to it as a means of convincing local communities that they will benefit. But the fact is that there is no supporting evidence.

Russell has argued that ecotourism might deliver, if the aspirations of local people and the particular circumstances of different initiatives were taken into account, and that there is a 'danger of throwing the out baby with the bathwater'.[67] This may be true. We should not abandon the idea just because

62 The *Telegraph*, Calcutta ,'Tiger tourism not to be banned: Jairam' 5 May 2010
63 Weaver and Lawton (2007): 1168 and 1176
64 Buckley (2009): 643
65 WTO (2001b) The British Ecotourism Market
66 Goodwin et al. (1997 a) Vol 1: 45–59
67 Russell (2007): 230, 225

we have not practically achieved it. Perhaps, by pursuing it more responsibly – by taking into account local priorities, conserving and avoiding damaging habitats and species, and making sure that the local community truly benefits financially – we can make it work. Ecotourism is an attractive idea, there have been substantial efforts in its name, but there is no evidence, yet, that it delivers its promise.

Sustainable tourism certification

As with ecotourism, sustainable tourism certification is attractive to donors. Yet, again, there is no evidence that it delivers its promise.

Certification can and should play a role in sustainability initiatives where the criteria are clear and public, and where the certificate carries a clear guarantee. The Blue Flag scheme certifies beaches using clear criteria, which are available on the Blue Flag Website: water quality; environmental management; environmental education and safety. The blue flag flies on the beach only when it meets all the mandatory criteria; again, on the website, there is a detailed list of beaches that meet the standard.[68] And, for the consumer, the Blue Flag proposition is very clear: the beach is safe, clean and it is safe to swim. There are no grey areas. The criteria are limited, clear and unvarying – although it is possible for local agencies to choose to apply even higher standards.

Turning to star ratings for hotels, the picture is very different. There is still no consensus about the difference between four- and five-star properties, and no quality-grading scheme with broad international support. This is for the good reason that different consuming cultures have very different expectations. National and regional quality-grading schemes reflect local priorities and consumer preferences – entirely to be expected in a diverse world. Similarly, sustainable tourism priorities vary from one environment to another: only greenhouse gas emissions have global impacts, while all other impacts are initially local, and issues vary in importance from place to place. If we have been unable to develop a global quality-grading standard for hotels, is it likely that a global green certification scheme can be developed for tourism? The dizzying range of issues, priorities, sustainability challenges, practical solutions and locations surely would render such a global certification meaningless. And, if it is meaningless, it will hardly capture consumer attention, let alone affect their purchasing.

---

68 www.blueflag.org

One scheme, the Green Globe standard, now has 41 criteria and 337 compliance indicators; the 'applicable indicators vary by type of certification, geographical as well as local factors'.[69] Clearly, this is not an easy consumer proposition. Green Globe has been certifying hotels for 15 years but the number of properties certified remains small.[70]

By contrast, the Green Tourism Business Scheme in the UK has more than 2000 members and now has sufficient market recognition to be a tie-breaker for consumers choosing accommodation in the South West.[71] Another successful example is ABTA's Travelife programme which, in the UK, quickly achieved recognition amongst consumers because it is being used by established brands in the UK to make their supply chain more sustainable and they are marketing the certified products. TUI surveyed its Thomson and First Choice customers in late 2009 and found that 73% would like to be able to identify a green holiday easily.[72] In Cape Town, the authorities have prioritised a short-list of sustainable tourism issues: these are the local priorities for action and are being applied across businesses and government in the city. With a long list of issues, businesses are free to pick and choose which are the easiest for them to address. It should be up to local authorities and local stakeholders to plan and choose their priorities, how these will be recognised and how they will gain traction with consumers.

Given the very large number of sustainable tourism certification schemes operating around the world, there is surprisingly little evidence of their market value. There is no published evidence that justifies the Tourism Sustainability Council's use of donor funds to accredit certification schemes, schemes that offer 'a common understanding of sustainable tourism and the adoption of universal sustainable tourism principles and criteria'.[73] There is no evidence of demand for international certification amongst businesses or among consumers. Consensus has been built amongst certifying agencies and NGOs around 37 criteria, some of which are based around process, and some around performance. The much more difficult task of attaching weightings to the criteria and determining the degree of sector and location flexibility has not yet been achieved.

---

69 Press release 17 August 2010 www.greenglobe.com

70 www.greenglobe.com/certified_hotel.html

71 Consumer research in the South West undertaken in 2009 reports that 4% of consumers look for GTBS businesses when looking for accommodation and a further 23% would chose a GTBS over a similar one. Research Department Southwest Tourism (2010): 72

72 TUI (2010): 31

73 www.sustainabletourismcriteria.org/index.php?option=com_content&task=view&id=266&Itemid=483 accessed 22 August 2010

The danger with large international certification schemes is that businesses score well by tackling lots of issues, ticking lots of boxes. They avoid prioritising the things which would make the biggest difference locally, and with no local accountability their accomplishments are sometimes only tokenistic. With a long list of issues, businesses are free to pick and choose which are the easiest for them to address. By contrast in Cape Town the city council and tourism businesses have agreed seven priorities and are working towards them.

Sustainable tourism is not simple – as we have seen, there are lots of issues to think about and to address. Mostly, for the consumer, a certification label is opaque, with neither the consumer nor the funder knowing what the business has achieved. It requires us to trust it, even though we know no specifics. For example, we do not know how much water or greenhouse gas emissions have been reduced through certification. The guest's experience will not be enhanced by certification in the same way as by experiencing a New Forest breakfast or visiting a sewage treatment reed bed and its wildlife – those experiences create stories which will be told and retold, encouraging repeats and referrals.

The Tourism Sustainability Council approach for example, seeks to impose supranational priorities over national and local ones. But, as we have seen in previous chapters, there is no global marketplace for tourism. Travellers come from diverse consuming cultures and they arrive in diverse destinations, each originating culture and destination with its own set of sustainability priorities. Even nationally the major issues will have different saliences in different places. As Sharpley has argued 'tourism development can only be considered from the perspective of the destination, not within 'one-size-fits-all', top-down planning frameworks'.[74] Responsible Tourism recognises, encourages and celebrates diversity: we need transparent reporting about what businesses are doing and about they are increasing their positive and reducing their negative impacts. Responsible Tourism requires consumer engagement and the companies who have made the most progress have involved their travellers and guests in achieving it. Sustainable tourism requires that producers and consumers take responsibility for achieving it. It cannot be reduced to a set of tick boxes.

A global sustainable tourism certification scheme makes sense for the NGOs and consultancy firms who will benefit from it: they hope it will create work for them and secure funding from donors sponsoring the setting up of the scheme. The diverse nature of the global market has resulted in the

---

74 Sharpley (2009a): 177

development of a wide diversity of schemes which reflect the local conditions. The new global Tourism Sustainability Council scheme imposes additional accreditation costs on existing national and local schemes, which may exclude or disadvantage those who cannot afford the certification process or to renew their existing membership. In most viable local schemes, businesses gain more from the advice they receive on making their business more sustainable (and also reducing costs) than from the marketing value of the certificate. The fact that there is significant churn in the membership of the schemes, as people join and leave, may reflect both the efficacy of the advice, sufficient for a number of years, and the failure of the logo to bring additional business. It is very difficult to see what added value the new Tourism Sustainability Council brings other than creating another layer of administration with the associated costs.

In all this there is a danger of green-washing. Third-party certification or verification may offer a guarantee of integrity, but where the inspectors are directly employed by the certified business, the integrity may be less than where inspection is conducted by staff employed by a second-party purchaser, a 'mystery shopper' who is able to check the quality independently. Too often, there is no redress or accountability in certification schemes. Whereas a consumer is able to seek recompense for failure to deliver sustainability elements offered when the booking was made, if a certified property is profligately using water or over-riding the key-card switches to run the air-conditioning before the guest arrives, the consumer can seek recompense from neither the hotel nor the certifier.

Once again tourism is in its silo, self-referencing, pursuing its own solutions, oblivious to what else is going on in destinations. Destination sustainability cannot be reduced to greening tourism businesses and their suppliers. Consumers and regulators should demand – and are demanding – transparent reporting of performance on water, waste and carbon efficiency. That is the future.

Responsible aviation

Aviation is, perhaps, the issue that looms largest in consumers' minds when the words 'responsible tourism' are uttered. Yet few have any idea how to sensibly and responsibly deal with flying. Some individuals have decided not to fly at all, and plenty more are flying less. Yet we should not forget that the majority of the world's population does not fly because they do not have the opportunity to do so – they cannot afford it. To reduce greenhouse gas emissions, people need to fly less and to fly in a more carbon-efficient, less carbon-intensive way.

Aircraft operators need to be encouraged to operate in a more carbon-efficient way. Perhaps the only way of doing this is for consumers to be enabled to make more carbon-efficient choices, choices which will then cause the airlines to operate in more fuel efficient, and therefore more carbon efficient, ways. . Charter flights and the new budget airlines offer point-to-point flights on newer, more fuel-efficient aircraft with higher load factors,[75] and operators such as Thomas Cook Scandinavia[76] have years of experience of reducing their environmental impacts. Flying point-to-point reduces the number of take-offs and landings to get from place to place, which, all other conditions being equal, reduces the greenhouse gas emissions for the journey. There is a bewildering range of ways in which a flight can be made more fuel efficient, from carrying fewer duty-free goods to using the latest fuel-efficient engines; passengers can carry less baggage and fly economy; pilots can operate the aeroplane in a more carbon-friendly way; governments can remove cost penalties in their airspace, removing cost incentives to fly around them and allowing airlines to fly directly on the most fuel efficient routing; airports can run their operations more fuel efficiently and reduce taxiing… to name but a few. The IPCC expects improved airframe and engine technology to reduce emissions by 20% between 1997 and 2015, and by up to 50%, over 1997 levels, by 2050.[77] Air-traffic management improvements could, by reducing congestion and optimising flight paths, reduce fuel consumption by 10%.

Aside from consumer pressure, there is one major incentive for airlines to improve their performance. Fuel is increasing in price, and now constitutes 20–25% of direct operational costs: the higher the price of fuel, the greater the incentive to use it efficiently. As fuel goes up, the number of flights will decrease; each will be more productive and more fuel efficient. There is much hype about alternative fuels but there is no evidence yet of the successful development of new engines. Biofuels, for example, can currently only be used in a low-mix ratio. To reduce carbon emissions they would need to burn more efficiently than current fuels. In addition, they compete with food production for use of arable land and the seas.

---

75   The fuel efficiency savings are in the 20–30% range per passenger km. Boeing's 787 Dreamliner is 20% more fuel efficient than existing commercial jets

76   Thomas Cook Airlines Scandinavia Environmental Report 2009/2010 available at http://viewer.zmags.com/publication/850d84aa#/850d84aa/1

77   Penner et al. (1999)

Recessions, the hassle of airport check-in and security, and consumers exercising choice also all help to reduce flight emissions. The British Social Attitudes Survey asks each year whether people agree or disagree with the statement 'The price of a plane ticket should reflect the environmental damage that flying causes, even if this makes air travel much more expensive.' In 2004 36% agreed; by 2008 46% agreed.[78] Offered the opportunity to use a Carbon Friendly Flight Finder to choose a more carbon efficient carrier, 57% of users exited the site having chosen to check out the carbon friendly option. Those willing to do so paid an average 19% more for their flight.[79]

Carbon offsetting has not been successful with consumers, although it was popular with NGOs and others who saw it as a business opportunity. There has been increasing scepticism from all quarters about carbon offsetting,[80] and some argue that it resembles the medieval practice of purchasing a pardon in order to continue with sinful business as usual.[81] ResponsibleTravel.com abandoned carbon offsetting in late 2009. The consumer proposition is weak: it neither salves the consumer's conscience nor applies pressure on the airline to improve its performance. Consumers have seen through the offsetting proposition. Air Passenger Duty charged per passenger similarly fails to place any pressure on the airline to improve its environmental performance and the money raised goes into the general pot of government expenditure. It is not a green tax.

A tax on fuel would create considerable pressure on the airlines to improve their efficiency of operation. It would fairly and squarely adhere to the 'polluter pays' principle, and it would have the added advantage of covering freight. It would be paid by the economically wealthy, whether flying internationally or domestically. If they chose to fly on the most efficient carriers, they would pay less and contribute to a reduction in pollution. A tax on fuel would also be responsible in that it would go some way to addressing inequality: the money could be hypothecated for adaptation for vulnerable communities in the developing world, so the economically wealthy would be contributing to benefit the economically poor – those who are most affected by climate change, which is in part caused by flights. Finally, airlines would have a strong incentive to pollute less.

---

78 British Social Attitudes Survey, available on line at www.britsocat.com

79 Based on a sample of 10,000+, unpublished preliminary results. GDS Global Travel Market, the company which ran the Carbon Friendly Search Engine, went into liquidation for reason unconnected with FlySmart, www.flysmart.org

80 Bullock, Childs and Picken (2009)

81 For a fuller discussion of this issues see Goodwin and Walmsley (2010) 'Indulging indulgence. Tourism, carbon offsetting and climate change'. ICRT Occasional Paper No.20.

In all these scenarios, individuals and businesses can make a difference.[82] But the bigger challenges of water, waste and human-induced climate change can only be addressed by collective action organised and enforced by governments. The travel and tourism sector is responsible for 5% of global greenhouse gas emissions. If it were a state it would come, on 2005 figures, fourth on the list of largest polluters, above India, but after the USA, China, and the European Union. Investment decisions being made now are determining operating costs for buildings which will be operating in very different circumstances in 15 to 25 years' time. The environmental problems confronted by the species and the sector are intractable: they are with us now, and they will become more acute. The risks need to be managed – but tragedy of the commons risks can only be managed collectively. Tough decisions and regulation will be required.

---

82   New Zealand www.responsibletourism.co.nz/ecowise.php UK Outbound www. reducemyfootprint.travel

References

Angelakis, A.N., Bontoux, L. and Lazarova, V. (2003) 'Challenges and prospects for water recycling and reuse in EU countries', *Water Science and Technology: Water Supply*, **3** (4), 59–68.

Bauer *et al.* (2002). Barriers to Good Environmental Practice in the Hotel Sector in the Biodiversity Hotspots: Cebu, Philippines unpublished: 7

Becken, S. (2008) 'Developing indicators for managing tourism in the face of peak oil', *Tourism Management*, **29** (4), 695–705.

Becken, S. and Hay, J. (2007) *Tourism and Climate Change – Risks and Opportunities*, Clevedon, Somerset: Channel View Publications.

Beddington J 2009 'Food, Energy, Water and the Climate: A Perfect Storm of Global Events?' Speech at Sustainable Development UK 09, 19 March 2009.

Bell, A. (2009) *Peak Water*, Edinburgh: Luath.

Bonner, R. (1993) *At the Hand of Man: Peril and Hope for Africa's Wildlife*, London: Simon & Schuster.

Bullock, S., Childs, M. and Picken, T. (2009) *A Dangerous Distraction: Why Offsetting is Failing the Climate and People: the Evidence*, London: Friends of the Earth.

Canadian Tourism Commision (2010) *Global Tourism Watch Year 3 Summary Report 2009*, Vancouver: Canadian Tourism Commission.

Cape Town Conference (International Conference on Responsible Tourism in Destinations – ICRT) (2002) *Cape Town Declaration*, Cape Town: ICRT and Western Cape Tourism.

Colchester, M. (1997) 'Salvaging nature: indigenous people and protected areas', in Ghimire, K. and Pimbert, M.P. (eds), *Social Change and Conservation*, London: Earthscan, pp. 97–130.

Diamond, J. (2005) *Collapse: How Societies Choose to Fail or Succeed*, London: Allen Lane.

Dingle, P.A. (1993) *Green Audit Kit*, Exeter: West Country Tourist Board.

EUHOFA/IH&RA/UNEP (2001) *Sowing the Seeds of Change*, Paris: UNEP.

Garcia, C. and Servera, J. (2003) 'Impacts of tourism development on water demand and beach degradation on the island of Mallorca (Spain)', *Geografiska Annaler: Series A, Physical Geography*, **85** (3–4), 287–300.

Ghimire, K. (2001) *The Native Tourist: Mass Tourism within Developing Countries*, London: Earthscan.

Ghimire, K. and Pimbert, M.P. (1997) *Social Change and Conservation*, London: Earthscan.

Goldstein, N.J., Cialdini, R.B. and Griskevicius, V. (2008) 'A room with a viewpoint: using social norms to motivate environmental conservation in hotels', *Journal of Consumer Research*, **35** (3), 472–482.

Goodwin, H. (1996) 'In pursuit of ecotourism', *Biodiversity and Conservation*, **5** (3), 277–291.

Goodwin, H. (2000) 'Tourism and natural heritage: a symbiotic relationship', M. Robinson, J. Swarbrooke, N. Evans, P. Long and R. Sharpley (eds), *Environmental Management and Pathways to Sustainable Tourism*, Sunderland: Business Education Publishers, pp. 97–112.

Goodwin, H. and Walmsley, A. (2010) 'Indulging indulgence: tourism, carbon offsetting and climate change', ICRT Occasional Paper 20, International Centre for Responsible Tourism, Leeds.

Goodwin, H. and Walters, K. (2007) 'No water, no future', report for the World Travel Market and ICRT, London.

Gössling, S. and Nilsson, J.H. (2009) 'Frequent flyer programmes and the reproduction of aeromobility', *Environment and Planning A*, **42** (1), 241–252.

Gössling, S., Peeters, P. and Scott, D. (2009) 'Consequences of climate policy for international tourist arrivals in developing countries', *Third World Quarterly*, **29** (5), 873–901.

Iglesias, A., Gattotte, L., Flores, F. and Moneo, M. (2007) 'Challenges to manage the risk of water scarcity and climate change in the Mediterranean', *Water Resources Management*, **21** (5), 775–788.

IPCC (Intergovernmental Panel on Climate Change) (2007) *Climate Change 2007: Synthesis Report*, Geneva: IPCC.

Kalogirou, S.A. (2001) 'Effect of fuel cost on the price of desalination water: a case for renewables', *Desalination*, **138** (1–3), 137–144.

Krippendorf, J. (1975) *Die Landschaftsfresser: Tourismus und Erholungslandschaft, Verderben oder Segen?*, Schönbühl, Switzerland: Hallwag

Liu, Z. (2003) 'Sustainable tourism development: a critique', *Journal of Sustainable Tourism*, **11** (6), 459–475.

Mathieson, A. and Wall, G. (1992) *Tourism: Economic, Physical and Social Impacts*, Harlow: Longman.

McNeely, J. (1994) 'Lessons from the past: forests and biodiversity', *Biodiversity and Conservation*, **3**, 3–20.

Muir, J. (1912) *The Yosemite*, New York, NY: The Century Company.

New Zealand (2007) *New Zealand Tourism Strategy 2015*, Wellington: Ministry of Tourism.

Patterson, T.M., Niccolucci, V. and Bastianoni, S. (2007) 'Beyond "more is better": ecological footprint accounting for tourism and consumption in Val di Merse, Italy', *Ecological Economics*, **62** (3–4), 747–756.

Penner, J., Lister, D.H., Griggs, D.J., Dokken, D.J. and McFarland, M. (1999) *Aviation and the Global Atmosphere: A Special Report of the IPCC Working Groups I and III*, Cambridge: Cambridge University Press.

Radwan, R.I., Jones, E. and Minoli, D. (2010) 'Managing solid waste in small hotels', *Journal of Sustainable Tourism*, **18** (2), 175–190.

Roe, D., Leader-Williams, N. and Dalal-Clayton, B. (1997) *Take Only Photographs, Leave Only Footprints: The Environmental Impacts of Wildlife Tourism*, London: International Institute for Environment and Development.

Russell, A. (2007) 'Anthropology and ecotourism in European wetlands: bubbles, babies and bathwater', *Tourism Studies*, **7** (2), 225–244.

Sharpley, R. (2009a) *Tourism Development and the Environment: Beyond Sustainability*, London: Earthscan.

Sharpley, R. (2009b) 'Tourism and development challenges in the least developed countries: the case of The Gambia', *Current Issues in Tourism*, **12** (4), 337–358.

Solomon, S. (2010) *Water: The Epic Struggle for Wealth, Power, and Civilization*, New York: Harper.

Sule, S. (2004) *Mumbai's Water Supply*, Mumbai: Bombay Community Public Trust.

UNWTO/UNEP (2008) *Climate Change and Tourism: Responding to Global Challenges*, Madrid: UNWTO.

UNWTO Davos Declaration (2007), Second International Conference on Climate Change and Tourism, *Climate Change and Tourism Responding to Global Challenges*, Davos, 3 October. Available at: www.unwto.org/pdf/pr071046.pdf

US Department of Commerce (2010) *The State of the Climate Highlights,* National Oceanic and Atmospherical Administration, Washington, DC: US Department of Commerce.

Wall, G. and Mathieson, A. (2006) *Tourism Change, Impacts and Opportunities,* Harlow: Pearson.

Weaver, D.B. and Lawton, L.J. (2007) 'Twenty years on: the state of contemporary ecotourism research', *Tourism Management*, **28**, 1168–1179.

WEF (World Environment Forum) (2009) *The Travel & Tourism Competitiveness Report 2009*, Geneva: WEF.

WTO (2001) *The British Ecotourism Market*, Madrid: WTO.

WTTC (2010) *Travel and Tourism Economic Impact – Executive Summary*, London: WTTC.

Zubair, S., Bowen, D. and Elwin, J. (2010) 'Not quite paradise: inadequacies of environmental impact assessment in the Maldives', *Tourism Management*, **32** (2), 225–234.

8 Conclusion

We have learnt, rather too late, that action comes, not from thought, but from a readiness for responsibility.

Dietrich Bonheoffer[1]

This has been a personal journey, one that has enabled me, with many others, to explore the concept of responsibility, to apply it in the context of tourism and to explore its relevance in a number of different societies.

I have sought to report here on the development of a broad movement in thinking about how to address the consumption of tourism, and how responsibility can be taken by individuals and groups in businesses and local government, encouraged and supported by their peers. Above all, I have tried to emphasise that with opportunity comes the responsibility to act. In many other areas of concern from banking and politics to fishing and farming we need more responsible approaches. Responsibility is free, we can have as much of it as we can handle: we can all take some, we can all take more; we should all take some.[2]

The experience of pursuing the Responsible Tourism agenda has frequently reminded me of the socio-cultural and religious diversity of our world and that it is individual people who make our species more sustainable. There are global problems and issues, but solutions are generally local, although we can learn from each other and translate solutions from one place to another. There are few if any global solutions, although there are global threats in our finite world.

During my years as a tourist and tour leader, I felt a mounting unease about the experience of tourism – which is what drove me to research and teaching on tourism. My disquiet stemmed from the chasm between claims about the benefits of ecotourism and the reality, so I began to look into the impacts of tourism in and around national parks in Africa and Asia. The result was empirical confirmation that the benefits of ecotourism were not to

---

1   Letters and Papers from Prison

2   I am grateful to Denis Wormwell, of Shearing Group for formulating this so powerfully. It is also used in the title of a paper by John Peters

be found in the destinations and that there was little point in dealing with the niche of ecotourism. In destinations, ecotourists are indistinguishable from all the others. The challenge was how to manage all forms of tourism to make them more sustainable, and many individuals had to take responsibility for that. At the Durrell Institute of Conservation and Ecology I met national park wardens who clearly had very little understanding about how tourists arrived at the park gates – I realised that, if they did, they would have a better chance of managing both the tourists and their impacts. The resulting courses we developed on tourism and conservation were designed to empower national park managers. Participation in the VSO and Tearfund campaigns, and subsequent work with Association of Independent Tour Operators, led me to the realisation that Responsible Tourism offered an approach which could engage all the stakeholders – and this also led me to the discovery of Krippendorf.

In the course of debate in the classroom Greenwich University in 2000, the Masters students identified three objectives for the development of Responsible Tourism, three things we aspired to see achieved: the creation of a marketplace for Responsible Tourism products; a charity to support people in destinations in managing tourism for the benefit of their community and their place; and awards to provide recognition and encouragement for those businesses which were changing. I co-founded ResponsibleTravel.com with Justin Francis in 2001[3] and in 2004 we launched the Responsible Tourism Awards. The Travel Foundation emerged out of the government's Sustainable Tourism Initiative and TravelPledge was launched in 2007 with another of our alumni, Nick Chaffe. Scores of students[4] of the International Centre for Responsible Tourism now work in the field of Responsible Tourism – they work for UK outbound operators, tourist boards, governments, NGOs, tourism businesses, trade associations and consultancies around the world.

My work on tourism and poverty reduction grew out of a request from the UK's Department for International Development for a working paper on tourism and poverty elimination. Those were heady days; but the 2002 WTO policy paper, of which I wrote the initial draft, committed only to alleviation. The foundation of the Pro-Poor Tourism Partnership was remarkably productive and demonstrated the value of open access publication on the Web, although there was considerable disappointment in the unwillingness of donors to demand evidence that the interventions which they funded had made people less poor.

---

3   I subsequently sold my shares.

4   There is a list of current students and alumni at www.artyforum.info/ICRTAlumni.html

Work with the Department of Environmental Affairs and Tourism in South Africa on their guidelines for Responsible Tourism led to the first International Conference on Responsible Tourism in Destinations, now held annually, and the Cape Town Declaration. The conference defined the characteristics of Responsible Tourism and the concept was subsequently taken up by the World Travel Market for their World Responsible Tourism Day, which is supported by UNWTO. My work on national tourism policy in South Africa, the Gambia, Bhutan, Rwanda and Oman, and discussion with our predominantly mid-career students from around the world, has reinforced the importance of recognising and working with the world's diversity: local priorities and narratives are of crucial importance.

The ethic of responsibility

At the core of the Responsible Tourism movement is the ethic of responsibility, a willingness to take responsibility for achieving sustainable development through tourism. Tourism takes place in diverse destinations and each is unique. Destinations are sometimes similar but they are never identical. Each unique location has a particular geology and geography, social structure, history and cultural heritage and a diversity of views will exit about the place, about what issues need to be addressed and how. Responsible Tourism was not defined in the Cape Town Declaration nor is it defined here. It is an ethic of responsibility, applied to tourism, which engages with those who recognise their objectives in the Cape Town Declaration characteristics of Responsible Tourism[5] and who support its principles:

♦ All forms of tourism can be more responsible

♦ The world is diverse, we should recognise and celebrate that it is and respect it

♦ We should resist the commodification of tourism , it undermines value.

♦ Circumstances alter cases, in different places, communities have different priorities and different environmental issues are salient

♦ Responsible and sustainable tourism will be achieved in different ways in different places

♦ Progress and achievements should be reported transparently and with evidence

♦ Stakeholders have different, albeit interdependent, responsibilities – partnerships are generally required achieve significant and lasting change;

---

5   See above p. 28

♦ Tourism can only be managed for sustainability at the destination level although businesses and consumers in the originating market can make a significant contribution

♦ In a finite world and one in which we are increasingly aware of our vulnerability to extreme climate events and to the consequences of food and raw material shortages, we need to foster resilience.

♦ Responsible Tourism involves more than compliance with minimum standards, certification is opaque and carries little meaning for consumers, it focusses on effort rather then achievement.[6]

♦ It is about determining what is important in a particular place, what can be done about it, and doing it with others

To accept responsibility is to accept risk, and to encourage others to take responsibility is inherently political – non-party political, but political nonetheless. Responsibility also means accepting that there will be scrutiny of the efficacy and efficiency of the approach or intervention. It is to accept that the outcomes will be judged against the objectives and the resource costs of achieving the objectives. It also means accepting that good intentions are not enough, that the road to hell is paved with good intentions, and that what matters is the outcomes, intended and unintended. It is an ethic that calls for action.

A Responsible Tourism movement?

The concept of responsibility and the idea of Responsible Tourism are not new. They were not new when Krippendorf, reflecting on his experience, concluded that the holidaymaker could have a better experience and realise their leisure purpose in a more fulfilling way if, as critical consumers, they assumed responsibility: '… it is not a bad conscience that we need to make progress but positive experience, not the feeling of compulsion but that of responsibility'.[7] The exercise of responsibility can be fulfilling, implying the exercise of choice, self-actualisation and adulthood. I share this perspective with Krippendorf, along with the sense that one should respond, that we need rebellious tourists and rebellious locals, that if we are able we should take response-ability.

---

6   See above, o. 231

7   See Krippendorf (1987): 132, 133 and 109. Krippendorf was familiar with the work of the World Council of Churches and O'Grady cited in Krippendorf (1987):133–134

Krippendorf was amongst the first to recognise that the expectations of holidaymakers were changing and that they sought more real and authentic experiences and that this broad consumer trend created fertile ground for Responsible Tourism. Many holidaymakers are increasingly seeking opportunities to engage with local people, their traditions and culture – their way of life. Responsible Tourism is able to deliver experiences which meet their aspirations for satisfying holidays of which the sustainable elements are a significant part.

The other usage of responsibility is more passive, and in some cultures predominates. There is often a willingness to take the salary and the position of responsibility, but to avoid being held accountable – to avoid being the *response-able* person in control: the person in charge who may be held to account for something. If it is possible to hold a position of power and authority, to have status and remuneration, without taking responsibility, it is rational to do so. It is also irresponsible and common amongst the powerful. This may be why they rose to a position of power and authority: they became skilled at avoiding responsibility and, having done nothing, are blameless and rise to the top.

Sustainability is an altogether safer concept: it is an abstract noun lacking definition, it does not mean much. It carries no emotion and no imperative to act. As we have seen, the oxymoronic concept of sustainable development seeks to balance recognition of our plight in a finite world with the moral and political imperative of enabling those billions living in economic poverty to have better lives. All too often, the concepts of sustainability and sustainable tourism[8] are used in-operatively; there is no real intent to apply them.

Claims of sustainability are too often unsubstantiated: the concept has utility for securing funding or a regulation but it is not tested against a sustainability objective. They are used to legitimate an approach or policy, but they are not applied to operations. In the area of pro-poor tourism, practitioners think it odd that they might be expected to define their targets and report the impacts of their initiatives: it apparently never crosses the minds of the donors to expect any report of impacts or outcomes. Rarely is any effort made to define the resulting contribution to sustainability or sustainable development in the particular situation. They appear not to care; it is enough that the money

---

8   The sustainable development discourse is based on Western notions of conservation and development. It can be vague and ambiguous, and used to disguise hypocrisy and foster delusions – that development can be sustained within biophysical limits. It often avoids issues of power, exploitation and privilege. See Sharpley (2009a): 65–67

is spent and accounted for. Donors call the shots and distort local priorities, often empowering unaccountable groups, but rarely the marginalised. The landlord of my local pub gets it: 'the words *we've got funding* strike fear...'[9]

Sustainability is best understood as an aim, too general to have utility unless a context-relevant objective or target is defined in order to determine whether the objective has been achieved. The process of achieving the objective is a process of responsibility: individuals take responsibility for achieving defined outcomes.

A sustainability objective[10] is the outcome, responsibility is the process.

Sustainability without a target, without responsibility for achieving it being attributed to individuals or groups of individuals, is rarely more than wishful thinking. Too often sustainable development means business as usual. Change requires that people feel their responsibility to act.

The challenge, then, is to get people to take responsibility: As we become more aware of the limits to growth the importance of action to ensure resilience will grow.[11] It is people who exercise responsibility, or who fail to do so. They do so within a culture, as consumers in the originating market or as producers and locals in the destination. In seeking to make change, we ignore the importance of culture and local priorities at our peril. Companies too are changed by individuals. When I taught political science to adult students, I used to explain the importance of recycling glass (it was a long time ago). If individually we avoid buying drinks in non-returnable bottles (it was a very long time ago!), we are exercising some degree of influence as consumers. If we drive to the recycling centre each weekend we are taking individual responsibility, and probably doing more harm than good with our emissions. Recycling is now available in the supermarket car park – less emissions. We begin to have a greater impact when, rebelliously, we start to encourage friends and family and the local council to recycle: at that point we have begun to engage in political action, changing the behaviour of others.

In order to encourage people to change their behaviour, whether as producers or consumers, we need a compelling narrative. Change requires a shared definition of the problem, agreement that it is a problem about which something should be done, and agreement on what steps should be taken.

---

9   Chris Maclean, landlord of the Railway Hotel, Faversham

10   The objective(s) should be SMART: Specific, Measurable, Actionable, Realistic and Time-framed (although the language used to express this may vary).

11   See above p. viii

However, the issue will not be addressed unless it is prioritised by the different stakeholders. This is inevitably a political process, one carried out by individuals. Individuals need to persuade others that there is a problem that something can be done about it, that something should be done about it and what should be done about it. That is a powerful narrative, but the issue needs to be more engagingly defined than the mere abstraction of 'sustainability'. We must focus on and engage with livelihoods, water, saving the reef or a piece of rainforest.

Success requires that the other stakeholders accept your diagnosis and cure:[12] that they have accepted your definition and analysis of the problem and your exposition of how practically to address it, in the particular situation, in order to achieve a result which is at least acceptable to you and the other stakeholders.[13] This is, more often than not, difficult. It is even more difficult if others who are not contributing to addressing the issue are going to gain from the efforts of those who are: the free-rider problem. It is even more difficult if the free riders are likely to more than offset any gain resulting from the intervention you seek. This undermines the essential 'we can make a difference' argument. If no difference can be made, why try? There is an argument to be made for making an effort whatever the odds, but it is generally unattractive. Free-riding is generally dealt with by regulation in trade associations or by government, and needs to be more explicitly – and punitively – addressed.

If you are reading this, you are probably aware of the facts about the real global threats posed by climate change, poverty and social exclusion. But facts do not speak for themselves. Facts communicate very little: they need to be given meaning within a particular cultural context. As teachers, students, producers, consumers and human beings, we must make sense of them in our particular cultures and situations. Only a very few of us feel sustainability – it carries no imperative to action. But we can all feel responsibility. The stories we tell are important. A narrative explains why the facts matter, what they tell us. It defines the issue and explains not only what we could do about it, but why we should do something about it. Perhaps, most importantly, it provides us with a motivation to act: because we can make a difference, a difference we would like to see in the world. The end of the story gives meaning to our action, motivates us to take responsibility, the sense that we can make a difference. We need to be convinced that what we do will make a difference or make

---

12   See above pp 10 for a discussion of the importance of phronesis

13   The stakeholders need to be convinced that the action proposed will have desired, or at least tolerable outcomes: consequential thinking is essential to the construction of the narrative.

for a better experience: if not, why bother? Get this right and the message will spread virally and change results. We need to foster Positive Deviance, we need to find the better solutions and encourage their replication.[14]

Responsible Tourism is a social movement in that there is now a significant informal network comprised of a 'plurality of individuals, groups and/or organisations, engaged in a political and/or cultural conflict, on the basis of a shared collective identity'.[15] A social movement is a purposive effort by groups of people who share some common principles and approaches, resulting in a shared sense of direction, but which recognises diversity and local particularities. A movement is also identified by its antithesis, in this case irresponsible tourism – and that includes initiatives which may be labelled sustainable but which do not deliver, initiatives which waste energy, causing disillusion and 'stirring up apathy'.[16] It has been argued here that ecotourism, carbon offsetting and the Global Sustainable Tourism Criteria are examples of this form of irresponsibility, these approaches need to be challenged to demonstrate that they deliver what they promise.

Responsible Tourism refers to a willingness to respond, to do something to contribute to sustainability though tourism. The movement is formed of overlapping communities, communities in which people find like-minded individuals with whom they can discuss the particular challenges they face, recognising that whilst the issues they confront are local and specific in their manifestation, the experience of others can help them identify ways forward and potential solutions. In Cornwall, CoaST has developed a strong membership organisation, comprising tourism businesses, those in the tourism supply chain or tourism management in the county.[17] It provides peer-group support through its ambassador programme and encourages change. Communities such as this, be they geographically focused or issue-based, develop a shared language and understanding of the challenges and opportunities. At the heart of Responsible Tourism movement is the willingness to support others in the risks they take to achieve change, offering critical support to help ensure that the objectives are reached for, and are lauded when they are achieved.

The movement is young but it is significant, particularly in the UK, where to a greater or lesser extent most of the industry is engaging with the issues.

---

14   See Pascale et al (2010) www.positivedeviance.org

15   Diani (2000): 156

16   A phrase attributed erroneously to Willie Whitelaw speaking of the Labour government in 1974 – apparently he actually said 'They are going around the country stirring up complacency.' www.guardian.co.uk/politics/2006/oct/28/politics accessed 25 February 2011

17   www.coastproject.co.uk

Those readers tempted to dismiss the Responsible Tourism approach as having found uniquely fertile soil in Britain should recall that the Canadian Tourism Commission reported as recently as 2010 that the British were the least likely to aspire to choose an environmentally friendly travel option, less likely than the French, Germans, Japanese, Chinese, Korean, Australians, Mexicans, Canadians and Americans.[18] If this research had been available to us ten years earlier, we may have been too daunted even to try. What if there had been similar efforts in other significant originating markets? We can make a difference, and we must all try more.

What we can do

Responsible Tourism is about identifying the issues which matter and addressing them, in the destination or the originating market, as a tourist or traveller, as a tour operator, guide or driver, as hotelier, chef or concierge, as a builder, planner or tourism marketer. Those who have an opportunity to make tourism better have a responsibility to respond, to do what they can and to encourage others. The importance and salience of issues varies from destination to destination, the agenda is broad ranging from reducing negative social, economic and environmental impacts to enhancing positive impacts; engaging local people in decision making about how tourism can assist in making theirs a better place in which to live.

Responsible Tourism is about raising awareness of the importance of the issues in a particular place, demonstrating what each stakeholder can do to address the issue and encouraging, cajoling, campaigning, shaming individuals to take responsibility and to act, with others, to make a difference. It is about demonstrating what can be done and then encouraging more and more people to do it. It is about engaging people to respond and to act.

As Krippendorf understood, we need rebellious tourists and rebellious locals, people who think critically and who act to make better places for people to live in and for people to visit. For me, rebellious tourists and locals:

♦ Focus on things which matter to the people around them

♦ Speak up – they do not let other people define the issues to be tackled

♦ Recognise and applaud those holidaymakers and tourism businesses that are making a difference

---

18 Canadian Tourism Commission (2010). See above: p. 48

- Encourage other businesses, through their economic and political power, to emulate these good examples
- Loudly and openly criticise those who are not taking responsibility, holding to account those who are paving the road to hell with their good intentions, pursuing approaches which do not deliver what they claim and which in some cases distract from approaches which may not attract donor funding but which do deliver. [19]
- Communicate their ideas, and make Responsible Tourism infectious – it needs to go viral

The next 10 years

As with all social movements there is no hierarchy in the Responsible Tourism movement. Individuals and organisations engage in the network, the movement, to the extent that it has value for them. This may pose a problem: how do we decide where to go, and what to do? Who takes responsibility for suggesting how we act?

As we have seen tourism is a particular form of consumerism. Decisions are made within different consuming cultures as diverse as the destinations we visit. Change is achieved locally. Gandhi advised us to 'be the change you want to see in the world'. We need action.

These, from my particular vantage point, are the crucial, practical things we must all do in the next decade, to push the movement forward and make a real change to the sustainability of tourism – both as an industry and as a leisure activity. We must, in no particular order:

- Resist the commodification of tourism, maintain the linkages between the concept of a real holiday full of authentic experiences with Responsible Tourism, we must ensure that the holidaymaker tastes the difference and that Responsible Tourism continues to spread virally.
- Continue to critique certification and develop better ways of transparently reporting the positive and negative impacts of tourism and the efficacy and achievements of particular approaches and businesses.[20]
- Address the issues around particular activities, such as diving, skiing, golf, sailing and wildlife viewing

---

19   The website www.irresponsibletourism.info may be useful to those wishing to raise questions about irresponsible tourism and those paving the road to hell.

20   See for example the initiative of Jenn Bobbin, www.rtreporting.org

♦ Encourage positive deviance, work with rebellious executives and managers, potential leaders, who recognise the value of doing business differently, people who understand the importance of long term shared value and who have the vision and energy to pursue, and gain from, a different business strategy one based on value rather than simply volume.

♦ Understand what responsible cruising and responsible aviation look like and to identify ways of securing change

♦ Do more to address the access issues which disadvantage so many people

♦ Find partners in other consuming cultures with whom to work in translating and spreading the ideas;

♦ Work with local authorities and communities to manage tourism in destinations, to meet the aspirations and priorities of local people and to create better places for people to live in.

♦ Raise and address the issues about polar and 'last chance to see' travel and tourism.

♦ Continue to work on the business case to document examples where responsibility makes business sense – more work needs to be done to demonstrate the difference that responsibility makes to particular businesses.

And if you, as a reader, don't agree, then what do you think? It is your responsibility to think how you can make a difference, become response-able... *respond*. These are my ideas – what are yours?[21] There is scope to discuss and develop the Responsible Tourism agenda at the website associated with this book www.takingresponsibilityfortourism.info.

Tourism is no more, and no less, likely than any other human activity to be sustainable. There are places and communities which use tourism; others are used by it. Tourism is set to continue to grow rapidly fuelled by economic growth in China, India, Russia, Brazil and the other dynamic growth economies. Tourism has potential for good and ill, it can bring sustainable development or degradation and in our finite world Responsible Tourism becomes more important and more difficult. We can make a difference producers and consumers alike. Tourism is what we make it. It is not hopeless, though there is much still to be done. If we take responsibility we can make a difference.

---

21   There is a website and a forum for this on-going discussion at www. takingresponsibilityfortourism.info

References

Bonheoffer, D. (2001) *Letters and Papers from Prison*, London: SCM Press.

Canadian Tourism Commision (2010) *Global Tourism Watch Year 3 Summary Report 2009*, Vancouver: Canadian Tourism Commission.

Diani, M. (2000) 'The concept of social movement', in K. Nash (ed.), *Readings in Contemporary Political Sociology*, Oxford: Blackwell.

Krippendorf, J. (1987) *The Holiday Makers*, Oxford: Butterworth Heinemann.

Pascale, R. Sternin J. Sternin, M (2010) *The Power of Positive Deviance: How Unlikely Innovators Solve the World's Toughest Problems*, Harvard: HBS Press

Sharpley, R. (2009a) *Tourism Development and the Environment: Beyond Sustainability*, London: Earthscan.

Sharpley, R. (2009b) 'Tourism and development challenges in the least developed countries: the case of The Gambia', *Current Issues in Tourism*, **12** (4), 337–358.

Index